Social Media, Political Marketing and the 2016 U.S. Election

C000091094

Facebook, Twitter and Instagram create new ways to market political campaigns and new channels for candidates and voters to interact. This volume investigates the role and impact of social media in the 2016 U.S. election, focusing specifically on the presidential nominating contest. Through case studies, survey research and content analysis, the researchers employ both human and machine coding to analyse social media text and video content. Together, these illustrate the wide variety of methodological approaches and statistical techniques that can be used to probe the rich, vast stores of social media data now available. Individual chapters examine what different candidates posted about and which posts generated more of a response. The analyses shed light on what social media can reveal about campaign messaging strategies and explore the linkages between social media content and their audiences' perceptions, opinions and political participation. The findings highlight similarities and differences among candidates and consider how continuity and change are manifest in the 2016 election. Finally, taking a look forward, the contributors consider the implications of their work for political marketing research and practice.

The chapters in this book were originally published as a special issue of the *Journal of Political Marketing*.

Christine B. Williams is Professor of Political Science at Bentley University, USA, and holds a MA and PhD from Indiana University, USA. She is North American Managing Editor at the *Journal of Political Marketing* and serves on editorial boards for several other journals. Her publications focus on political communication, specifically new and emerging technologies and e-government.

Bruce I. Newman is Professor of Marketing as well as the Wicklander Fellow in Business Ethics at DePaul University, USA. He is one of the world's leading experts in political marketing and combines an expertise in marketing and politics with his knowledge of consumer psychology and statistical applications. He is the founding editor-in-chief of the *Journal of Political Marketing*. He has published more than 15 books and numerous articles on the subjects of political marketing and consumer psychology.

Social Media, Political Marketing and the 2016 U.S. Election

Edited by
Christine B. Williams and Bruce I. Newman

LONDON AND NEW YORK

First published 2018
by Routledge

2 Park Square, Milton Park, Abingdon, Oxfordshire OX14 4RN
52 Vanderbilt Avenue, New York, NY 10017

Routledge is an imprint of the Taylor & Francis Group, an informa business

First issued in paperback 2020

British Library Cataloguing-in-Publication Data
A catalogue record for this book is available from the British Library

ISBN13: 978-1-138-47706-3 (hbk)
ISBN13: 978-0-367-3104-1 (pbk)

Typeset in Garamond
by codeMantra

Publisher's Note
The publisher accepts responsibility for any inconsistencies that may have arisen during
the conversion of this book from journal articles to book chapters, namely the possible
inclusion of journal terminology.

Disclaimer
Every effort has been made to contact copyright holders for their permission to reprint
material in this book. The publishers would be grateful to hear from any copyright
holder who is not here acknowledged and will undertake to rectify any errors or
omissions in future editions of this book.

Contents

Citation Information

The chapters in this book were originally published in the *Journal of Political Marketing*, volume 16, issue 3–4 (2017). When citing this material, please use the original page numbering for each article, as follows:

Introduction
Introduction: Social Media, Political Marketing and the 2016 U.S. Election
Christine B. Williams
Journal of Political Marketing, volume 16, issue 3–4 (2017) pp. 207–211

Chapter 1
Empowering the Party-Crasher: Donald J. Trump, the First 2016 GOP Presidential Debate, and the Twitter Marketplace for Political Campaigns
Michael Cornfield
Journal of Political Marketing, volume 16, issue 3–4 (2017) pp. 212–243

Chapter 2
Understanding the Social Media Strategies of U.S. Primary Candidates
Joseph (Jun Hyun) Ryoo and Neil Bendle
Journal of Political Marketing, volume 16, issue 3–4 (2017) pp. 244–266

Chapter 3
Communicating Party Labels and Names on Twitter During the 2016 Presidential Invisible Primary and Primary Campaigns
Kate Kenski, Christine R. Filer, and Bethany A. Conway-Silva
Journal of Political Marketing, volume 16, issue 3–4 (2017) pp. 267–289

Chapter 4
The Image is the Message: Instagram Marketing and the 2016 Presidential Primary Season
Caroline Lego Muñoz and Terri L. Towner
Journal of Political Marketing, volume 16, issue 3–4 (2017) pp. 290–318

Chapter 5
Appeals to the Hispanic Demographic: Targeting through Facebook Autoplay Videos by the Clinton Campaign during the 2015/2016 Presidential Primaries
Edward Elder and Justin B. Phillips
Journal of Political Marketing, volume 16, issue 3–4 (2017) pp. 319–342

Chapter 6

Populism and Connectivism: An Analysis of the Sanders and Trump Nomination Campaigns
Michael J. Jensen and Henrik P. Bang
Journal of Political Marketing, volume 16, issue 3–4 (2017) pp. 343–364

Chapter 7

Intraparty Hostility: Social Identity, Subidentity, and the Hostile Media Effect in a Contested Primary
Aaron S. Veenstra, Benjamin A. Lyons, and İ. Alev Degim Flannagan
Journal of Political Marketing, volume 16, issue 3–4 (2017) pp. 365–385

Chapter 8

Role of Social Media in the 2016 Iowa Caucuses
Daniela V. Dimitrova and Dianne Bystrom
Journal of Political Marketing, volume 16, issue 3–4 (2017) pp. 386–406

For any permission-related enquiries please visit:
http://www.tandfonline.com/page/help/permissions

Notes on Contributors

Henrik P. Bang is Professor of Governance at the Institute for Governance and Policy Analysis, University of Canberra, Bruce, Australia.

Neil Bendle is Associate Professor of Marketing at Ivey Business School, Western University, London, Ontario, Canada.

Dianne Bystrom is Director of the Carrie Chapman Catt Center for Women and Politics, Iowa State University, Ames, Iowa, USA.

Bethany A. Conway-Silva is Assistant Professor, Communication Studies Department, California Polytechnic State University, San Luis Obispo, California, USA.

Michael Cornfield, a political scientist, is an Associate Professor of Political Management at The George Washington University Graduate School of Political Management and Research Director for the Global Center for Political Management, Washington, D.C, USA.

Daniela V. Dimitrova is Professor and Director of Graduate Education at Greenlee School of Journalism and Communications, Iowa State University, Ames, Iowa, USA.

Edward Elder is based at the School of Social Sciences, Politics and International Relations, University of Auckland, Auckland, New Zealand.

Christine R. Filer is a research analyst at Langer Research Associates, New York, New York, and a PhD candidate at the Department of Communication, University of Arizona, Tucson, Arizona, USA.

İ. Alev Degim Flannagan is based at the Department of Radio and Television Programing, Istanbul Ayvansaray University, Istanbul, Turkey.

Kate Kenski is Associate Professor at the Department of Communication, University of Arizona, Tucson, Arizona, USA.

Michael J. Jensen is Senior Research Fellow, Institute for Governance and Policy Analysis, University of Canberra, Bruce, Australia.

Benjamin A. Lyons is Postdoctoral Research Fellow, Annenberg Public Policy Center, University of Pennsylvania, Philadelphia, Pennsylvania, USA.

Caroline Lego Muñoz is Associate Professor of Marketing at the University of North Georgia, Oakwood, Georgia, USA.

Bruce I. Newman is Professor of Marketing as well as the Wicklander Fellow in Business Ethics at DePaul University, USA. He is one of the world's leading experts in political marketing and combines an expertise in marketing and politics with his knowledge of consumer psychology and statistical applications. He is the founding editor-in-chief of the *Journal of Political Marketing*. He has published more than 15 books and numerous articles on the subjects of political marketing and consumer psychology.

Justin B. Phillips is a PhD candidate at the School of Social Sciences, Politics and International Relations, University of Auckland, Auckland, New Zealand.

Joseph (Jun Hyun) Ryoo is based at Ivey Business School, Western University, London, Ontario, Canada.

Terri L. Towner is Associate Professor at Oakland University, Rochester, Michigan, USA.

Aaron S. Veenstra is Associate Professor at the School of Journalism, Southern Illinois University Carbondale, Illinois, USA.

Christine B. Williams is Professor of Political Science at Bentley University, Waltham, Massachusetts, USA, and holds a MA and PhD from Indiana University, USA. She is North American Managing Editor at the *Journal of Political Marketing* and serves on editorial boards for several other journals. Her publications focus on political communication, specifically new and emerging technologies and e-government.

Introduction: Social Media, Political Marketing and the 2016 U.S. Election

CHRISTINE B. WILLIAMS

This essay introduces the contributions of the volume "Social Media, Political Marketing and the 2016 U. S. Election." Using a variety of methodological approaches, the authors investigate the communication strategies of the Democratic and Republican candidates for president together with the responses of their audience. Collectively, this research offers insights into how new communication technologies are changing both political marketing and the ways candidates and voters interact.

Facebook, Twitter, and Instagram create new ways to market political campaigns and new channels for candidates and voters to interact. We can gauge the scale of social media's role in the 2016 presidential election from data reported by the Pew Research Center (July 18, 2016). According to their survey, 44% of the U.S. adults got information about the 2016 presidential election from social media. That is more than the percentage cited for either local or national print newspapers or for candidate websites and emails combined. And 24% got news and information from social media posts by Donald Trump and Hillary Clinton. Trump had almost 10 million Twitter followers to Clinton's seven million, and his nine million Facebook followers were about double her number. In May of 2016, the Pew study found that candidates averaged five to seven posts per day on Facebook and 11 to 12 per day on their Twitter accounts.

This volume investigates the role and impact of social media in the 2016 U.S. election, focusing specifically on the presidential nominating contest. That contest presents a unique case for study, with one author (Kurtzleben

2016) itemizing 65 ways 2016 was unprecedented! Notably, this was an open seat election that saw the largest field of candidates in the modern era and one that arguably splintered both political parties. A stop Trump movement associated with prominent Republican leaders and donors raised significant amounts of money for a negative advertising campaign. By way of example, one anti-Trump Super Political Action Committee (PAC), Lift Leading Illinois for Tomorrow, spent $9.9 million, allocating nearly all of it to digital media (Williams and Gulati 2017). Indeed, campaign financing broke several records: outside groups spent more than some candidates' own campaigns; a small number of donors raised unprecedented amounts of money; and a record number of female donors helped fuel Clinton's campaign. Both candidates and advocacy groups launched major outreach campaigns that targeted Latino and Asian voters. Not only voter registration but also turnout for Super Tuesday and other state contests reached new highs, primarily on the Republican side, and their first candidate debate rivaled that of major sporting events with an audience of 24 million. Yet despite this intense courting of the electorate and the level of interest generated by these events, a majority of voters disliked both nominees heading into the general election (Chozick and Thee-Brenan 2016).

The research compiled in this volume is further noteworthy for the wide variety of methodological approaches and statistical techniques used to probe the rich, vast stores of social media data now available. Through case studies, experiments, survey research, and content analysis, its contributors use both human and machine coding to analyze social media text and video content. The individual chapters examine what different candidates posted about and which posts generated more response. The analyses shed light on what social media can reveal about campaign messaging strategies and explore the linkages between social media content and their audiences' perceptions, opinions, and political participation. The findings highlight similarities and differences among candidates and consider how continuity and change are manifest in the 2016 election. Finally, taking a look forward, the contributors consider the implications of their work for political marketing research and practice.

Michael Cornfield sets the stage with his analysis of the first Republican debate, a notable opening foray in the 2016 presidential nominating contest. He illustrates how Donald Trump's insurgent marketing strategy encapsulated in his choice of words and targets dominated social media conversations, generating more likes, retweets, and growth in followers than any other candidate. Through his debate performance, Trump sets the agenda by defining which issues and character traits would become salient in the campaign. Cornfield concludes that social media have made the "invisible primary" visible and allow unaccredited people to register their support or opposition in a campaign phase previously limited to elites.

Joseph Ryoo and Neil Bendle investigate which topics candidates emphasize in their Twitter and Facebook posts and how that emphasis changes over time. They generate these themes using two methods: a supervised process based upon a predetermined list and an unsupervised topic modeling process Latent Dirichlet Allocation (LDA). Over time, Donald Trump increased the attention he paid to trade as well as his focus on himself, yet avoided mention of the abortion issue. By the conclusion of the nomination phase, Hillary Clinton increased her posts on Trump, but maintained a level focus on women's rights. In that same time frame, Bernie Sanders shifted emphasis from himself to the Democratic Party. The study demonstrates that social media posts constitute a rich repository of data, which can be mined for insights into a campaign's communication strategy.

Kate Kenski, Christine Filer, and Bethany Conway-Silva use computer-assisted content analysis to examine candidate tweets during the preprimary and primary phases of the presidential election. Party was more important than ideology in their messaging, with no difference between outsiders and establishment candidates in the emphasis placed on in-group affiliation. Candidates tweeted about themselves more than either their intra- or inter-party opponents. That said, Hillary Clinton mentioned Donald Trump more than he mentioned her, although other Republicans did criticize Trump and President Obama in their tweets. In contrast to expectations derived from social identity and reference dependence theories, social media are used primarily to boost name recognition in the initial stages of the campaign.

Caroline Munoz and Terri Towner categorize the visual framing of candidates' Instagram images during the presidential primaries. The ideal candidate frame is preferred to a populist one and generates the highest numbers of likes and comments from viewers. Its visuals include elected officials and patriotic symbols (statesmanship), the latter being frequently depicted in Donald Trump's images, and family (compassion), often depicted in those of Hillary Clinton. Candidates differed in the frequency of their posts and use of text overlays, and whether viewers engaged with a like or a comment depended on the image. This study is one of the first to describe and evaluate candidates' visual self-presentation strategy on social media.

In another study of visual marketing strategy and effectiveness, Edward Elder and Justin Phillips analyze the effectiveness of Facebook autoplay videos in targeting potential voters, specifically the coveted Hispanic demographic by the Clinton campaign. Her targeted videos attracted more likes from new supporters than untargeted ones. Moreover, live unedited event videos were more effective than those professionally produced, especially if paired with images of other Hispanics. On the other hand, videos focusing on Donald Trump did not attract new Hispanic support, which the Clinton campaign appears not to have recognized. More generally, this research confirms the effectiveness of a targeted political advertising strategy.

Michael Jensen and Henrik Bang investigate the different strands of populism reflected in the Facebook posts of Bernie Sanders and Donald Trump and their supporters' response to them. In their populist campaigns, both present themselves as champions of the people fighting the economic and political establishment. Nearly 25% of Trump's posts, however, reference himself and portray him in a hierarchical authority role: the strong leader who will come to the rescue and restore greatness. Sanders' posts instead emphasize the power of citizens to effect change or horizontal connectivism. These candidates' contrasting depictions are likewise reflected in comments on their respective posts. Trump's supporters reference the need for strong authority, which correlates with expressions of fear; Sanders' supporters express optimism with references to democracy and their own capacity to make a difference politically. Rather than de Tocqueville's fear that populism would give rise to despotism, Jensen and Bang see in connectivism a potential path forward for democratic politics.

Aaron Veenstra, Benjamin Lyons, and Alev Degim Fannagan conduct experiments to determine whether centrality, favorability, and social network homogeneity influence perceptions of media bias during the primaries and general election. The centrality and favorability of candidates to respondents influenced perceptions of candidate bias, but party support factors did not influence party bias. Postconvention, candidate favorability remained significant for candidate bias while social network homogeneity predicted party bias. While personalization could be the result of an unusually divisive nomination contest in 2016, long term, candidate-centered identity could undermine general election support from the losing candidates and from the voters who supported them. More broadly, social media communities fueled by media hostility could undermine the democratic role of the press.

Turning to behavioral impacts in the concluding chapter, Daniela Dimitrova and Dianne Bystrom investigate the effects of online and social media activity on participation in the Iowa caucuses. Active social media use through liking and sharing content positively impacts caucus attendance while passive use diminishes it. Social media is the strongest predictor of attendance among all information channels, followed by cable television viewing; late night TV comedy shows and radio are significant, negative predictors. The authors conclude that individual communication channels do not motivate participation as much as attention paid to the caucuses. The findings suggest that campaigns should redirect attention away from passive website viewing and develop social media content that will generate likes and shares.

Our special issue, "Social Media, Political Marketing and the 2016 U.S. Election," contributes to a growing literature focused on the data and role of this new technology in political campaigns. Its chapters illustrate how social media, like print and broadcast before it, offers insights into campaign communication strategy. Collectively, these studies also demonstrate that social media are well suited to measuring audience response to candidates' messages and thus the effectiveness of their marketing. This research showcases differences among the 2016 presidential candidates over the course of the campaign, although questions remain about differences among social media platforms, demographic subgroups, and electoral contexts. It is too soon to know the extent to which these findings reflect unique attributes of the 2016 election or are harbingers of a fundamentally changed electoral order. What is clear is that the internet has created a communication environment that is larger, faster, and more heterogeneous than ever before. Social media are a significant player in this new environment. This volume provides a timely exploration of its emerging impact on political marketing and the interactions that undergird the relationship between candidates and voters. As the early months of the Trump presidency bring the positive and negative potential of social media to the fore, this research agenda needs to keep pace and address its role and impact as a governing tool.

REFERENCES

Chozick, A., and M. Thee-Brenan. 2016. "Poll Finds Voters in Both Parties Unhappy with Their Candidates." Accessed July 17, 2016. https://www.nytimes.com/2016/07/15/us/politics/hillary-clinton-donald-trump-poll.html?mcubz=0&_r=0.

Kurtzleben, D. 2016. "The Most 'Unprecedented' Election Ever? 65 Ways It Has Been." Accessed July 3, 2016. www.npr.org/2016/07/03/.../the-most-unprecedented-election-ever-65-ways-it-has-been

Pew Research Center. July 18, 2016. "Election 2016: Campaigns as a Direct Source of News." http://www.journalism.org/2016/07/18/election-2016-campaigns-as-a-direct-source-of-news/

Williams, C., and G. Gulati. 2017. "Digital vs. Television Ad Expenditures by Outside Groups." In *The Internet and the 2016 Presidential Campaign*, Chapter 6, edited by J. Baumgartner and T. Towner, 127–47. New York, NY, US: Lexington Books.

Empowering the Party-Crasher: Donald J. Trump, the First 2016 GOP Presidential Debate, and the Twitter Marketplace for Political Campaigns

MICHAEL CORNFIELD

This article argues that an important political marketplace of keywords expands in social media around campaign events such as a debate; that rhetorical efforts to define the situation in which a campaign event occurs are met in this marketplace by user responses that more or less echo the keywords, thereby enhancing or diminishing the political power of their "caller" or speaker; and that social media monitoring platforms can enhance our understanding of public opinion influence competitions among candidates through the careful selection, tabulation, and inspection of words and phrases being voiced. In the case at hand, an analysis of Twitter volume data and a reading of a sample of 1200 tweets between July 30 and August 15, 2015, a period enveloping the first 2016 Republican presidential candidate debate on August 6, 2015, helps us understand how Donald J. Trump escaped political punishment from party and media elites for subverting Republican and U.S. norms of candidate behavior. Elite voices greatly disapproved of Trump's debate performance and conduct, a traditional augury of declining public support. But the presence of social media voices enhanced Trump's capacity to succeed with an insurgent marketing strategy, one he would continue into his election as president fifteen months later. Specifically, comparatively high user volume

Color versions of one or more of the figures in the article can be found online at www.tandfonline.com/wplm.

on a debate-oriented section of Twitter (i.e., posts with the hashtag #GOPDebate) for Trump's name, slogan, and Twitter address, and for such advantageous keywords as "political correctness," "Megyn Kelly," and "illegal immigration" relative to terms and phrases favoring other candidates and Republicans as a whole indicates the presence of heavy and active popular support for Trump. The contents of the corresponding tweet sample exhibit Twitter-savvy techniques and populist stances by which the Trump campaign solicited that support: celebrity feuding, callouts to legacy media allies, featured fan comments, a blunt vernacular, and confrontational branding. The contents also illustrate ways in which users manifested their support: from the aforementioned high keyword volume to imitative behavior and the supplying of evidence to verify Trump's contested claims during the debate.

"The funny thing is that even a critical story, which may be hurtful personally, can be very valuable to your business."
— *The Art of the Deal* (Trump and Schwartz 1987, 56–58).
"Almost universal support that 'Trump won the debate.' Only @FoxNews is consistantly [sic] fighting the Trump win, and I got them the ratings."
— August 8, 2015 tweet by @realDonald Trump,
with 2843 retweets and 8100 likes.

INTRODUCTION

The descriptive term "invisible primary" has become a misnomer. For decades, it served as the conventional name for the long stretch of presidential campaigning that precedes party primaries and caucuses. But the period is not invisible, it does not turn on voting, and the rise of social media has accentuated both counter-phrase developments.

Social media platforms have joined politics niche channels and publications in exhibiting a great deal of what candidates do and say in the many months before Iowa and New Hampshire. During this time, their public activity consists more of branding and auditioning to the politically attentive than it does persuading and mobilizing targeted segments of the electorate. Social media have expanded the ranks of those paying attention beyond party activists, political professionals, and campaign journalists. And they have brought the comments and shares of this enlarged community into public view as well. Accordingly, communications during the so-called invisible primary are now better understood as the activity of a political marketplace, in which millions of consumers of political messages choose among vendors and ratify their choices by echoing their words, so that more people hear them.

We can learn about what happens in this contemporary *agora* through quantitative and qualitative analysis of Twitter traffic. In this article, I present a method to conduct such research and use findings from tweets in and around the first 2016 Republican candidate debate to show how Donald J. Trump was able to neutralize adverse judgments of his performance by party elites through adroit social media marketplace behavior. He sold himself everywhere as a populist subversive. On Twitter, posters not only bought his act in high numbers but also provided him with resources to sustain it. Their voices validated Trump's approach and preserved his lead in the polls and media shares.

A Medley of Debate Judges and Judgments

On August 6, 2015, the Republican National Committee (RNC), in collaboration with media sponsors Fox News and Facebook, staged the opening debate among candidates for the party's presidential nomination. As with the previous 73 GOP presidential debates dating back to 1948, there were no set criteria by which candidates could be ranked on their performances and a winner could be designated. (Of course, the same fuzzy condition applies to Democratic debates as well.) Instead, a variety of self-appointed judges, relying on a variety of standards and methods, ventured forth assessments. These judges included the candidates and their campaign staffers and surrogates, the sponsor-designated newspersons who moderated the event and posed questions to the candidates, audience research organizations conducting polls and focus groups, journalists and commentators, and anyone making use of opportunities to express opinions in mass and social media. I shall refer to them collectively as "expressive attentives," to distinguish them from others watching and learning about the debate but not moved to comment in public.

The most authoritative winner–loser judgments were anchored in poll results, in that those provided a veneer of objectivity. Indeed, the debate organizers relied on poll standings to establish the roster of candidates eligible to participate. But the persons polled (and, more subtly, those writing the poll questions) nevertheless lacked firm and discrete judging criteria. Convenient heuristics to assist with their choices were scarce. Party identification figures heavily in picking winners in general election debates, but this was a competition within one party. It was also the very first debate, with no previous performances to help with the gauging. The mind-concentrating circumstances of intense localized campaigning and a pending vote choice were at least 6 months and six more scheduled debates away, and then available only to party activists residing in Iowa. To top it off, there were 16 candidates participating, in two groups. The double session supplied an ingoing suggestion, to be sure, along with the predebate judgments in media circulation and the podium assignments based on the poll standings. Still, this was no game, sport, award show, or election. The debate winners and losers were anyone and everyone's guess.

The first GOP debate of the 2016 presidential campaign is thus an exemplar of Lloyd Bitzer's concept of a "rhetorical situation," wherein "exigent" ambiguities press on a collection of people such that they become more susceptible to persuasion by someone who can provide a fitting and clarifying account, a lens through which they can see what's going on and act to their satisfaction (Bitzer 1992). The exigencies—"an imperfection marked by urgency," in Bitzer's formulation—lay not just in who would get a boost in the Republican race to be the next president, or nominee, or front-runner but also in what issues and what sort of character traits would be of prime importance as the race continued.

Hindsight helps us see the most significant outcome of the August 5, 2015 debate and raises a question in connection with a contrast evident among the judgments at the time. The eventual winner, Donald J. Trump, dramatically transgressed five norms of candidate debate behavior:

- He refused to pledge support to the eventual party nominee.
- He insulted women, notably moderator Megyn Kelly, the only woman on the stage, and actress/talk show host/activist Rosie O'Donnell. This provocation escalated during a televised interview the following night, when Trump alluded to Kelly's menstrual cycle as a source of her allegedly hostile attitude toward him.
- He stereotyped and exaggerated the threats to Americans posed by undocumented immigrants and blamed the government of the major nation of entry, Mexico.
- He proudly admitted to having curried favor through campaign contributions with government officials, liberals/Democrats as well as conservatives/Republicans, including those presidential candidates on stage with him and, most notably, the likely Democratic opponent, Hillary Clinton.
- He proudly admitted he manipulated investors while making money for himself when taking a few of his companies through the bankruptcy laws.

Even as he stirred emotions with these statements, Trump offered rationales for each of them:

- Not pledging support to the eventual nominee provided him with bargaining leverage against the other candidates, most of whom were part of corrupt and inept Washington, D.C.
- The insults were just kidding around; more important, he and the country did not have time for "total political correctness."

- He brought the problem of rapists and criminals coming through the Mexican border to everyone's attention; he had evidence to document the problem and a way to stop it (the wall); the media distorted what he said about Mexicans.
- He could not be bought, and he had used that weakness in politicians to get what he needed from them, including Hillary and Bill Clinton, who attended his wedding to Melania Knauss.
- He used the bankruptcy laws as other great businessmen have, to reduce costs and make money, and the loser investors were not really victims.

These aggressive statements, presented through a roguish persona, were emblematic of Trump's insurgent self-marketing campaign. They were show-stopping moments.

In making their instant judgments, political insiders rejected the arguments and downgraded the speaker. *Ballotpedia* conducted a snap online poll of "106 Republican operatives, strategists and party activists from around the country." (Barnes 2015) As can be seen in Table 1, they awarded "biggest winner" victory plurality to Marco Rubio (29%), followed by John Kasich (19%) Jeb Bush (18%), and Chris Christie (17%); Trump got 1% and Ted Cruz 2%. Meanwhile, 49% deemed Trump the "biggest loser," with Rand Paul next at 24%. (A parallel survey of 44 Democrats yielded similar results regarding the winners, favoring Christie, Kasich, and Rubio. But regarding the losers, they selected Bush (32%) and Paul (30%), with Trump tied with Walker for third biggest loser at 14%.)

Rubio impressed the Republican insiders with his forceful and aspirational statements. Kasich "sounded confident and reasonable." As for Trump, James A. Barnes summarized the comments thusly:

> "Too much anger, too many *non sequiturs*," said one GOP insider. "Peevish, scowling, thin skinned, shallow," said another. "Bombastic, offensive, and arrogant," echoed a third. Several of the GOP professionals were put off by Trump's declaration at the start of the debate that he could not rule out an independent run for the presidency if he did not win the party's nomination. "He alienated people on the very first question," said a party operative. "He showed this is all about him. He is more concerned about himself than our party or beating Clinton." Another GOP insider predicted, "He would lose a general election by 50 points."

The insider assessments differed from the preferences evident in polls and the distribution of express attention on Twitter. By those metrics, Trump continued to dwarf the Republican field. Bush, an early favorite, and Rubio, the insider-anointed debate winner, scarcely registered on Twitter. Carly Fiorina, excluded from both the prime time panel and the insider survey,

TABLE 1 Debate Winners and Losers by Three Metrics

	Twitter share of voice			Real clear politics poll average			Ballotpedia poll of republican insiders		
	Pre-Debate (%)	Post-Debate (%)	Change (%)	Pre-Debate (%)	Post-Debate (%)	Change (%)	Winner (%)	Loser (%)	Winner-Loser (%)
Trump	54	54	0	22	23	1	1	49	-48
Clinton	21	20	-1						
Cruz	8	8	0	6	6	0	2	5	-3
Carson	2	5	3	6	6	0	3	4	-1
Fiorina	3	5	2	0	0	0			
Bush	8	6	-2	13	12	-1	18	10	8
Rubio	4	3	-1	6	6	0	29	0	29

Almost no change in Twitter share of voice and poll standing despite insider declarations that Trump lost Bigly and Rubio won.

benefited from a boomlet of attention on Twitter, as did Ben Carson. However, neither candidates' rise came at Trump's expense.

For a presidential candidate to crash into a party's eminences, violate its norms, contest its consensus on issues and not pay a swift penalty in public standing runs afoul of some theoretical principles and historical patterns found in the study of presidential campaign communications and campaign debates in particular.

LITERATURE REVIEW

The August 2015 debate took place in the prevoting phase of the presidential election process, a "surfacing" period that also featured candidacy announcement speeches as events for rhetorical presentations and responses (Trent and Friedenberg 2008). The main objective of campaigners in these years (yes, it goes on for more than a year) has been to impress party and political media elites. These officials, staffers, big donors, pundits, and reporters evaluated candidates for their fitness to lead the party, win the election, and serve in the Oval Office. Journalist Arthur T. Hadley, whose account of the 1973–1975 prevote process gave it the enduring name "The Invisible Primary," theorized that elites scrutinized candidate psyches, staff, strategy, money, media presence, and volunteers (Hadley 1976). They awarded their favorites with endorsements, money, and favorable word of mouth, some of which made it into the media. Experience in gaining and serving in government office mattered. "Of course," wrote political scientists Polsby and Wildavsky (1984) in the sixth edition of their widely used and admired textbook on presidential elections, "to be 'taken seriously' by the news media a candidate should have won a statewide election for public office." (Polsby and Wildavsky 1984, 96). More recently, as data processing became faster, elites consulted surveys and other modes of audience research to inform their assessments. By the 1992 presidential debates, public opinion data were available as soon as fifteen minutes after the conclusion of a debate (Johnson 2017).

Debates stand out during the entire presidential campaign process as the only events in which candidates interact on television. Indeed, in the curious lingo of American politics, any format in which candidates interact on television is referred to as a "debate." For instance, Al Gore and Ross Perot once "debated" NAFTA on the Larry King talk show program. Although multiple candidates also attend state party dinners and donor conferences, these events are not called debates because the candidates speak one at a time. At one such conference, held a few days before the August 2015 GOP debate, five candidates (Bush, Cruz, Fiorina, Rubio, and Walker) were interviewed in sequence and mingled individually among megadonors and their surrogates convened by the Freedom Partners Chamber of Commerce, an organization founded by private energy moguls Charles and David Koch. Rand Paul attended an earlier Koch conference along with Cruz and Rubio (Vogel 2015). As will be discussed ahead, Trump not only did not attend but also took care to skewer those who did in his predebate tweeting.

Commercial television has hived off candidate debates to cable news channels. The specialization provides political and journalistic voices with more air time to judge debates. Since the cable news channels are part of media conglomerates, ad revenue imperatives to provide entertainment along with commentary remain in force. Candidate displays of emotion possess cross-channel value; when they materialize, clips can be replayed again and again and glossed with meaning as "turning points" in the horse race narrative that professional mediators resort to prolong and heighten audience interest in election campaigns (Patterson 1993). The clips and references show up, as well, on late-night comedy and mid-day talk programs.

Technology has enhanced the dramatistic milieu of a televised debate. The emotions on candidates' faces have become easier to read thanks to the advent of more fluid camerawork and high-definition picture resolution. Reaction shots, split screens, and graphics sharpen the perceptibility of conflicts. Switching the standard debate venue from television studios to large theaters and arenas has added still more affective power to the show; notwithstanding the obligatory admonition by the hosts to the audience to refrain from applause or booing, they issue spontaneous judgments for all to hear.

Television business imperatives make it more reasonable to regard candidate debates as auditions or early rounds in an elimination game reality series than as an Oxford-style issue discussion of the sort that public television aired on such programs as "Firing Line" and "The Advocates," and CNN's "Crossfire." Accordingly, media consultants and other members of debate prep teams help candidates formulate and rehearse quippy comebacks to anticipated attacks and vulnerable claims by opponents. Such toppers can yield "defining moments" that last until some other clip comes along, which sometimes also lodge in public memory as synecdoche for the debates, the elections, and the careers of those involved (Clayman 1995). There is an appropriate look to go along with a pithy riposte: a study of 37 one-hour issue debates in Denmark found that an intense gaze at the right moment "to emphasize specific, crucial features of content" worked persuasively with audiences (Jorgensen, Kock, and Rorbech 1998).

For every Lloyd Bentsen who prevails in a defining moment, there is a Dan Quayle who gets saddled with the role of being the foil or victim. Unforced errors and unfortunate visages have beset incumbent presidents in debates from Gerald Ford to Barack Obama. (Jamieson and Birdsell 1990, Schroeder 2008.) The consulting industry niche of crisis communications, geared to helping companies and their executives handle scandals, has developed a subspecialty to mitigate and forestall humiliating exchanges in debates. These advisers have a lot of tactics to choose from in making their recommendations, from blame-shifting to apologizing, hair-splitting to isolating, professing good intentions to claiming everyone does it (Benoit 2015).

Televised debates and their assessments now occur in the context of a digital media system which blends direct and online with mass communication forms. Participant practices, norms, and formats are being "hybridized," in Andrew Chadwick's term. (Chadwick 2013.) Television clips can be watched on demand; one-liners fly through cyberspace on hashtag wings; transcripts come with annotations; in short, every piece of debate content can be archived, shared, and appended with comments. A standard of hybridizing excellence was set in 2007 with the CNN/YouTube presidential debates, especially the democratic debate. Citizens posed questions to candidates by video and a few of them were permitted to follow up live from seats in the audience, and campaigns got time for their own videos to be screened. But the political parties and television networks have yet to adopt digital media fully. In the first GOP debate of 2015, more than 40,000 questions posted on Facebook were culled, abridged, teased, and voiced by the Fox News panel, with no follow-ups from the handful of posters whose queries were chosen. It was as though a red rope had been installed around the stage to prevent the questioners from interacting with the stars. While debate viewers increasingly monitor a second screen to skim and engage in social media communication, with the effect of converting "political moments into pop culture fodder," the organizations in charge of presidential debates and the questioners and candidates who participate in them have not, for the most part, accepted social media users into the event (Ricke 2014).

Insulating debate players from the digital crowd is not just a *status quo* power move; they need protection from change as well as the crowd. Adapting to social media necessitates adjustments in communication habits and styles which can be jarring, demanding, and deleterious. Kerric Harvey, editor of a three-volume encyclopedia on social media and politics, has pointed out that while social media are "technologically organized as one-to-many transmissions," users experience communication on a one-to-one, peer-to-peer basis. Tweets "feel personal," "create a sense of community," tend to be "short, pointed, and often extremist" in content, and while often fun, can result in dangerous repercussions. Harvey also noted how social media messages "proliferate organically according to their salience for social network users and their perceived relevance to topics of the day." (Harvey 2014) Institutions can affect this distribution dynamic through adept and alert tactics. But no one can will a social media message into or out of virality. Just because an account's followers' numbers in the tens of millions does not guarantee that a particular post will be viewed and absorbed by a significant percentage of them.

Still, political campaigners try to reach and persuade people through all available media, and that includes digital stabs at virality. From the countdown clocks and the spin rooms to Facebook news feeds and text alerts, marketing pitches suffuse candidate debates.

Students of political marketing mine insights by applying core business marketing concepts to campaign situations (Cwalina, Falkowski, and Newman 2011). A political marketplace can be said to exist where (1) advertising and other promotional expenditures help, (2) sales pitches (3) in competitions for consumer attention for one brand of a situational definition over others. Often these pitches engender a would-be leader promising to solve a problem in service to a cause and vision of life. A marketplace setting contrasts with, on the one hand, political forums and arenas in which rules of evidence and procedure are in greater force regulating communication, and, on the other hand, socializing locales in which less purposive communication occurs. Notwithstanding the power of images and numbers, the basic currency in a political marketplace consists of words. The transactions consist of calls that meet with echoes of affirmation, contestations, and silence, evidence of which marketing teams may use to adjust subsequent messages and performance techniques.

In his provocations and pitches, Trump portrayed himself as a campaign outsider taking on the political establishment on behalf of "forgotten" Americans. He thereby projected an economic and cultural nationalist persona long familiar as a staple of populist rhetoric. Populism is profitably understood in the U.S. context as a rhetorical style adopted under certain circumstances for certain goals, as opposed to an ideology with relatively fixed positions on issues and in parties. Bonikowski and Gidron (2016) show how presidential candidates have varied in their use of populist ideas and keywords depending on their incumbency status; Dwight Eisenhower and Bill Clinton, for example, ran for open seats with much more populist language than they did as incumbents four years later. In their choice of villains, Republican populists have tended to focus on government elites and Democrats corporate elites, but the thematics are similar: I'm with you, the ordinary guys and gals, not the special interests and power structures; together, we will purify Washington on behalf of American values and its victimized citizens (Bonikowski and Gidron 2016). Opposition to immigrants has been another signature feature of populism.

Several notable candidates ran as populists in previous presidential campaigns. The most direct antecedents to Donald Trump were Pat Buchanan (1992 and 1996), H. Ross Perot (same years, but as a third-party candidate), and George Wallace (also third-party, in 1968 and 1972). In 2016, Trump competed for the Republican nomination against two other outsiders making their debut in electoral politics, Ben Carson and Carly Fiorina. The track record of outsiders, populist and otherwise, has been poor: Buchanan won a primary, but he along with Pat Robertson, Alan Keyes, Steve Forbes and Morry Taylor in 1996, Gary Bauer in 2000, and Herman Cain in

2012 did not come close to winning the Republican nomination (Kondik and Skelley 2015).

So it was reasonable to presume, as elite judges on television did, that the odds were steep against Trump retaining his lead in the polls.

Trump Heading into the Debate

Donald J. Trump brought decades of self-marketing experience to the debate stage and its surrounding media venues. The only other GOP candidate there with remotely comparable experience in branding himself was Ben Carson, who, like Trump, was taking up electoral politics as a third vocation, in his case after stints in surgical medicine and vending self-help literature. Trump began his career selling and managing real estate while working for his father in New York City. Negotiating with financiers, builders, and government officials was crucial to success. Trump learned over the years to use his fame to grease the deals for property acquisition and facility construction. Over time, the Trump brand itself became his principal sales item, licensed to others who managed properties and then consumer products with his name on them (Kranish and Fisher 2016).

The television series *The Apprentice*, which aired with Trump as host from Trump Tower between 2004 and 2015, added a self-referential dimension and global reach to his brand. As a celebrity, Trump had already grown accustomed to a polarized entertainment press that either acted obsequiously to win story access or ruthlessly to vacuum up dirt. Show-runner Mark Burnett persuaded Trump to take on the role in part by arguing that having his own show would give him greater brand control, providing direct access to a mass audience and, as an executive producer, greater income. Trump's opening voice-over to each episode declared: "I've mastered the art of the deal and have turned the name Trump into the highest quality brand. And as the master, I want to pass along some of my knowledge to somebody else."

For his presidential race, Trump placed his brand into conflict with establishment politics, government, and media. He was at once an exponent of populism, a famous businessman, and a successful social media marketer. On the day Trump announced his candidacy, June 16, 2016, he had almost three million followers on Twitter. By comparison, Jeb Bush, who announced the day before, had 198,340 and Marco Rubio, who announced on April 13, had 706,910.

Trump descended to his campaign rallies in a Boeing 757 reconfigured down from 200 to 43 seats with gold-plated seat belt buckles and, of course, his name emblazoned on the outside (D'Antonio 2015). In his speeches and tweets, as journalist Mark Danner has written:

> "His assertions, framed in simple, concrete, direct language, are not policy statements so much as attitudes, the tireless ranting of the man on the barstool beside you…" (Danner 2016)

Even barstool experts have their day. Trump's depiction of an America besieged by undocumented criminals was borne out two weeks after his announcement address when on July 1 Kate Steinle, a young white woman, was murdered by a Hispanic man who had been deported five times in San Francisco, a sanctuary city and symbol of progressive politics.

On July 17, at a Family Leadership Summit in Iowa where nine other Republican candidates also appeared before 3,000 conservative activists, Trump said that John McCain was not a war hero because he had been taken captive. This political sacrilege drew rebukes from candidates Jeb Bush, Rick Perry, Marco Rubio, and Scott Walker, 2012 GOP nominee Mitt Romney, and RNC spokesman Sean Spicer. To some commenters and party elites, Trump seemed to have crossed a red line. The remark certainly projected a socially imagined dividing line between the New Yorker and his rivals.

The television audience for the debate would draw 24 million viewers, the biggest nonsports live audience in history of cable television. One-tenth as many tweets, 2.46 million, sported the hashtag #GOPDebate on August 6 and 7. These may be productively studied as the Twitter section of the marketplace where the candidates and their campaigns sought and to significantly varying degrees received responses from expressive attentives.

RESEARCH APPROACH

Propositions

The following research propositions informed my data selection and analysis.

P1: Social media marketplaces for politics expand around and during campaign events. The enlarged numbers of users and expressives constitute good opportunities for campaigns to cultivate audience attention and project branded keywords.

P2: High volumes of branded keywords in event sites designated as neutral indicate campaign success in advantageously defining a political conflict. Branded keywords may be identified for investigation through contextual analysis of the campaign environment: the players, processes, issues, and ideologies informing an event. In retrospective analysis, additional keywords may be drawn from dramatic exchanges and remarks evident in event transcripts and tapes.

P3: Social media monitoring metrics can enhance understanding of event impacts on political situations. Investigators can tabulate the volume of keyword mentions and examine samples of posts to see how they were used. The findings augment what can be learned from polls, focus groups, and dial-response data about audience reactions to political rhetoric.

Data Sources

Twitter text data and tabulations come from the media monitoring platform and archive company Crimson Hexagon. Quotes from the debate come from the UCSB American Presidency Project transcript: Presidential Candidates Debates: "Republican Candidates Debate in Cleveland, Ohio," August 6, 2015. http://www.presidency.ucsb.edu/ws/?pid=110489.

Methodology

The method I employed to conduct research in light of these propositions has four basic steps:

1. Select a political event, identify a well-trafficked and neutrally defined event-related hashtag (often a top Trending Topic at that time), and use the event as a center-point to set a date range, thus **bounding a marketplace** where keyword calls and echoes occurred. Additional marketplaces may be examined as warranted by research questions.
2. Use relevant literatures to determine event contexts, stakes, and norms, and then in combination with an informed reading of the event transcript/tape, **generating a starter list of keywords** with likely rhetorical power.
3. **Examine marketplace volumes of keywords**.
4. **Examine randomized samples of posts** for specific calls, echoes, marketing techniques, and audience/user responses.

I selected #GOPDebate on the assumption that people who included that hashtag in Twitter posts between July 30 and August 15, 2015 wanted to be heard mainly by the general political community, not just by supporters of a particular party or candidate. I selected @realDonaldTrump on the assumption that people who included that candidate Twitter address in the same time period wanted to be heard mainly by the candidate himself, his campaign team, and supporters. I drew three random samples of 200 posts from each virtual venue. The first, #GOPDebate, a trending topic at the time, constituted the primary rhetorical arena under scrutiny. Pulls from the second, @realdonaldtrump, permitted me to see marketing techniques and responses in greater detail. The three time periods sampled consisted of the week preceding the debate, the two days of the debate and immediate aftermath, and the week following those two days. Two marketplace venues times three intervals times two hundred posts yielded a sample of 1,200 posts.

FINDINGS

Post Volume Data

Figures 1 and 2 present the frequency of posts over time on Twitter with another hashtag, the event-spanning #2016 Election. Figure 1 shows a

Events Stimulate Chatter

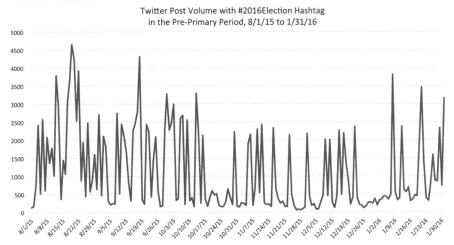

FIGURE 1 Events stimulate chatter.

comb-like pattern of many spikes occurring in the pre-primary period between August 1 2015 and January 31, 2016. This on/off dynamic suggests that events and news stimulated tweeting in bursts as people (and their bots) were moved to send messages beyond the communities constructed by shared political views, interests, and preferences. The range is fairly stable,

Talk-Sparkers in August 2015

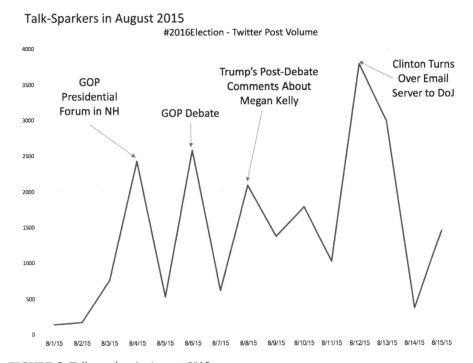

FIGURE 2 Talk-sparker in August 2015.

TABLE 2 Debate Winners and Losers by Tweet Volume

	Pre-Debate	Debate	Post-Debate	Total
	7/30 to 8/5	8/6 to 8/7	8/8 to 8/15	7/30 to 8/15
#GOPDebate	40,392	2,463,240	135,045	2,638,677
@realDonaldTrump	347,477	470,911	879,216	1,697,604
@HillaryClinton	135,798	110,666	301,169	547,633
@MegynKelly	25,874	234,520	217,582	477,976
@BretBaier	8,965	31,322	21,969	62,256
#ChrisWallace*	42	2,042	702	2,786
@TedCruz	55,571	96,399	116,362	268,332
@CarlyFiorina	19,358	131,857	86,915	238,130
@JebBush	54,076	59,718	96,564	210,358
@RealBenCarson	14,012	74,763	72,593	161,368
@MarcoRubio	26332	72,042	41,437	139,811

*There is another Chris Wallace on Twitter.
Trump, Clinton, and Kelly addressed the most; others up as well.

with 42 spikes between 1500 and 4700 posts on big days, and fewer than 600 on other (off) days, including, not surprisingly, the Christmas fortnight.

Figure 2 focuses on #2016 Election posts in the period under scrutiny, from August 1 to 15, 2015. The first spike of that month occurred on August 4, the day after fourteen major Republican presidential candidates participated one at a time in a "Voters First Republican Presidential Forum" on the campus of St. Anselm College in Manchester, New Hampshire. (Three candidates appeared by videolink; Huckabee and Trump did not take part.) The next, slightly larger spike corresponds to the day after the August 6 debate, followed by a smaller spike in the wake of Trump's post-debate interview comments about Megyn Kelly. The biggest spike of the period was sparked by news that Hillary Clinton turned over her private email server to the Justice Department.

The saw-toothed pattern evokes neither a power law curve nor a steady line. With each spike in posts, the frequency of words and signifiers (e.g., "@" and "#") increases proportionally thanks to the 140-character limit. The absence of long posts makes it easier to discern any hierarchies in usage. That is, it is reasonable to infer that a high post count corresponds to a high number of people using a term.

Table 2 displays a player-oriented breakdown of the Twitter marketplace for attention-getting related to the debate. It can be seen that the use of the event-designated topical hashtag #GOPDebate mushroomed to nearly 2.5 million tweets in the two days of the debate and instant spin. The table includes some of the same "share of voice" data presented in Table 1, with the names of the three debate moderators added. The data depict who received the most publicity via Tweeting in this central locale through the relative popularity of addressable names. Traffic with the address of Trump's campaign more than doubled in the week after the debate from the preceding week, and Clinton's nearly tripled at a lower level of volume. But the biggest gainer of the debate principals examined from pre- to post- debate was the address of Megyn Kelly, with a ten-fold increase during the event sustained for a week thereafter. Carson and Fiorina also jumped by a sizable percentage but well below the volume levels of Trump, Clinton, and Kelly. What these data suggest is that Kelly and her conflict with Trump took away potential Twitter-poster mindshare from the other GOP candidates.

Thus far the data show a pronounced preference of interest for Trump over the others. Only a dive into the content can disclose what that entailed and rested upon. Content examination also illustrates good and weak practices in how to market a candidate around a scheduled high-profile event through Twitter, and helpful ways in which tweet consumers respond.

Keywords of the Debate: A Contextualized List for Investigation

What keywords spoken during the debate could have elicited politically significant responses from Twitter users? I have boldfaced the words I chose to examine in the following rhetorically-oriented recap of the event as a competition for attention and contest definition. I looked in particular for words that signaled unique selling propositions, as well as those that sought to depict current and perennial issues of interest to Republicans in a light favorable to the candidate, and finally, names and memes that could generate social buzz. The most echoed keywords, along with my selection rationales for each, appear in Table 3.

At the start of the event, ten men identified by voice-over as a **businessman**, a **neurosurgeon**, three governors, two former governors, and three US Senators walked onto a television stage at Quicken Loans Arena in Cleveland. They took places facing the audience and, in the foreground, three Fox News personalities who would act as questioners and moderators: **Bret Baier, Megyn Kelly**, and **Chris Wallace**.

The show began with an aggressive flourish: Bret Baier conducted a visual loyalty test, asking any candidate "unwilling *tonight* [emphasis added] to **pledge** your support to the eventual nominee of the Republican party and pledge to not run an independent campaign against that person." Trump alone raised his hand. Baier followed up as the audience booed. Trump played along with Baier's elongation of the moment. He said he "fully understood" that he was standing on the stage where the nomination would be accepted nearly one year later, and said it again when Baier pointed out that "experts say an independent run would almost certainly hand the race over to Democrats and likely another Clinton." Thus, boxed into a seeming act of betrayal, Trump tried to extricate himself by saying he had to respect whoever won the nomination, and that making such a double pledge *at this time* [again, emphasis added] would cede leverage without a concession to a candidate he would want to negotiate with.

TABLE 3 Selected Debate Keywords by Frequency (8/1 to 8/15/15)

Keyword	Total #GOPDebate	Total@ realDonaldTrump	Beneficiary	Search terms	Rationale
Top terms					
MAGA	178,642		DJT	"Make America Great Again" "MakeAmericaGreatAgain" "MAGA"	The slogan
Megyn Kelly	92,939	146,840	DJT	"Megyn Kelly" "MegynKelly" "@MegynKelly"	Star of the show; top confrontations and defining moments
Ronald Reagan	61,266		GOP	"RonaldReagan" "Ronald Reagan"	The party patriarch
Abortion/Pro-Life	39,824		GOP		Perennial issue
Political correctness	24,443	37,410	DJT	"Political correctness" "Politically correct" "PC"	Culture war trigger phrase
ISIS	23,757		GOP		Current issue.
Illegals and illegal immigration	19,138		DJT	"Illegals" "Illegal Immigrants" "Illegal Aliens" "Undocumented" "Illegal Immigration"	Current issue "introduced" into campaign by Trump
Obamacare	9,784		GOP		Current issue.
Business	8,380	17,004	DJT	"Business" "Businessman"	A unique selling proposition for Trump. (With Fiorina not present)
Mexico	7,960		DJT		Trump singled out for attention
Leader	7,887		GOP		Standard evaluation term for candidate debates
Sexist	5,592		DJT		Accusation against Trump
Racist	5,155		DJT		Accusation against Trump, (re: Hispanics)
Pledge	4,996		DJT		Opening gimmick of debate
Amnesty	3,980		Cruz		Immigration controversy trigger phrase
Blood	2,977	8,877	DJT		Controversy between Kelly and Trump
Tells the truth	2,091		DJT		Popular claim about Trump

22

[Terms below 2k posts]		
Sanctuary cities	1,525	Aspect of immigration issue
National security	1,425	Perennial issue; clash between Christie and Paul
Terror	1,279	Perennial issue
Entitlements	1,217	Perennial issue
Annual/ economic growth	1,149	Perennial issue
Privacy	789	Clash between Christie and Paul
Temperament	27	Charge against Trump

In jumped Rand Paul: "This is what is wrong!" Trump buys and sells politicians, the senator exclaimed, and he's hedging his bets. Trump flicked away the challenge with a wisecrack: "Well I've given *him* plenty of money." Paul, a self-branded "**different kind of Republican**," received no applause for his interjection on behalf of his party. Nor did he intervene later when Trump spoke about his campaign contributions to politicians of both parties.

A firestarter of a question block commenced under the stated rubric of electability. The three moderators endeavored to embarrass each candidate and in a few instances goad them to attack one another. When Bush's turn arose, he was asked to differentiate himself from his presidential brother and father. Alluding to the classic film "The Godfather," he bragged that he had earned the nickname "**Veto Corleone**" while Governor of Florida. This self-nickname, like Paul's slogan, generate no discernible echoes on the Twitter venues under examination.

It was Baier's turn to ask an electability question of Trump, but Kelly did instead. Following a left-handed compliment to Trump as a man beloved for speaking his mind, she elicited nervous laughter and gasps from the audience by reciting a few insults Trump had been heard levying at women. "Your Twitter account," she continued, but Trump interrupted, wise-cracking that he had insulted "only **Rosie O'Donnell**," and the laughter lightened and expanded. Kelly demurred: "No it wasn't." He conceded "Yes I'm sure it was." Kelly quoted a longer and cruder example from the Trump corpus, and asked him if that sounded "like the **temperament** of a man we should elect as president." She closed by predicting that Clinton would press this charge of vulgarity against Trump, which turned out to be the case.

Trump, his hands chopping the air in sync with his staccato cadence, replied that he didn't have time for "total **political correctness**." The country was in big trouble, we don't win anymore, we lose to **China** and **Mexico**, what I say is fun, kidding. And then he all but dared Kelly to persist:

> "And honestly Megyn, if you don't like it, I'm sorry. I've been very nice to you, although I could probably maybe not be, based on the way you have treated me. But I wouldn't do that."

This was an unprecedented exchange for a presidential debate. It crystallized sexist remarks as a test of presidential character in a race expected to conclude with a man running against a woman. Many of the other candidates auditioning for the role of opposing Clinton as Republican nominee did so by attacking her record, ideology, party, and ties to Obama. Trump alone was attacked by a Clinton proxy in the form of Megyn Kelly, a blonde lawyer with superstar television status, prosecuting a case with morally incriminating quotations. None of the other candidates invoked a celebrity outside politics, as Trump did by citing Rosie O'Donnell.

The second round dealt with immigration. Bush went first, and summarized policy positions in his book about the issue: earned legal status, reunited families, drive **economic growth**, eliminate sanctuary cities, no **amnesty**. It sounded comprehensive at the expense of ready memorability. Then Chris Wallace turned to Trump, whose words about the Mexicans that their government was sending over the border Bush had called "extraordinarily ugly." Wallace asked Trump to explain that charge face to face with Bush and share any evidence Trump said he possessed to substantiate it.

Trump began his response with the valid assertion that "if it weren't for me, you wouldn't even be talking about **illegal immigration**, Chris." Dishonest reporters didn't cover what he had said. We need a **wall**. "And I don't mind having a big beautiful door in that wall so that people can come into this country legally. But we need, Jeb, to build a wall, we need to keep illegals out. [*cheering and applause*]" Bush did not respond. Wallace reiterated his request for evidence; Trump sourced the Border Patrol. No one called him on it. Indeed, John Kasich, queried next, tacitly validated Trump's leadership in bringing the crisis to the nation's attention by crediting him with hitting a nerve in this country.

In the following debate block Kelly introduced the entwined topics of **terror, national security**, and **privacy** by pitting Paul against Christie regarding the National Security Agency's bulk collection of Americans' phone records. The longest and most heated candidate exchange of the night ensued; Kelly closed it by thanking the pair for an "interesting exchange." Next, Cruz, Bush, Walker, and Carson talked about how to stop **ISIS.**

"Gentlemen," said Bret Baier, "the next series of questions deals with **ObamaCare** and the role of the federal government." Baier tried to pin Trump on having changed his position about single-payer health care systems. Trump explained that he favored a private version; Paul interrupted again and got a similar put-down from his target: "You're having a hard time tonight," Trump riposted, earning applause.

But then, instead of heading the pair and other candidates into a discussion about health care, Baier veered away to the topic of Trump's ideological inconstancy and his donations over the years to the likes of Hillary Clinton and Nancy Pelosi. "You explained away those donations saying you did that to get business-related favors."

The debate went back into Trump's wheelhouse: money-begging politicians against him, the man who would blow up the "broken system" of favor-trading he knew oh so well. Several candidates started talking at once. Some jokingly asked Trump for money while others denied that they had ever received it from him. Pressed about what he got in return from Clinton and Pelosi, he noted that he got the former to come to his (third) wedding in exchange for his giving to a foundation that is supposed to be doing good when he didn't know it would be used "on private jets going all over the world." The implication was that Trump had successfully manipulated

Clinton in the past and could be counted on to do the same in the 2016 general election.

Following a segment pitting Christie against Huckabee on what to do about **entitlements**, Wallace charged at Trump once more: "Your companies have gone bankrupt four times and your lenders lost money, so why should you be trusted to run the nation's business? Trump said he'd "used the laws of this country just like the greatest people that you read about every day in business … and I have never gone bankrupt." In a follow-up accusation Wallace added a category of victim: "Trump Entertainment Resorts, which went bankrupt in 2009. In that case alone, lenders to your company lost over $1 billion and more than 1,100 people were laid off….Is that the way you'd run the country?"

Trump ignored the invocation of layoffs:

"First of all, these lenders aren't babies. These are total killers. These are not the nice, sweet little people that you think, OK? [*laughter and applause*] You know, I mean you're living in a world of the make-believe, Chris, you want to know the truth. [*applause*]"

As with the exchange involving Clinton and favor-trading, there was an implicit parallel for audiences to draw: what Trump did to these investors he could do to foreign investors in America and apply his business dealmaking prowess to protect the national family.

There was no "second of all." Wallace did not pursue a defense of the employee layoffs.

Several candidates bashed the Obama deal with Iran. After a break, they all opposed **abortion**. Trump was asked about his position on abortion in the context of a withering attack from Kelly:

KELLY: Even in this campaign, your critics say you often sound more like a Democrat than a Republican, calling several of your opponents on the stage things like clowns and puppets. When did you actually become a Republican? [*catcalls*]

Trump broke the fourth wall like the veteran actor he was and delivered an aside directly to the audience, telling them "I don't think they (the moderators) like me very much." He went on:

TRUMP: I'll tell you what. I've evolved on many issues over the years. And you know who else has? **Ronald Reagan** evolved on many issues. And I am pro-life.

The candidates gave largely autobiographical closing statements, which provided Trump the chance to sound two of his favorite phrases, that "We don't **win** anymore" and to correct that he would "**make America great again**."

————

The following evening, August 7, Trump phoned into CNN for a half-hour interview. He called Kelly a "lightweight" who asked "all sorts of ridiculous questions. You could see there was **blood** coming out of her eyes, blood coming out of her wherever. In my opinion, she was off base." Attributing Kelly's questions to a physical condition was the epitome of sexism. Trump added that he was thinking about not showing up for the next debate hosted by Fox, laying ground for negotiations with Fox News Chairman and CEO Roger Ailes.

Keyword Frequency Analysis

Table 3 compares the frequency of the boldfaced keywords in tweets with the event-oriented hashtag #GOPDebate.

The data show that, by far, the most popular keyword was Trump's campaign slogan. While this is hardly a surprise, the tremendous margin of volume attests to the extent of his support network at this early stage of the race.

The second highest keyword was Megyn Kelly's name. This worked to Trump's benefit since it was his exchanges with Kelly that accounted for the most compelling dramatic moments of the event, including the reference to it by Trump the night after the debate, which generated a rise in the use of the word "blood" as well. The volume is especially high associated with Trump's Twitter handle. Both the journalist and the outsider candidate crashed the party event. Their battle made the rest of the debate, including the drama-provoking electability auditions of the other candidates, seem dull by comparison.

It's worth noting in connection with the popularity of the Kelly–Trump feud as a debate topic that social media expressive attentives tweet unconstrained by any sense of obligation to performing as debate judges. In contrast to the Ballotpedia elites, focus group participants, and poll respondents, they could but were not directed to select winners and losers, much less rely on traditional criteria of evaluation. They could veer away from comparing the roster of candidates and offer comments in the context of a celebrity clash, a battle of the sexes, a tilt between journalist and politician. And they were free as well to use whatever vulgar language that passion brought to mind. This is one reason why a multiplicity of contexts should be consulted in compiling keyword lists. In social media forums for political talk, digressions, diversions, and unconventional perspectives are participant features which researchers should take pains not to convert into analytic bugs.

Third in frequency of #GOPDebate mentions was Ronald Reagan's name, a talisman for Republican candidates and party stalwarts alike. It would spark a batch of candidate efforts to associate themselves with the fortieth president in the succeeding debate, staged at his presidential library in September 2015. On this occasion, no one was favored by a Reagan coupling.

The fourth highest keyword echo was abortion, a perennial issue of concern in American politics (Lenz 2012). This also worked to no candidate's favor, absent a differentiating or dramatic invocation. The same applies to the sixth most frequently posted keyword, ISIS, and the eighth, Obamacare. There was not a lot of distance among the candidates on these issues, and no one came up with an inspiring usage.

The fifth highest keyword by volume, "political correctness," would be invoked by numerous candidates and commentators over the course of the election campaign. It served as an oblique but emotionally powerful allusion (or "dog whistle") signaling objection to encouragement of diversity by liberals. To be PC meant bending over backwards to the sensitivities of minority group views at the expense of an unappreciated and heretofore silenced white and often male majority which felt intimidated from airing grievances for fear of being called sexist or racist.

Trump did not coin the term. It served as the ironized name of a Bill Maher talk show from 1993 until 2002 ("Politically Incorrect"), and Rush Limbaugh has inveighed against it for decades (Hess 2016). However, Trump was the first and only candidate to inveigh against political correctness in this debate. He was able to do so, in classic debate fashion, as a retort. He did not use the "ugly" sexist terms first *on this show*, Kelly did by quoting him, so he was justified in his comeback. Moreover, he coupled PC with national security, arguing that it made Americans less safe from crime and terrorism.

The seventh highest keyword count, "illegal immigration," ratified Trump's claim that he brought the issue to public attention. It built upon a populist rhetoric lineage which Trump took to a coarse extreme in the context of acceptable campaign discourse.

"Business" and "Pledge" referents from other Trump skirmishes with the moderators, traded in lower but still appreciable volume with Twitter users in the #GOPDebate "market," as did the critical terms "sexist" and "racist." Only Cruz broke through into the top usage list with "amnesty," like "PC" a common term he staked out first in the debate series.

Meanwhile, "national security" "terror" "entitlements" and "economic growth," stock issue categories that were awarded debate blocks of questions and answers, did not garner significant usage by comparison. Other bold-faced terms in the recap section failed altogether in being echoed.

Without data from subsequent time periods it is unwarranted to estimate the extent of influence that accrued to Trump as a result of these Twitter echoes of his keywords. But the rhetoric-response phenomenon is on display.

By turning to the sample pulls, we can see techniques Trump used almost exclusively among the candidates to market his campaign brand. We can also see ways that debate consumers responded there. Since I was looking for techniques, I inspected examples from both marketplace venues, #GOPDebate and @realDonaldTrump.

Pre-Debate Content: Pumping a "Trump Vs. the Politicians" Showdown

As it was before social media, the underlying strategic goal of pre-event tweeters is to frame the debate in a manner that can build public understanding from a perspective favorable to their views. Understanding encompasses expectations of performance, appreciation of stakes, issue priorities and positions, and ways of expressing support.

Among the tweets sporting the #GOPDebate hashtag the week before the event was one from Forward.Us. (@FWD.us), a pro-immigration advocacy group founded in 2013 by high-tech titans including John Doerr, Bill Gates, Reid Hoffmann, and Mark Zuckerberg. On August 5 Forward.us tweeted that:

> We're excited to launch 2 new tools – just in time for the #GOPDebate: bit.ly/1OQx4SK #Election2016.

The "Presidential Candidate Tracker" enabled users to track quotes in real-time. The "GOP Future" tool allowed them to adjust Latino, Asian American, African American, and White support levels for a party nominee state by state in a simulation of the Electoral College outcome. These facilitated civics knowledge but not political action. The tweet garnered one retweet and one like.

Trump benefited from promotional assistance provided by media allies such as Sean Hannity of Fox and Breitbart News. They trumpeted the front-runner and themselves simultaneously:

> "The #GOPDebate is tomorrow and all eyes will be on front-runner @realDonaldTrump. We discuss NOW on #Hannity!" RT @BreitbartNews EXCLUSIVE @realDonaldTrump tells #Breitbart he hopes #GOPDebate stays on high level but will go negative if attacked."

The Breitbart tweet prepared debate viewers to expect a fight and for Trump to assume the role of a reluctant but invariably triumphant participant. That conforms with traditional constructs of leaders as alpha males.

Trump supporters on Twitter not only waited for a fight but knew what it would be about. Austin Anderson, a junior at Montana State, echoed awareness of the populist contrast Trump would state and enact:

> I'm super excited to see @realDonaldTrump versus the politicians in the #GOPDebate on Thursday.

Trump advanced that frame with this popular (6524 retweets, 9642 likes) dollop of sarcasm directed at his competition on August 2:

> I wish good luck to all of the Republican candidates that traveled to California to beg for money etc. from the Koch Brothers. Puppets?

Trump often retweeted tributes he received, a tactic three political scientists confirmed as associated with populism (Crigler, Just, and Hua 2016). On July 31 Trump bestowed a garland of Twitter fame onto a poster whose tribute to him was consistent with the campaign's one-against-many marketing frame:

> @blindtothetruth Trump is polling well because he speaks his mind. Not like some of the career politicians he's running against. Cowards. [941 retweets, 2029 likes]

This portrayed the candidate as the people's truth-teller waging a successful battle against cowards.

There was heavy retweeting in the @realDonaldTrump sample of a strange post quoting the Rolling Stones song "It's Only Rock and Roll But I Like It." Trump used Stones songs at rallies; perhaps this was an online equivalent, a way to psych up readers.

None of the tweets in the #GOPDebate sample supporting other candidates and opposing Trump used these techniques of allying with sympathetic media channels, framing the upcoming debate as a one-against-many populist battle against career politicians, and featuring validating tweets sent to the candidate's Twitter handle. Instead, they tended to take the form of news releases.

Debate and Spin Day Content: Trump's Top Challenger Turns Out to be Kelly

As the second column of Table 2 makes plain, Trump's confrontational exchanges with Megyn Kelly evoked many Twitter responses. Many of these matched the emotional intensity of the debate combatants. One tweeter, posting while watching, wrote that "Megan [sic] angrier than Rosie on a diet," referencing O'Donnell. A man from the state of Georgia oared against the tide:

> Trump is so angry. While we're doing the Ronald Reagan comparisons, it's worth noting that Reagan was *never* this angry. Ever.

Another, following Trump's lead, sought to counter the verdict of a televised convener of an instant focus group:

> RT @realDonaldTrump "@FrankLuntz: I'm getting a lot of @MegynKelly hatemail tonight. ?? #GOPDebate" She is totally overrated and angry. She really bombed tonite.

None of the other candidates had mentioned, much less attacked, a celebrity outside the domain of politics in the debate. Jeb's relationship with his father and brother did not come into play.

Numerous candidates received tweet plaudits and staked victory claims at #GOPDebate. Yet few included campaign Twitter handles or chimed campaign themes. Instead, in brick-and-mortar spin room fashion, they cited polls and news sources in a neutral tone of voice. It was noted, for example, that NRO (*National Review Online*) declared Carly Fiorina the winner of both debates. Another pointed out that *USA Today* praised Mike Huckabee's closing statement. Favorably quoted sound bites surfaced on behalf of Ted Cruz (a consistent conservative), Ben Carson (the skin doesn't make them who they are), Fiorina (not close to the Clintons like Trump), Huckabee (the purpose of the military is to break things and kill people), John Kasich (America is a miracle country), Rand Paul (we need to quit sending money to countries that hate us), Scott Walker (people not the government create jobs) and Jeb Bush (they called me Veto Corleone). But sound bites are not hashtagged slogans, persuasion frames, exclamatory cheers, or replays of defining moment drop-mic comebacks.

Trump's social media director Dan Scavino Jr. was the only named spin-meister in the sample. At 4:37 am eastern time the morning after the debate, in a model of fervent concision, Scavino posted results from three instant polls to declare Trump the winner, adding the Trump twitter handle after each count of participants:

> #GOPDebate Winner! Drudge 50% (187K) @realDonaldTrump TIME 46% (25K) @realDonaldTrump FOXSD 49% @realDonaldTrump [1800 retweets, 2200 likes]

The tweet included a screen shot (which, by Twitter rules, do not count against character counts) of the *Time* poll. Unbound by survey research conventions, Scavino did not point out that all three polls were self-selected. But then, Twitter posts are tabulations of a self-selected universe as well, and presidential debates have no institutionalized standards of judgment.

Trump supporters rose to their candidate's defense at #GOPDebate. For example, while Trump did not stand out from the panel in opposing abortion, several tweeters called attention to the fact that Trump was "the only one who mentioned the killing of Christians overseas tonight," including

Kristan Hawkins, President of Students for Life of America (studentsforlife. org), "Abortion Abolitionist," with 3700 followers. Trump's weak response to Chris Wallace's insistence that he substantiate his claim about Mexican illegals inspired a RT from @WarriorsHart444, a closed-to-the-public Twitter page with 11,000 followers. It referred the curious to an August 5 story in *The Daily Caller*: "Illegal Alien Arrested Four Times in Two Years Allegedly Beat California Woman with Hammer, Raped Her."

More "proof positive" emerged as tweeters posted a photo of the Clintons and Trumps from the wedding Trump mentioned in his discussion of campaign contributions. The photo, very common across media channels, showed all four people smiling; now, in the context of the debate, the smiles could be seen as an implicit sign of Trump's dominance over the Clintons and other purchasable politicians.

On occasion Trump defenders sparred with skeptics. When "4Q2" addressed Trump, Kelly, FoxNews, "WYVeteran" and "ElvisFever" to ask "where's your evidence that the Mexican Govt is sending illegal immigrants," "Rosemary" shot back "Where is your proof that it is not happening."

Post-Debate Content: Celebrity Business

By August 8 #GOPDebate tweeters could take recourse to the first wave of statistically significant survey research results and attendant punditry. But these went mostly unused at least in this location, where posters declined sharply in number. I did not see any claims that Trump had peaked or become unstoppable. Instead, the focus in this small section lingered on imagined and intimated next rounds in the feud between Trump and Kelly. "Can somebody send me the link." asked one, "to keep @megynkelly from ever doing any Debates @FoxNews #petition @realDonaldTrump." A secondary topic was the success of Carly Fiorina among second-tier participants. Trump's own tweets played off both story lines, and reprised the motifs of reluctant gunslinger and populist crusader sounded in his big debate moments.

Supporters echoed him. On #ThePatriot143, with 105K followers, Cris posted a screen shot of an ABC news take-out of Trump's quote about sparking the immigration discussion. A couple of commenters demurred, saying Santorum and Cruz spoke about it first. But as another put it, Trump said it the loudest.

By August 11, the MAGA hat was on sale in the campaign shop, "selling fast!" 978 RTs.

Scavino posted a thirteen-second clip of Trump on *Oprah* in 1988, saying he'd run for president if things got real bad:

RT @DanScavino 1988 @realDonaldTrump told @Oprah (36 million followers), he would not rule out a run for #POTUS, if it got really bad! He held to his word.

This celebrity back story depicted Trump on an heroic national rescue mission. Tweeters compared him to Clint Eastwood, "not scared of American terrorists." Trump recycled a plaudit for him as businessman, and that reverberated among expressives: "RT @felberjosh 5 Things #DonaldTrump Can Teach #Entrepreneurs About Success #JoshFelber.com @realDonaldTrump"

DISCUSSION

The evidence presented here confirms that event-tagged spaces on Twitter balloon with posts which include marketplace-like pitches and reactions emblematic of competitions to define of a rhetorical situation. At #GOPDebate during early August 2015 Trump-centric content dominated among Twitter writers and readers. Trump and his social media director cultivated support, and Trump supporters rose to their spurs, lures, and entreaties. Together they prevailed in this space as celebrity, agents, and fans unified as outsiders against insiders.

The sampled tweets from #GOPDebate and @realDonaldTrump illustrate several sales and purchasing techniques in play. The campaign and candidate relied on:

1. *Celebrity feuding.* When Trump engaged in hostile communication with Megyn Kelly and mentioned Rosie O'Donnell, that caught the eyes of their large Twitter followings and made news. Styled as a feud instead of a single exchange sowed expectations of further retorts, which occurred spectacularly the following night and beyond.
2. *Media ally callouts.* Trump and Scavino cited and communicated with favorable news outlets in their tweeting. This validated their debate interpretations and put dissenters on notice to audiences enlarged through hyperlinked references.
3. *Featured fan comments.* Retweeting favorable if not outright fawning comments from the people reinforced the claim to a populist mantle.
4. *Blunt vernacular.* Tweeting in a conversational voice, as contrasted with the disembodied voice of a news release and the stentorian tone of a formal debater, reinforced the populist theme while encouraging responses in kind.
5. *Confrontational branding.* Trump and Scavino constantly depicted the candidate as ready to fight against a corrupt and double-talking establishment which had drained American greatness for its own purposes. Their exclamatory messaging took to an extreme the conventional candidate strategy of accentuating contrasts in order to advance a unique selling proposition.

In response, supporters tweeted Trump's name, his Twitter address, and his hashtagged campaign slogan in much higher volume than the other candidates, as Tables 1 and 2 document. They repeated keywords favorable to his cause well out of proportion to words favoring his competition and the party as a whole, as evident in Table 3. The samples are rife with imitative behavior: respondents scrapping with critics, supplying citations in support of Trump's contested claims, and amping up the enthusiasm and anger he displayed both in the debate and online.

In keeping with P2, this helps explain how the self-styled party crasher, the verbal scourge of establishment politicians, retained his lead in the polls despite debate moments that in earlier cycles would have triggered a drop in the standing of his candidacy. The social media volume and content quickly made clear that Trump was not going to be a flash in the pan like Cain, Gingrich, or Bachmann. After the first debate, cable began carrying his rallies live, his tweets were read on the air, he was allowed to participate in interviews by phone (Kranish and Fisher 2016). The issue positions he brought to the fore, tighter border controls and revamped trade as means to national restoration and job recovery, remained as potent as they were distinctive. Economic growth and religious liberty receded from relevance as issues. The echoes affirmed the campaign's depiction of Trump as an aggressive leader who would bring business smarts to the presidency. To be sure, both Trump's signature issue and melodramatic persona generated intense opposition as well at #GOPDebate. But as he advised in *The Art of the Deal*, bad PR is still PR. This seems especially so when attention-grabbing matters, as it did in the opening interactive phase of a battle to land the lion's share of first impressions among a swollen roster of candidates.

CONCLUSION

Social media have altered the structure and environment of campaigning by giving unaccredited people (including purveyors of bots) a means to register feedback before a public audience. Debate judgments now range across a larger and broader population. This expansion contributed to the upset result of the first GOP debate of the 2016 campaign: the showiest candidate won despite –even on the strength of– being a Joker-type provocateur.

I have relied on the metaphor of a political marketplace to include social media debate comments along with the traditional verdicts of journalists, party elites, and polls. Such a marketplace resembles a regular marketplace in that consumers choose among products vended by sales agents. The product is rhetoric, words and images intended to convince people that the world in which they live would be improved were they to agree to see it as depicted. In this metaphorical context, echoing an agent's keywords on Twitter represents a down payment toward his or her success in the depiction competition. The selected @ and # spaces are agoras where transactions occur in common view.

Detecting politically significant responses to campaigns in social media requires careful and transparent filtering of what surfaces there. Much of social media content nominally about politics consists of trivial chatter, from an influence perspective. Comments of the "did you hear/see that" variety matters to those engaged in it (Papacharissi 2015), but not as part of the competition to define the world at large in terms of character, issues and process. At the same time, as noted earlier, some pertinent comments about politics originate in a broader context than conventional rules and norms of an event suggest. Multicontext-sensitive keyword selection supplies a filter that can screen out those tweets which are the textual equivalent of nodding, cheering, booing, and chanting, while retaining those which may figure into attention-getting, persuasion, and mobilization. The method in use for this essay constitutes a systematic and replicable means of word-into-keyword filtration.

The method can be enriched. Investigators can analyze tabulations of likes and photos along with mentions and sample content. Sentiment analysis may pan out as a useful metric, too with the help of natural language processing and external coding validation of how positive, negative, and neutral valances are assigned. Properties of social media voices can be identified in the aggregate, preserving personal privacy; the most salient identifications would be party, voting record, and voting location, which is to say the data in public voter files. A long-term goal would entail the construction and testing of a unit of influence that accounts, roughly but equivalently, for changes in audience brand recognitions, resource contributions, and situation readings –in other words, the comparative extent of campaign success in achieving name recognition, support mobilization (money and volunteers), and persuasion. With such a unit we could institutionalize social listening as a full-fledged method of political research integratable with surveys, focus groups, dial-response, and experimental testing, and amenable to predictive and historical modeling. In the meantime, the method at hand enables us to tell fuller stories of campaign marketing with the Twitter response data we have.

The framework and method deployed in this study can be applied to a series of debates, and to an entire campaign process. As this occurs, the potency of certain techniques and responses may change as the number of contestants declines and persuasion and mobilization become more urgent than name recognition. The approach may also be adapting to the study of other types of political events: protests, trials, hearings, summits, policymaking. Today Twitter responses to rhetoric are aspects of all of these processes.

In 1987, when Donald Trump published and promoted The Art of the Deal, much of the pre-primary stage of presidential campaigning that he was considering entering was indeed not visible to many people. Nearly three decades later, Trump tested a contention from that book before a broader and more variegated audience; as reproduced in the first epigraph to this article, he posited that even critical news coverage was a boon to business. That testing is exemplified in the second epigraph: a Tweet chiding Fox for resisting his spin of the debate as a victory. He was able to proclaim his judgment and call out the network in public by himself, in fewer than 140 characters, and then see results in the form of retweets and likes, all for free. The social media marketplace for politics is a remarkable development.

ACKNOWLEDGMENTS

I am grateful to Dr. Michael D. Cohen for advice and assistance in the data compilation and interpretation. This research was funded in part through a bequest from Mark R. Shenkman.

REFERENCES

Barnes, J. A. 2015. "Ballotpedia's Insiders Poll." August 7, 2015. Ballotpedia.org.

Benoit, W. L. 2015. *Accounts, Excuses, and Apologies: Image Repair Theory and Research*. 2nd ed. Albany, NY: SUNY Press.

Bitzer, L. F. 1992. "The Rhetorical Situation." *Philosophy & Rhetoric* 25:1. Originally published in 1968.

Bonikowski, B., and N. Gidron. 2016. "The Populist Style in American Politics: Presidential Campaign Discourse, 1952–1996." *Social Forces* 94 (4):1593–1621. doi:10.1093/sf/sov120

Chadwick, A. 2013. *The Hybrid Media System: Politics and Power*. New York: Oxford.

Clayman, S. E. 1995. "Defining Moments, Presidential Debates, and the Dynamics of Quotability." *Journal of Communication* 45 (3):118–46. doi:10.1111/j.1460-2466.1995.tb00746.x

Crigler, A., M. Just, and W. Hua. 2016. "Populist Disruption: Sanders and Trump Tweets in the 2016 US Presidential Primaries." Paper prepared for presentation at the annual meeting of the American Political Science Association, Philadelphia PA.

Cwalina, W., A. Falkowski, and B. I. Newman. 2011. *Political Marketing: Theoretical and Strategic Foundations*. Armonk, NY: M.E. Sharpe.

Danner, M. 2016. "The Real Trump." New York Review of Books, December 22, 2016.

D'Antonio, M. 2015. *Never Enough: Donald Trump and the Pursuit of Success*. New York: St. Martin's.

Hadley, A. T. 1976. *The Invisible Primary: The Inside Story of the Other Presidential Race: The Making of the Candidate*. Englewood Cliffs, NJ: Prentice-Hall.

Harvey, K. 2014. "Introduction." In *Encyclopedia of Social Media and Politics*, edited by K. Harvey, Xxxv. Los Angeles: Sage.

Hess, A. 2016. "How Political Correctness Went From Punch Line to Panic." New York Times Magazine, July 24, 2016.

Jamieson, K. H., and D. H. Birdsell. 1990. *Presidential Debates: The Challenge of Creating an Informed Electorate*. New York: Oxford.

Johnson, D. W. 2017. *Democracy for Hire: A History of American Political Consulting*. New York: Oxford.

Jorgensen, C., C. Koch, and L. Rorbech. 1998. "Rhetoric That Shifts Votes: An Exploratory Study of Persuasion in Issue-Oriented Public Debates." *Political Communication* 15:283–99. doi:10.1080/105846098198902

Kondik, K., and G. Skelley. 2015. "Eight Decades of Debate: A brief history of presidential primary clashes." Sabato's Crystal Ball, July 30th, 2015. Centerforpolitics.org.

Kranish, M., and M. Fisher. 2016. *Trump Revealed: An American Journey of Ambition, Ego, Money and Power*. New York: Scribner.

Lenz, G. S. 2012. *Follow the Leader? How Voters Respond to Politicians' Policies and Performance*. Chicago: Univeristy of Chicago.

Patterson, T. 1993. *Out of Order*. New York: Knopf.

Papacharissi, Z. 2015. *Affective Publics: Sentiment, Technology, and Politics*. New York: Oxford University Press, p. 71.

Polsby, N. W., and A. Wildavsky. 1984. *Presidential Elections: Strategies of American Electoral Politics*. 6th ed. New York: Scribner's.

Ricke, L. 2014. "Debates." In *Encyclopedia of Social Media and Politics*, edited by K. Harvey and K. Harvey, 353–55. Los Angeles: Sage.

Schroeder, A. 2008. *Presidential Debates: Forty Years of High-Risk TV*. New York: Columbia.

Trent, J. S., and R. V. Friedenberg. 2008. *Political Campaign Communication: Principles & Practices*. 6th ed. Lanham, MD: Rowman & Littlefield.

Vogel, K. 2015. "Koch Brothers Summon Bush, Cruz, Rubio, and Walker to SoCal Confab." Politico, July 25, 2015. Note how the headline writer excluded the non-officeholding non-male Fiorina.

Understanding the Social Media Strategies of U.S. Primary Candidates

JOSEPH (JUN HYUN) RYOO and NEIL BENDLE

This paper examines the social media strategies of candidates seeking their party's nomination for the 2016 U.S. presidential election. We use textual analysis to understand what candidates focused on. We assess eight themes covered in Twitter posts. For example, Clinton focused on GUN CONTROL, while Sanders focused on climate change. Using Facebook data, we introduce a topic modeling approach, latent Dirichlet allocation, to the political marketing literature. This allows us to uncover what topics the candidates focus on without researcher intervention and, using a dynamic model, show how this changes over time. We note that Clinton's focus on Trump increases toward the end of the primary campaign.

The U.S. primary system is a fascinating example of political choice (Johnson 2006; Bendle and Nastasoiu 2014). Intraparty bickering, which elsewhere occurs behind closed doors, e.g., UK parliamentary selections, plays out in the midst of massive media interest. Theoretically, U.S. primaries are fascinating—candidates have personal styles and ideas sometimes quite distinct from the party they seek to represent, causing potential headaches for party management (Bendle, Ryoo, and Nastasoiu 2017). Largely absent is central control over the party brand (Scammell 1999; Knuckey and Lees-Marshment 2005; Marland 2016). Donald Trump, in particular, used

Color versions of one or more of the figures in the article can be found online at www.tandfonline.com/wplm.

the direct access Twitter allowed him to bypass his party's establishment (Heffernan 2016).

Primaries have a vital role in intraparty competition (Teorell 1999), bringing fissures into the open. Candidates can take their own positions free from party whips or policy platforms, allowing for a unique interplay between policy pronouncements and communications strategy. This makes the topics candidates choose to focus on enlightening about the concerns of the candidate and what the public is thought to care about (Bendle and Cotte 2016). Past research suggests that what a candidate talks about is a key strategic decision (Bendle 2014). A candidate must gain the public's interest, often by saying newsworthy things, but do this while not giving hostages in case they should win. The idea of pivoting and changing policy between the primary and general election, the logical application of the median voter theorem (Hotelling 1929; Downs 1957), is fraught with danger (Bendle, Ryoo, and Nastasoiu 2017). In this work, we analyze the themes/topics in primary candidate pronouncements to see what candidates chose to address. An especially interesting aspect of primary campaign strategies are their dynamic nature. Momentum matters, and bandwagon effects can impact campaign success (Abramowitz 1989; Abramson et al. 1992). Our topic modeling approach allows us to see how the messages sent by the candidates change over time.

Our broad research questions are thus as follows:

1. Which topics/themes do candidates choose to focus on in the primary?
2. How does the focus change over time, including when they cease to be candidates?

This research is possible because of changes in the way campaigns are conducted. The Internet is now central to campaign strategy and we look at two widely used social media platforms. Our first medium, Twitter, encourages pithy (140 characters or fewer) communications direct to millions of followers at, essentially, no variable cost per tweet (Jackson and Lilleker 2011; Aharony 2012; Conway, Kenski, and Wang 2013; Bode and Dalrymple 2015). Our second medium, Facebook, accepts lengthier messages while also allowing access to voters unfiltered by the traditional media. Done especially well, or especially badly, social media earn traditional media mentions. For example, Donald Trump's controversial tweets about the other candidates, debate moderators, and even the Pope, garnered widespread television and newspaper coverage (Lee and Quealy 2016). Social media allow for greater interactivity, but is this what we see (Stromer-Galley 2000a, 2000b)?

Traditionally, political marketing research uses case studies (Miller 2013), interviews (Parsons and Rowling 2015), and manual coding (Graham et al. 2013). We advance political marketing by employing both supervised text mining and automated topic modeling. Our key methodological contribution is the use of dynamic latent Dirichlet allocation (LDA). This allows us to understand candidate communications strategies and the differences between these (Pfau 1988; Enli and Skogerbø 2013). We assess which topics are relatively popular with each candidate by comparing the popularity of terms within a given candidate's postings against the popularity of terms in the entire corpus of all the candidates' postings. In examining social media messages, we see what the campaigns think is important to communicate with the voters.

OUR DATA

We text-analyze the candidates' Twitter feeds and Facebook messages. We used Twitter to assess the themes in candidates' messages using a supervised process focusing on a predetermined list of themes. For the Facebook data, we used a more advanced dynamic topic modeling technique. This method could be more effectively applied to the Facebook data given the lengthier messages used on this social medium.

Twitter

We captured the Twitter activity of six candidates for the nomination of the two major U.S. political parties, that is, Republicans and Democrats, from January 25 to May 4, 2016. January 25 was chosen as it is the first full day of trading on the Iowa Electronic Markets and a week before the first vote of the primary season. The final date, May 4, is when John Kasich, Donald Trump's last rival in the Republican primary, suspended his campaign, in effect conceding Trump's victory. At this point, while there were still states to vote, it also seemed nearly certain that Hillary Clinton had secured the Democratic nomination.

We look at the Twitter feeds of candidates who have their own contract price on the Iowa Electronic Markets. This is a prediction market where people can effectively bet on the winner and has been shown to have good predictive properties (Berg, Nelson, and Rietz 2008). The candidates we choose were seen by the market makers as being relatively likely to secure the nomination, which allows us to focus on stronger candidates. Selecting the two Democrats—Hillary Clinton, the eventual winner, and Bernie Sanders, her main rival—would have been a relatively easy choice after the vice-president, Joe Biden, declared that he was not running (Collinson 2015). The Republican primary was more uncertain, but by January 2016 several initially plausible candidates appeared very unlikely to win, for example, Jeb Bush, the early favorite (Leonhardt 2016). John Kasich did not have a contract price but his campaign never seemed to have a plausible path to victory through the votes of rank-and-file Republicans. (He won only his home state of Ohio.) The four Republican candidates with contract prices, that is, plausible winners, were Donald Trump (the eventual winner), Ted Cruz, Ben Carson, and Marco Rubio.

Candidates have differing numbers of Twitter accounts. For example, while Donald Trump had one Twitter handle (@realDonaldTrump) at the time of data collection, Marco Rubio had two (@marcorubio and @SenRubioPress). We collected data only from the candidate handles (i.e., @marcorubio), which generally have the most followers. The keyword analysis is sensitive to the absolute frequency of words and so we wanted to use the same number of handles for each candidate. We assumed that the messages tweeted by the candidate handle should be representative of the candidates' campaign messaging on social media, whereas governmental handles have wider aims (e.g., including constituent engagement).

Our data collection process involved using the R program and REST APIs. These are programming interfaces that are publicly available to Twitter developers but impose a maximum search limit of the 3,200 most recent tweets per profile. To avoid missing tweets, we capture data at regular discrete intervals. Even so, our data do omit a small number of tweets posted, and deleted, between collections. While this is a possible source of bias, tweet deletion is relatively rare and should not overly impact our analysis of the entire corpus.

The basic descriptive data (Vergeer, Hermans, and Sams 2011; Table 1) show each candidate's Twitter activity. Ted Cruz was the most active, followed by Bernie Sanders. Cruz specialized in pithy tweets, but Sanders

TABLE 1 Descriptive Data: Candidate Twitter Use

	Democrats		Republicans			
	Hillary Clinton	Bernie Sanders	Ben Carson	Ted Cruz	Marco Rubio	Donald Trump
Number of followers~	6,112,796	2,092,378	1,311,590	1,089,765	1,350,812	7,908,579
Total tweets~	5,456	8,285	3,031	16,571	5,426	31,830
Date joined Twitter	April 2013	November 2010	February 2013	March 2009	August 2008	March 2009
Suspended campaign	NA	NA	March 4th	May 3rd	March 15th	NA
Tweets in our data	1,865	2396	539	3512	884	1406
Tweets per day^ (101 days in data)	18	24	5	34.8	9	14
Words in our data*	16,327	21,510	4,486	22,408	6,558	11,885
Words per tweet	8.75	8.98	8.32	6.38	7.42	8.45
Standard deviation	3.17	3.14	3.41	3.17	2.68	4.25
% of tweets original content	81%	67%	71%	35%	69%	96%

Note. ^Includes period after suspending campaign for Rubio, Carson, and Cruz. *After removing URLs, non-words, and stop words (uninformative words, e.g., "the") ~as of May 4, 2016; data accessed using http://www.trackalytics.com/.

TABLE 2 Descriptive Data: Candidate Facebook Use

Candidate	Number of posts	Words published	Words/ post	Standard deviation	No. of fans of page on 07/12/2016 from track analytics	Posts/day	% as status	% as links	% as photos	% as videos
Bush	672	10,476	15.59	13.19	Missing	4.80	4%	31%	20%	46%
Carson	1,144	40,520	35.42	60.36	Missing	4.83	25%	28%	30%	17%
Christie	515	6,224	12.09	19.25	Missing	4.52	3%	23%	31%	43%
Clinton	2,196	44,511	20.27	26.23	4,367,915	8.01	3%	38%	30%	29%
Cruz	1,483	25,728	17.35	26.96	2,135,738	6.62	3%	46%	21%	30%
Fiorina	348	17,310	49.74	62.61	Missing	2.10	13%	24%	15%	48%
Huckabee	1,456	80,978	55.62	65.68	1,957,611	5.52	16%	67%	10%	7%
Kasich	1,150	20,604	17.92	12.03	Missing	4.73	6%	24%	42%	28%
O'Malley	136	3,368	24.76	23.11	Missing	1.53	10%	32%	23%	33%
Paul	1,302	31,767	24.40	35.21	2,145,374	5.07	7%	39%	26%	28%
Rubio	435	7,959	18.30	15.92	1,383,668	3.78	4%	56%	11%	29%
Sanders	1,321	40,582	30.72	27.13	4,393,366	4.84	7%	29%	39%	23%
Santorum	311	6,749	21.70	29.90	Missing	2.47	5%	46%	23%	25%
Trump	1,917	39,756	20.74	32.68	Missing	7.10	25%	20%	41%	13%

tweeted most words per message. Ben Carson was the first of these candidates to drop out, and his activity dried up as his campaign petered out.

Facebook

Facebook data of the political candidates were captured from October 13, 2015, to July 12, 2016, and includes a total of 14,386 posts for 376,532 words. The Democratic primary contest lasted the longest, so we focus on dates relevant to that contest to assess the online activity of candidates. The first Democratic primary debate was held on October 13, 2015, and Sanders publicly endorsed Hilary Clinton for president on July 12, 2016.

We deliberately analyzed a wider range of candidates in our Facebook data, compared to our Twitter data, including many candidates who made little impression on the results of the primary. The candidates we analyzed include all Republicans invited to their first debate of 2016, the Fox Business debate, which included both a main and a secondary debate. Our full list of candidates consists of Jeb Bush, Ben Carson, Chris Christie, Hillary Clinton, Ted Cruz, Carly Fiorina, Mike Huckabee, John Kasich, Martin O'Malley, Rand Paul, Marco Rubio, Bernie Sanders, Rick Santorum, and Donald Trump.

The data were collected using commercially available software from Next Analytics. The multipurpose software is licensed and enables the user to scrape data across a variety of social media platforms, such as Twitter, Facebook, and Instagram. We used this to scrape publicly available Facebook posts of a given public page (the posts are either status, event, link, photo, or video) and their associated details, such as time stamps, type of post, and reaction counts.

Public posts within our initially specified time window were scraped from each of the candidates' Facebook pages that were verified by Facebook as officially associated to the public figure (the page name is marked by a blue checkmark). Table 2 shows the descriptive data.

SOCIAL MEDIA STRATEGY

Modern political marketing (O'Cass 1996; Lees-Marshment 2001a, 2001b, 2004, 2009; Marland, Giasson, and Lees-Marshment 2012) has been criticized as advocating strategic repositioning in response to voter preferences (O'Shaughnessy 2001; Savigny 2008). Yet in many ways the old-fashioned idea of the selling of political candidates (McGinniss 1988) is alive and well on social media; our candidates speak at least as much as they listen. Television-age candidates seem to have transferred their top-down communi-cation approaches to social media. Social media hold the promise of genuine interactivity (Lilleker and Jackson 2010), but our evidence suggests that this is yet to be fully embraced (Stromer-Galley 2000a, 2000b). Despite recycling others' material being Twitter's most common relational activity (Cook 2016), primary candidates favored broadcasting their own messages, see Table 1, presumably because original tweets give more control over content. Ted Cruz is the only candidate to retweet other peoples' content more than producing his own tweets. Adopting a sales orientation seems true even of reality-television star, and arguably the first "Twitter candidate," Donald Trump.

From the level of activity, we can theorize about the attention that candidates pay to social media. The Democrats, Clinton and Sanders, posted regularly on Facebook and saw a relatively high level of activity that lessened somewhat over time. In line with theoretical advice (Abramowitz 1989; Abramson et al. 1992), Sanders' supporters continued to emphasize that he could win, but as time passed it became harder to mathematically support a Sanders victory. The lessening of activity may represent intensity draining from the campaign.

The most obvious feature of the social media data is the precipitous fall in activity of candidates leaving the race, with the notable exception of Mike Huckabee. (For campaign funding reasons, leaving the race is formally described as "suspending" the campaign.) When a candidate drops out they typically take drastic actions to reduce campaign spending, and staff who manage social media are likely to find themselves out of a job.

To understand tweeting style, we checked the number of words in Tweets and found that those generated by Donald Trump have a noticeably higher variance compared to those of the other candidates; see the descriptive data in Table 1. Levene's test failed to reject that the variances for Clinton, Sanders, Cruz, and Carson are equal. The variance of words in Trump's tweets was significantly higher (<.001), while Rubio's was significantly less (<.001), compared to the other four candidates. The higher variance for Trump may be evidence of a more engaging and varied Twitter style. Alternatively, it may suggest multiple writers with unique approaches, including Trump himself, managing the Twitter account with limited overall style control. Supporting the latter suggestion, on June 20 Donald Trump's campaign manager changed and the press noticed a more unified voice to Trump's tweets (Berenson 2016). Our data end on May 4, 2016, so we leave it to future research to explore this suggestion.

UNDERSTANDING THE THEMES IN CANDIDATES' TWITTER DATA

A key element of analyzing any text, such as tweets, is removing uninformative characters. These include URLs, characters that do not form words, and stop words. Stop words are common and uninformative words present in nearly all writing that do not distinguish between texts. These include words such as "the" and "and." Lists of stop words are provided by commonly available text-mining packages for R. We used the 'tm' package, which accesses the dictionary provided by the *Journal of Machine Learning Research* (Lewis et al. 2004). Our text cleaning leaves us with a list of words but no grammatical structure. As we lose the order of the words in a tweet, such approaches are often referred to as analyzing a "bag of words," as compared to analyzing text with a beginning, middle, and end.

Candidates might actively manage what they talk about in an attempt to nudge the political agenda (Sayre et al. 2010), what the public thinks matters to other people (Mutz 1989), or what the media covers (Shapiro and Hemphill 2016). To see what the candidates discuss on Twitter we used what is known as a supervised process. We drew up a short list of the election's eight major themes from a *New York Times* article (Andrews and Kaplan 2015; we modified "Syrian refugees" to "Syria"). For each theme—immigration, gun control, climate change, Syria, health care, abortion, death penalty, and taxes—we developed a list of associated words. Our R code searched 2,000 of the latest public tweets in live time that contained both the theme and "America." We gathered lists of words especially likely to be found in these tweets after removing words common to all tweets, e.g., "NRA" was especially likely to appear only in gun control–themed tweets. From this list, we manually selected six to nine words commonly associated with each theme, see Table 3.

We recorded mentions of these "associated" words in each candidate's tweets. Mentions were then grouped into months and divided by the total words tweeted by each candidate that month. This procedure yielded rough estimates for a candidate's focus upon a specific theme in the given month. Figure 1 shows the themes that each candidate focused on.

Both Democrats focused heavily on words associated with health care, this being an important theme to them and perhaps less so to the Republicans. This is interesting because the theme is one which the Republicans had campaigned on heavily since Obamacare/the Affordable Care Act was passed in 2010. We do not have previous data to compare to

TABLE 3 Topics and Words Associated With Each Topic

Topics	Words associated with topic
Immigration	Immigration, Islamic, Muslim, illegal, immigrant, immigrants, Mexican, border
Gun control	Gun control, guns, rifle, NRA, shooting, violence, amendment
Climate change	Climate change, fracking, energy, ice, fuel, gas
Syria	Syria, Syrian refugee, terrorist, terrorism, terrorists, ISIS, crisis, Islam
Health care	Health care, insurance, Obamacare, health, social, policy
Abortion	Abortion, parenthood, prolife, prochoice, reproductive, right
Death penalty	Death penalty, capital punishment, innocent, trial, justice, murder
Taxes	Tax, taxes, offshore, evading, business, money, rich, economy, jobs

Note. The dictionary of terms is chosen by the researchers prior to the analysis (supervised method).

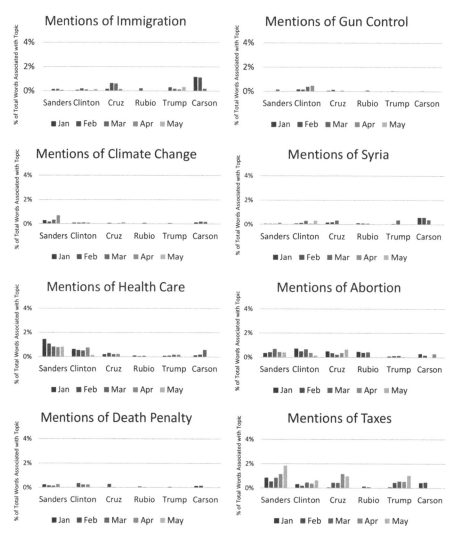

FIGURE 1 Candidate focus on topics on Twitter (supervised method).

but one conjecture is that the Republicans may have been slightly shifting their focus away from health care this cycle.

We can see differences between the candidates within a party. Hillary Clinton seems to have focused more on gun control compared to Bernie Sanders, who spoke more about climate change, despite both of these topics being important to Democrats. Ben Carson, arguably the most atypical candidate, seemed especially willing to focus on sensitive and contentious themes that were relatively important to the Republican base such as immigration and Syria.

A notable limitation of the keyword analysis is that it treats each mention as equal in weight, measuring only the frequency of the chosen keywords. Clearly not all tweets are equally important. Furthermore, the discussion of abortion highlights further strengths and limitations. Abortion is a relatively important topic across the U.S. political spectrum and we show that all the candidates used words relevant to the topic of abortion. However, our analysis cannot reveal exactly what the candidates were saying about abortion. Sanders and Cruz seem to show similar levels of focus on this topic but, given abortion's divisive nature, they likely have said quite different things, which is not picked up. Notable is Donald Trump's relative avoidance of discussions of abortion. It is likely that Trump wanted to avoid this and focus on what he perceived as his strengths.

ANALYSIS OF FACEBOOK DATA

Given the staccato nature of tweets, we turn to Facebook data for our formal topic modeling of social media posts. Facebook's longer posts provide an advantage when using more advanced statistical procedures to extract topics mentioned by the candidates. In doing this we analyzed the Facebook feeds of fourteen candidates for their party's nomination. Figure 2 shows word clouds created from the postings of all the candidates, (after removing uninformative words; details below). Perhaps the most interesting feature is the shared focus on Trump. Both parties agree that the word "president" is key to the campaign, but Trump is not far off in usage from both sides.

Our previous analysis allowed insight into themes referred to by candidates but required the external specification of themes and the words associated with each theme. Modern text analysis allows investigations that do not require such a heavy hand from the researcher. We, therefore, turn to an unsupervised (by the researcher) process. Such processes, at the

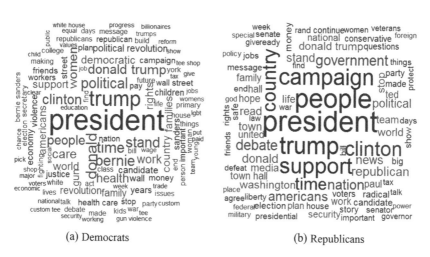

(a) Democrats   (b) Republicans

FIGURE 2 Word clouds from Facebook posts by word count.

expense of some efficiency, limit the potential for researchers' bias to impact findings.

Topic Modeling: Delving Further into Topics

To conduct this unsupervised analysis, we use a form of topic modeling called LDA (Tirunillai and Tellis 2014; Wang et al. 2015; Bendle and Wang 2016). The main advantage of this method is that it works with massive amounts of unstructured data. LDA is a procedure that uncovers the latent topics from a data set (Griffiths and Steyvers 2004) and has similarities to the principal components methods in that it extracts common underlying attributes.

LDA is part of a wider class of statistical models called topic models. These models attempt to reverse-engineer a writer's thinking. From the words used, we infer the topics the writer considered. (The precise number of topics we determine by minimizing what is known as "perplexity"; details later). To understand the intuition behind LDA, imagine that each candidate's Facebook content was generated randomly by drawing words from a given hidden structure. The LDA model assumes that each document, for example, here a Facebook post, is a mixture of the uncovered topics. The hidden structure can be represented as buckets per topic that each contain words relevant to the topic. Ted Cruz might consider a topic such as his main rival. (The model does not name the topic but we might name the topic "Trump.") When thinking of this topic, Cruz might use words like "Donald" or "Trump." The hidden structure that LDA uncovers specifies the proportions of topics, for example, how often Cruz thinks about Trump, and the likelihood that any given word in a topic is used. For example, "Donald" is used whenever Cruz considers Trump.

How does LDA uncover the hidden topic structure of the documents? The model tests all the possible hidden structures that could exist given the number of topics the analyst decides fits the data best. The model then determines the likelihood that each hidden structure could have created the data observed using the Dirichlet distribution, a distribution often used to represent estimated multivariate probabilities. The hidden structure found to have the highest probability of having created the data is then identified as being the underlying hidden structure. Note that in LDA, each unseen topic has a probability distribution over a fixed word vocabulary, so when Hillary Clinton discusses the topic that we have labeled "women rights," she might mention "rights" or "health" at a given probability. LDA estimates the length of the piece of user-generated content using a distribution of the lengths of content. This is important because Facebook posts can vary widely in length. For each post, LDA then samples from the topics and the list of words associated with that topic.

While LDA has great potential to aid research, there are a couple of key limitations to note. These include the bag of words assumption—as in our

Twitter analysis of themes, we throw out the order of words before conducting the research. Finally, while the researcher does not choose the topics, the researcher names the topics from the list of words associated with the topic so each researcher's choice of name might be different.

Number of Topics

To clean the data, we have removed stop words, URL links, hashtags, greetings (e.g., "good morning," "good night"), and time indicators (e.g., "year," "day," "week"). Also, we have used part-of-speech tagging to identify and remove uninformative words, such as personal pronouns and pre-determiners, to emphasize important words, such as nouns, verbs, and adjectives. Finally, the term frequency–inverse document frequency (or how atypical it is to use that word) was calculated for the corpus, and the bottom quartile of words were deleted.

There are many approaches to determine the optimal number of topics (Chang et al. 2009). We minimize perplexity—the trained topic model's surprise when predicting unforeseen data. The intuition is that of cross-validation in that we create a model from a subset of the data. Then, we test how well the model performs in fitting the unforeseen words from the testing data set with the uncovered topics from the training data set. For each possible number of topics, this process is repeated ten times and the average score is taken. A lower perplexity score means a better-performing model.

It is not uncommon for topics, each symbolized as a list of words, to be incomprehensible to the human researcher. Additional steps are taken to increase comprehensibility to allow the researcher to manually give a name to each topic uncovered. Such steps involve removing context-specific words (e.g., "Christmas," "birthday"), overused nouns (e.g., names of states), and unrecognizable names (e.g., "Tom") in increments and re-estimating the model.

We treat the Facebook posts of each candidate as a body of data that contains a unique set of latent topics distinct from those of the other candidates. This means that the perplexity analysis suggests different numbers of topics for each candidate. Martin O'Malley, an unsuccessful Democratic candidate (data not shown), was best described as using eight topics, while Donald Trump was best described by only three.[1]

The Topics Discussed

Next, we provide lists of topics discussed by selected major candidates in their Facebook feeds; see Table 4 for the Democrats and Table 5 for the Republicans. Comparing the results across candidates, it is interesting to note the topics. For example, Cruz has a topic dealing with the subject of radical Islam, as did Santorum (data not shown; note that we labeled the topics in

TABLE 4 Topics Discussed by Selected Democrats

Hillary Clinton		
Topic 1	Women's rights	Women, rights, care, health, shop, custom, pick
Topic 2	Trump	Trump, Donald, Donald Trump, job, trumps, plan, republican
Topic 3	Campaign	President, Clinton, campaign, bill, house, friends, making
Topic 4	People	People, country, families, Americans, time, gun, stand
Bernie Sanders		
Topic 1	Bernie	Bernie, political, political revolution, revolution, Sanders, Trump, Bernie Sanders
Topic 2	Justice	Time, family, social, justice, end, women, work
Topic 3	Democrats	President, democratic, Clinton, support, workers, world, important
Topic 4	Wall Street	Street, health, wall, stand, Wall Street, money, care

Note. In latent Dirichlet Allocation (LDA) the researcher names the topics to aid understanding. Generated by the automated procedure, LDA (unsupervised method).

TABLE 5 Topics Discussed by Selected Republicans

Ben Carson		
Topic 1	Government	Time, people, questions, government, life, question, plan
Topic 2	America	Nation, God, town, work, stand, picture, number
Topic 3	World	President, country, world, united, Americans, national, refugees
Topic 4	Carson	People, Carson, campaign, political, Ben, debate, continue
Ted Cruz		
Topic 1	Nation	People, time, stand, nation, conservatives, country, hope
Topic 2	Trump	Trump, Donald, Donald Trump, Republican, ready, debate, stop
Topic 3	Ted	Ted, campaign, conservative, support, congressman, supporting, state
Topic 4	Radical Islam	President, radical, Islamic, states, ill, united, radical Islamic
John Kasich		
Topic 1	General election	Clinton, leader, Republican, campaign, endorsement, Americans, made
Topic 2	Experience	Check, experience, case, jobs, job, election, guest
Topic 3	Messages	Town, hall, town hall, ready, time, message, show
Topic 4	Team	Team, nation, defeat, things, family, days, business
Topic 5	Support	News, support, read, country, polls, primary, volunteers
Marco Rubio		
Topic 1	Policy	People, check, country, foreign, policy, stop, conservative
Topic 2	Messages	Century, time, security, news, GOP debate, nation, start
Topic 3	Campaign	Debate, campaign, team, hope, debate contest, contest, life
Topic 4	President	President, agree, read, senate, goal, support, Clinton
Topic 5	Plan	Plan, family, agree, fundraising, midnight, attacks, national
Donald Trump		
Topic 1	Trade	Clinton, people, president, country, jobs, special, trade
Topic 2	Thanks	Support, time, safe, amazing, Ted, big, honor
Topic 3	Trump	Trump, Donald, campaign, Donald Trump, Republican, united, Mr. Trump

Note. Generated by the automated procedure, latent Dirichlet allocation (unsupervised method).

line with the candidates' use of terminology, not our own). Clinton has a topic that seems to deal with issues related to women's rights. Sanders has a topic dealing with somewhat similar issues that we have labeled as justice, given that it contains this term as a keyword.

Words in each candidate's topics are not equally likely. Figure 3 shows the relative importance of words in Hillary Clinton's topics; dots nearer the right of the graph are more important. When focusing on the campaign she often mentioned president, and when focusing on women's rights she focused on health a moderate amount.

Of interest, some topics are much harder to name than others. Partly this is a function of the method—some topics are simply less clear. Part of the challenge, however, may reflect elements of a candidate's communication style. Jeb Bush's topics (data not shown) were especially hard to label. One might conjecture that this shows a lack of clarity in his topics that may be connected to the messaging problems that he faced.

How Topics Change Over Time

Finally, we turn to an especially interesting application of the topic model: to estimate a dynamic model that shows how topics change throughout the election. Given the large number of different words that can be associated with a certain topic, LDA can more accurately illustrate dynamic change in topic use across shorter time intervals than a keyword analysis, such as that

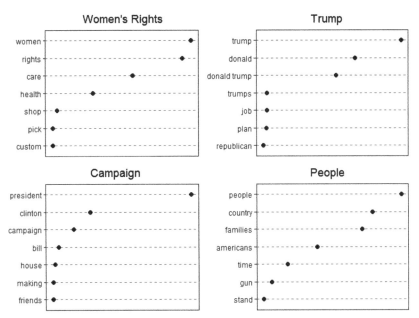

The weights of the words for each topic are generated from LDA.

FIGURE 3 The relative importance of words: Hillary Clinton's topics.

we used for our Twitter data. Our dynamic model provides more detail on the changing online social media strategies of the political candidates.

To do this, we use the posterior distribution of the topics uncovered from the LDA model and plot the average probabilities of each topic being mentioned per day. Cubic splines fit the model and allow us to visualize the rise and fall of topics focused on by the candidates. Here we focus only on selected major candidates for reasons of space, see Figure 4 through Figure 7.

Clinton's topic focusing on Trump increases toward the end of the time window. It may be inferred from Clinton's Facebook posts that toward the end of her primary with Sanders, she shifts focus onto Trump. The topic of women's rights seems level across time, indicating that this topic is consistently important to Clinton's social media campaign.

Sanders' topic that deals with himself decreases, while that of Democrats increases, over time. This may relate to party dynamics, as he subtly concedes to Clinton over time, perhaps alarmed by Trump securing the Republican nomination. The topics of justice and Wall Street both oscillate but remain core issues addressed by Sanders' social media campaign.

On the Republican side, it is clear that over time topics dealing with the campaign and related messages tend to decrease, often likely due to the candidates dropping out of the race. Some topics increase over time, including Ben Carson's focus on the world, which includes refugees. Although the candidates have dropped out of the race, their social media campaigns continue to highlight these issues.

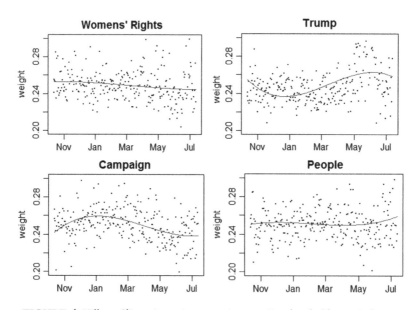

FIGURE 4 Hillary Clinton's topics over time on Facebook (dynamic latent Dirichlet allocation).

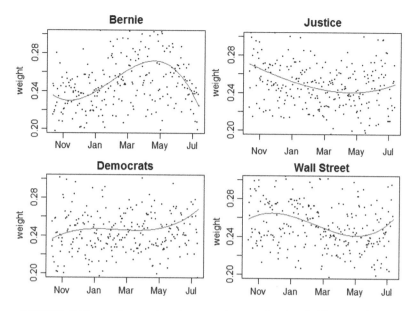

FIGURE 5 Bernie Sanders' topics over time on Facebook (dynamic latent Dirichlet allocation).

Looking at Trump's topics specifically, it appears that the topic of trade increases over time, while the topic regarding thanks decreases. This may be due to the fact that Trump has shifted focus from establishing rapport with primary voters to focusing on issues that resonate with his core general election voters as his presidential nomination became more certain. It is

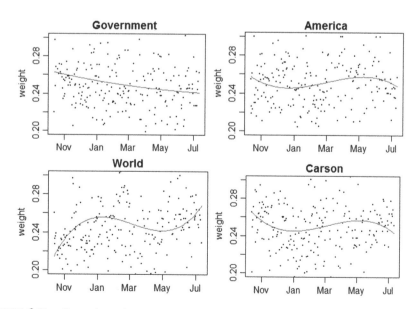

FIGURE 6 Ben Carson's topics over time on Facebook (dynamic latent Dirichlet allocation).

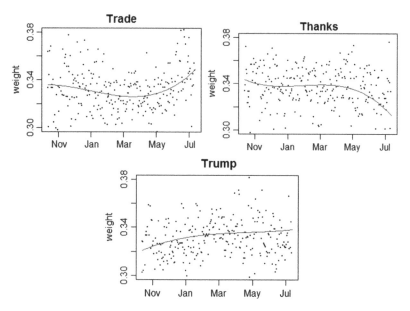

FIGURE 7 Donald Trump's topics over time on Facebook (dynamic latent Dirichlet allocation).

perhaps unsurprising that the topic related to Trump himself remains popular throughout, if anything only increasing with his ego-boosting primary victories.

CHALLENGES AND FURTHER RESEARCH

Social media provide a wonderful repository of data for the researcher. A campaign's messages are recorded and easily accessed. Such work allows insights into communication strategy not possible in the past. That said, our data are far from perfect to assess campaign strategy. Traditionally, campaigns may have undervalued their online communications. Remnants of this could leave social media communications unrepresentative—perhaps an intern did the posting. This is unlikely in the major political campaigns that we study but may remain the case for more minor campaigns, for example, for state senator, and more details would be welcome.

U.S. primary election campaigns are major operations and one might expect that staff would be employed to tweet on the candidate's behalf. Indeed, the variance of words in Trump's tweets may point to multiple authors (or simply an erratic personality). Indeed, the sheer volume of activity of the candidates suggests that each candidate must receive assistance. It is hard to imagine how Ted Cruz could personally conduct his volume of social media activity even if he wished to do so. This means that some posts from a candidate's account must only be approved by, rather than written by, the candidate—either through formal sign-off on each tweet or simply security limitations placed on who can access the candidate's account. While who composes the messages is an interesting organizational question, we would suggest that it does not matter too much for our analysis. We are interested in campaign strategy as revealed by the messages. Any staffer composing tweets in effect speaks for the candidate. Writers adopt the tone of the candidate and highlight topics the candidate wants to discuss. Even though a candidate does not literally type every word, the candidate is still responsible for the output. If a writer diverged from the candidate's desired approach, then they would soon be brought back into line. Thus, throughout this research we maintain the fiction that candidates write their own messages mainly for ease of exposition.

Candidate online strategies may diverge from their offline strategies, and indeed even online the Facebook strategy might diverge from the Twitter strategy. That said, we suggest that modern U.S. presidential primary campaigns are run by professional staffers who work on ensuring a consistent approach across media. Although any message might be tailored somewhat to the strengths of any medium, our data suggest that tailoring may be surprisingly limited. Twitter is used mostly simply to send messages, an approach similar to other media, such as paid TV advertising. Many of the topics we see being embraced resonate with the general communication strategy of the candidate: Health care was an important policy priority for the Sanders campaign, which was reflected on Twitter. While further research comparing different types of strategy from the same candidate would be useful, our current research is a step toward better understanding modern candidate communication.

Methodological Limitations

One of the reasons we use two different approaches to get at the topics/themes on social media is that methods vary in their effectiveness with different data sets. LDA requires very large amounts of text to automatically extract topics. This makes it relatively less effective on the large, but not very large, Twitter data set that we have. Here supervision by the researcher—for example, specifying the words associated with the themes before the analysis is conducted—has benefits. The researcher and political consultant when analyzing text will typically find that the larger the data set, the more appropriate it is to use a less supervised process. Supervision by the researcher essentially gains efficiency of analysis in extracting the insights from text but risks introducing bias, for example, because we specified the themes/words in advance. As the data set gets larger, the need for efficiency of analysis in extracting insights becomes less important and so paying the price of supervision, introducing possible bias, becomes less appealing.

Of course, no method is perfect. While LDA can be very useful, it works based upon a number of assumptions. Not least of these is the bag of words assumption: Context is somewhat lost. The LDA method that we outline has great potential to automate some textual analysis, but a trained reader is often able to analyze small amounts of text more thoroughly.

Implications for Political Marketers

Textual analysis is a booming field and political marketers can now use these tools. This could even help generate the sort of interactivity that appears to be missing in campaigns. Even ignoring the obvious problems of some social media comments—for example, unpleasant, not constructive—political marketers find manually comprehending all the comments on their websites nearly impossible. A supervised process, like our Twitter analysis, has potential but can be challenging. For instance, it is almost impossible to develop a dictionary to capture all the many ways writers spell, and misspell, relevant terms. LDA can quickly extract the topics in a large amount of text without much researcher input. For example, it can uncover the topics in comments on a policy position. LDA can hope to give a quick understanding of large amounts of textual data: a potential boon in gaining a read on public opinion in time-sensitive campaigns.

Political Marketing Research

We show the topics/themes that candidates choose to focus on in the primary using two different textual analysis methods. The first, using a dictionary of terms associated with themes, allowed us to see the focus on health care in both parties. We also saw differences within the party, with a greater focus on gun control for Clinton and climate change for Sanders. Ben Carson proved the most willing to tackle hot button issues that might appeal to his party's base, for example, immigration.

The second process we used is LDA, an unsupervised automated procedure that extracts topics from very large amounts of text. This allowed us to see the Republican's focus on what they might term radical Islam. The use of the dynamic model is particularly exciting as it uncovers how candidates change communications over time. It allows us to see how the focus of campaigns changes over time, including when a candidate ceases a campaign. Toward the end of the campaign, we see Clinton turning her focus toward Trump, effectively preparing for the general election. Meanwhile Sanders seems to move his focus from himself to the Democrats more generally, perhaps subtly conceding the primary and preparing his supporters to rally against the Republicans in the general election.

There is great potential for further research in this area. Investigations could build on the idea that social media interactivity seems yet to be fully embraced by candidates. Researchers may be able to provide advice on improving this, driving campaigns toward a more responsive marketing strategy. It is also easy to see how the LDA method could be used to better understand other very large research data sets, e.g., manifestos and policy positions, text-heavy websites, and political autobiographies. Automated textual analysis has a bright future in research.

CONCLUSION

We have provided an overview of the social media strategies of the major candidates in the 2016 primary elections. This involved gaining a greater understanding of the basic details of the campaigns, such as number of tweets, and the strategic approaches used. We looked at the themes addressed in the candidates' tweets. Introducing a dynamic topic modeling method to political marketing (LDA), we uncovered the topics in candidates' Facebook messages and showed how these changed over time. Overall, we suggest that social media not only provides candidates with a way to communicate with potential voters but also an interesting source of data for better understanding communication strategy.

NOTE

1. We generated the perplexity score for two to ten and fifteen topics. Testing the performance of fifteen topics for each candidate gives us confidence that we are not caught in a local minimum below ten. Further details on this technical element of the analysis are available from the authors on request.

REFERENCES

Abramowitz, A. I. 1989. "Viability, Electability, and Candidate Choice in a Presidential Primary Election: A Test of Competing Models." *The Journal of Politics* 51 (4):977–92. doi:10.2307/2131544

Abramson, P. R., J. H. Aldrich, P. Paolino, and D. W. Rohde. 1992. "'Sophisticated' Voting in the 1988 Presidential Primaries. *The American Political Science Review* 86 (1):55–69. doi:10.2307/1964015

Aharony, N. 2012. "Twitter Use by Three Political Leaders: An Exploratory Analysis." *Online Information Review* 36 (4):587–603. doi:10.1108/14684521211254086

Andrews, W., and T. Kaplan. 2015. "Where the Candidates Stand on 2016's Biggest Issues." The New York Times, Accessed August 12, 2016.

Bendle, N. T. 2014. "Reference Dependence in Political Primaries." *Journal of Political Marketing* 13 (4):307–33. doi:10.1080/15377857.2012.721738

Bendle, N. T., and J. Cotte. 2016. "Assumptions of Rationality in Political Marketing: The Case of the Republican Autopsy." *Journal of Nonprofit & Public Sector Marketing* 28 (1):66–83. doi:10.1080/10495142.2016.1131481

Bendle, N. T., and M.-A. Nastasoiu. 2014. "Primary Elections and US Political Marketing." In *Political Marketing in the United States*, edited by J. Lees-Marshment B. Conley and K. Cosgrove 85–111. New York, NY, USA: Routledge.

Bendle, N. T., J. Ryoo, and M.-A. Nastasoiu. 2017. "The 2016 U.S. Primaries: Parties and Candidates in a World of Big Data." In *Political Marketing in the United States 2016*, edited by J. Gillies 65–80. London: Plagrave Macmillan.

Bendle, N. T., and X. Wang. 2016. "Uncovering the Message from the Mess of Big Data." *Business Horizons* 59 (1):115–24. doi:10.1016/j.bushor.2015.10.001

Berenson, T. 2016. "Donald Trump's Tweets are Getting More Polished." Time, Accessed October 3, 2016.

Berg, J. E., F. D. Nelson, and T. A. Rietz. 2008. "Prediction Market Accuracy in the Long Run." *International Journal of Forecasting* 24 (2):285–300. doi:10.1016/j.ijforecast.2008.03.007

Bode, L., and K. E. Dalrymple. 2015. "Politics in 140 Characters or Less: Campaign Communication, Network Interaction, and Political Participation on Twitter." *Journal of Political Marketing* 15:311–32. doi:10.1080/15377857.2014.959686

Chang, J., J. L. Boyd-Graber, S. Gerrish, C. Wang, and D. M. Blei. 2009. "Reading Tea Leaves: How Humans Interpret Topic Models." *NIPS (Neural Information Processing Systems)* 31:1–9.

Collinson, S. 2015. "Joe Biden Won't Run for President." CNN, Accessed 08/11/2016.

Conway, B. A., K. Kenski, and D. Wang. 2013. "Twitter Use by Presidential Primary Candidates during the 2012 Campaign." *American Behavioral Scientist* 57:1596–610. doi:10.1177/0002764213489014

Cook, J. M. 2016. "Are American Politicians as Partisan Online as they are Offline? Networks in the U.S. Senate and Maine State Legislature." *Policy & Internet* 8 (1):55–71. doi:10.1002/poi3.109

Downs, A. 1957. *An Economic Theory of Democracy*. New York: Harper & Row.

Enli, G. S., and E. Skogerbø. 2013. "Personalized Campaigns in Party-centred Politics Twitter and Facebook as Arenas for Political Communication." *Information, Communication & Society* 16 (5):757–74.

Graham, T., M. Broersma, K. Hazelhoff, and G. van't Haar. 2013. "Between Broadcasting Political Messages and Interacting with Voters." *Information, Communication & Society* 16 (5):692–716. doi:10.1080/1369118x.2013.785581

Griffiths, T. L., and M. Steyvers. 2004. "Finding Scientific Topics." *Proceedings of the National Academy of Sciences of the United States of America* 101 (Suppl. 1):5228–35.

Heffernan, V. 2016. "How the Twitter Candidate Trumped the Teleprompter President." Politico Magazine, Accessed July 18, 2016. http://www.politico.com/magazine/story/2016/04/2016-heffernan-twitter-media-donald-trump-barack-obama-teleprompter-president-213825#ixzz4EkUsIY7P.

Hotelling, H. 1929. "Stability in Competition." *The Economic Journal* 39 (153): 41–57.

Jackson, N., and D. Lilleker. 2011. "Microblogging, Constituency Service and Impression Management: UK MPs and the Use of Twitter." *The Journal of Legislative Studies* 17 (1):86–105. doi:10.1080/13572334.2011.545181

Johnson, D. 2006. "First Hurdles: The Evolution of the Pre-primary and Primary Stages of American Presidential Elections." In *Winning Elections with Political*

Marketing, edited by P. Davies and B. B. Newman 177–210. New York: The Haworth Press.

Knuckey, J., and J. Lees-Marshment. 2005. "American Political Marketing: George W. Bush and the Republican Party." In *Political Marketing: A Comparative Perspective*, edited by D. G. Lilleker and J. Lees-Marshment 39–58. Manchester, UK: Manchester University Press.

Lee, J. C., and K. Quealy. 2016. "The 250 People, Places and Things Donald Trump has Insulted on Twitter: A Complete List." The New York Times. Accessed August 10, 2016.

Lees-Marshment, J. 2001a. "The Marriage of Politics and Marketing." *Political Studies* 49 (4):692–713. doi:10.1111/1467-9248.00337

Lees-Marshment, J. 2001b. *Political Marketing and British Political Parties: The Party's Just Begun*. Manchester, NY: Manchester University Press. [Distributed exclusively in the USA by Palgrave].

Lees-Marshment, J. 2004. *The Political Marketing Revolution: Transforming the Government of the UK*. Manchester: Manchester University Press.

Lees-Marshment, J. 2009. *Political Marketing: Principles and Applications*. Oxford: Routledge.

Leonhardt, D. 2016. "Jeb Bush is Still the Favorite, the Markets Say." The New York Times. Accessed 08/11/2016.

Lewis, D. D., Y. Yang, T. Rose, and F. Li. 2004. "RCV1: A New Benchmark Collection for Text Categorization Research." *Journal of Machine Learning Research* 5:361–97.

Lilleker, D. G., and N. A. Jackson. 2010. "Towards a More Participatory Style of Election Campaigning: The Impact of Web 2.0 on the UK 2010 General Election." *Policy & Internet* 2 (3):67–96. doi:10.2202/1944-2866.1064

Marland, A. 2016. *Brand Command: Canadian Politics and Democracy in the Age of Message Control*. Vancouver, BC: UBC Press.

Marland, A., T. Giasson, and J. Lees-Marshment. 2012. *Political Marketing in Canada*, edited by A. Marland T. Giasson and J. Lees-Marshment. Vancouver, BC: UBC Press.

McGinniss, J. 1988. *The Selling of the President*. New York, NY: Penguin Books.

Miller, W. 2013. "We Can't All be Obama: The Use of New Media in Modern Political Campaigns." *Journal of Political Marketing* 12 (4):326–47. doi:10.1080/15377857.2013.837312

Mutz, D. C. 1989. "The Influence of Perceptions of Media Influence: Third Person Effects and the Public Expression of Opinions." *International Journal of Public Opinion Research* 1 (1):3–23. doi:10.1093/ijpor/1.1.3

O'Cass, A. 1996. "Political Marketing and the Marketing Concept." *European Journal of Marketing* 30 (10/11):37–53. doi:10.1108/03090569610149782

O'Shaughnessy, N. 2001. "The Marketing of Political Marketing." *European Journal of Marketing* 35 (9/10):1047–57.

Parsons, M., and M. Rowling. 2015. "Social Media and the Paradox of Fear: An Exploratory Study of Political Relationship Marketing Within South Wales." *Journal of Political Marketing* 1–3. https://doi.org/10.1080/15377857.2015.1039746

Pfau, M. 1988. "Intra-party Political Debates and Issue Learning." *Journal of Applied Communication Research* 16 (2):99–112. doi:10.1080/00909888809365276

Savigny, H. 2008. *The Problem of Political Marketing*. New York: Continuum International Publishing.

Sayre, B., L. Bode, D. Shah, D. Wilcox, and C. Shah. 2010. "Agenda Setting in a Digital Age: Tracking Attention to California Proposition 8 in Social Media, Online News and Conventional News." *Policy & Internet* 2 (2):7–32. doi:10.2202/1944-2866.1040

Scammell, M. 1999. "Political Marketing: Lessons for Political Science." *Political Studies* 47:718–39. doi:10.1111/1467-9248.00228

Shapiro, M. A., and L. Hemphill. 2016. "Politicians and the Policy Agenda: Does Use of Twitter by the U.S. Congress Direct New York Times Content?" *Policy & Internet* 9:109–32. doi:10.1002/poi3.120.[Online 4A].

Stromer-Galley, J. 2000a. "On-line Interaction and Why Candidates Avoid It." *Journal of Communication* 50 (4):111–32. doi:10.1093/joc/50.4.111

Stromer-Galley, J. 2000b. "Democratizing Democracy: Strong Democracy, US Political Campaigns and the Internet." *Democratization* 7 (1):36–58. doi:10.1080/13510340008403644

Teorell, J. 1999. "A Deliberative Defence of Intra-party Democracy no Title." *Party Politics* 5 (3):363–82. doi:10.1177/1354068899005003006

Tirunillai, S., and G. Tellis. 2014. "Mining Marketing Meaning from Chatter: Strategic Brand Analysis of Big Data Using Latent Dirichlet Allocation." *Journal of Marketing Research* 51 (4):463–79. doi:10.1509/jmr.12.0106

Vergeer, M., L. Hermans, and S. Sams. 2011. "Online Social Networks and Micro-blogging in Political Campaigning: The Exploration of a New Campaign Tool and a New Campaign Style." *Party Politics* 19 (3):477–501. doi:10.1177/1354068811407580

Wang, X., N. T. Bendle, F. Mai, and J. Cotte. 2015. "The Journal of Consumer Research at 40: A Historical Analysis." *Journal of Consumer Research* 42 (1):5–18. doi:10.1093/jcr/ucv009

Communicating Party Labels and Names on Twitter During the 2016 Presidential Invisible Primary and Primary Campaigns

KATE KENSKI and CHRISTINE R. FILER

BETHANY A. CONWAY-SILVA

This study investigated the use of party and ideological labels and candidate names in major party candidate tweets (N = 94,310) during the 2016 presidential preprimary and primary campaigns to understand the extent to which candidates focused on intraparty and interparty themes as a part of their marketing strategies. The results show that the candidates and their campaigns did not engage in heavy partisan labeling to cultivate their social media identities. Outsider candidates were not more likely to use party or ideological labels in their tweets than insider candidates were. The candidates focused on self-advocacy in their tweets.

The prevalence of social media use by presidential candidates has changed significantly over the past three campaign cycles. Social media in general and the platform Twitter specifically are relatively new in presidential campaign politics, utilized somewhat in 2008 and frequently but not consistently across campaigns in 2012 (Conway, Kenski, and Wang 2013). By 2016, presidential campaigns harnessed these platforms with greater purpose than in previous election cycles. In the present study, we investigate social media use via Twitter by the major presidential primary candidates during the "invisible" primary and primary phases of the campaigns, focusing on the ways in which the candidates invoked party labels and candidate names to establish their identities and market themselves to their respective voter constituencies. Understanding the use of partisan labels is important because for citizens, "partisan messages can serve as a primary means of becoming familiar with and developing opinions about political matters" (Jarvis 2017).

We explore the 2016 surfacing phase and primary campaign tweets ($N = 94,310$) of the major party candidates to gauge the extent to which the candidates focused on intraparty or interparty themes as part of their marketing. We consider two theoretical frameworks that offer insight into label invocation: social identity theory (Tajfel and Turner 1979) and reference dependence (Bendle 2014). Social identity theory (Tajfel and Turner 1979) contends that one's identity is based in large part on group membership; perceptions of that identity can be strengthened by attacking outgroups. Reference dependence in political primaries (Bendle 2014) suggests that labels and names are used most successfully in primaries by moderate candidates to pivot against the extreme candidates running for nomination within their party, thus establishing their electability over those extreme candidates. The results of this study show that candidates and their campaigns did not engage in heavy thematic use of party and ideological labels to cultivate their social media identities. Rather, candidates focused on self-advocacy.

PARTY LABELS

Party and ideological labels are often important to the success or failure of political organizations and candidates. Jarvis (2005) explains that "names serve as shortcuts for citizens that help them make sense of politics, particularly as Americans move into an overcommunicated information age" (11). Increased messaging has expanded the "clutter" in the media environment, which can threaten the effectiveness of advertising messages (Webb and Ray 1979). We are at a unique point in history, when people are bombarded with messages more than ever before. Consequently, labeling in political life helps people orient themselves to actors in the political system and what they represent. Research suggests that the mass public understands what ideological labels mean, although their understanding is not as nuanced as that of political elites (Herrera 1996–1997).

A comprehensive content analysis of data from 1948 to 2000 conducted by Jarvis (2005) shows variance over time in how frequently political speeches and news included party labels, but there is no question that political elites used party labels in each election. Party labels appeared frequently in the news, albeit less often than candidate names, which increased in frequency across time (Jarvis 2005). Even as personalization has increased in news (Bennett 2012), party labels continue to be utilized (Jarvis 2005). Jarvis observes that labels and brands reside "in a dynamic message environment that is littered with connotations of the past, of the present, and from the opposition" (197). So while their meaning to the populace may change over time, their presence as an organizing mechanism for understanding political life remains.

In an information age that inundates citizens with messages, political branding helps manage identities, including branding that involves party labels. Political candidates and their campaigns may also create brands that do not use party labels, favoring instead labeling that plays up anti-establishment, "outsider," or independent sentiments. Jarvis and Jones (2005) find that Republican presidential candidates are more comfortable negotiating their roles as candidate-centered campaigners than are Democratic presidential candidates. Although the use of party labels has decreased over time, they are now more contentious when used (Jarvis and Jones 2005). Jarvis (2005) shows that in general elections, the candidate of the party mentioned most frequently in the news is the candidate more likely to lose than his or her counterparts. Candidates, however, who do not mention party much are criticized as being too candidate-centered. Consequently, candidates must navigate a balance between acknowledging party politics, lest they get criticized by the press, but they must not overstate party identification, which may alienate voters. How candidates use party and ideological labels in social media during the preprimary and primary campaigns is in an open question.

SOCIAL IDENTITY THEORY AND REFERENCE DEPENDENCE THEORY

Two theories offer insight into how candidates may implement party labels in campaign messaging: social identity theory and reference dependence in political primaries. Social identity theory (Tajfel and Turner 1979) maintains that group affiliation often serves as a way that people understand themselves; people may increase their self-image through social identification with an ingroup and social comparison with an outgroup. Although not developed to understand political situations specifically, social identity theory can be applied to the political domain (Greene 2004). Reference dependence in political primaries (Bendle 2014) contends that reference effects can change preferences in primaries by changing the standards by which voters evaluate their options. At their cores, both of these theories purport that social comparison is an important tool for forging identification.

Employed in the political context, social identity theory suggests that candidates benefit by attacking the outgroup. In campaigns, the most important group categorization is partisan identification. Hence, the most important outgroup is often the opposing party. Current research on U.S. voting indicates a rise in "negative partisanship" whereby members of each party have come to embrace increasingly negative views of the opposing party (Bafumi and Shapiro 2009; Iyengar, Sood, and Lelkes 2012; Pew Research Center 2014; Abramowitz 2015). Focusing, therefore, on party labels and themes of "negative partisanship" (e.g., attacking the outgroup party) may be an effective way for primary candidates to demonstrate their commitment to their ingroup party and garner support.

Allport (1954) maintained that one's sense of belonging could be strengthened through hostility toward outgroups. According to Brewer (1999), "[s]ocial differentiation provides the fault lines in any social system that can be exploited for political purposes. When trust is ingroup-based, it is easy to fear control by outsiders; perceived common threat from outgroups increases ingroup cohesion and loyalty" (437–438). One way that primary candidates may exhibit that outgroup hostility is by attacking the opposing party, the sitting president if he is a member of the opposing party, and/or well-known candidates in the opposing party. We therefore expect primary candidates to reference the opposing party and its members in campaign discourse.

Although social identity theory does not speak directly to primary campaign communication, one may assume that the public expression of social identity is pertinent for those candidates who do not have long histories or experiences with the party in which they are running. The expression of outgroup hostility may be particularly important for outsider candidates—those candidates who have never been elected to office under the party from which they are trying to secure the presidential nomination—as a way to establish that they are real members of the ingroup. Thus, this behavior should be prominent among outsiders.

Reference dependence in political primaries assumes that electability, that is, whether or not a primary candidate has a good chance of winning the general election if selected as the party's nominee, is a motivating factor to primary voters (Bendle 2014). If moderate candidates in primary campaigns compare themselves to extreme candidate options within their party, it is assumed that primary voters will be more likely to consider the electability of the candidates as a factor in their vote choice, rather than necessarily cast their ballot for the candidate that they like most. This theory, therefore, suggests that the names found in moderate or well-established primary candidate discourse, such as tweets, will be those of the more extreme, and thus perceived as less electable, primary candidates, as more moderate candidates reference them in a strategic manner.[1]

Both of these frameworks suggest that names and party labels matter, as they are often used to structure how voters think about the candidates and evaluate them. The frameworks are not necessarily in competition with one another, as it is possible that primary candidates attack the outgroup and stress electability through the admonishment of outsiders. Indeed, in their analysis of advertisements in the 2004 and 2008 presidential primaries, Ridout and Holland (2010) found that interparty attacks (those against the opposing party) were just as frequent as intraparty attacks against co-partisans. As applied to names and labels, social identity theory predicts that candidates will mention the opposing camp to increase their self-image within their party, while reference dependence predicts that when it comes to references within their party, moderate candidates will do more naming and will specifically mention the more extreme candidates to promote the primary voters' thinking about electability, as moderate candidates are presumed to be more palatable to the electorate overall than extreme party candidates.

ATTACK POLITICS AND THE 2016 CAMPAIGN ENVIRONMENT

Attack advertising is a consistent feature in American political campaigns (Jamieson 1992, 1996), and attack strategies influence voters (Pfau and Kenski 1990). Benoit's (2017) functional theory of political campaign discourse argues that candidate speech falls into three general categories: acclaim, attack, and defense. "Acclaims address a candidate's strengths or advantages. Attacks expose an opponent's weaknesses or disadvantages. Defenses respond to, or refute, attacks against a candidate," explains Benoit. Although attacks are common, candidates often use the beginning of the campaign season to define themselves through biographies and advocacy or acclaim advertisements. Benoit's (2007) analysis of advertisements from 1952 to 2004 revealed that primary candidate advertisements tend to be relatively positive, although the 2012 candidates departed from this pattern by attacking as much as they acclaimed (Benoit and Compton 2014).

Given three major changes to the 2016 campaign environment, it is unclear whether candidates maintained their general tendency to minimize attacks during the beginning of the election cycle. The major changes include increased polarization, expansion of the preprimary phase, and the rapidity of information transference. First, scholars have documented increases in polarization among elites (Fiorina, Abrams, and Pope 2006) and citizens, which may stem in part from selective exposure to like-minded political content (Taber and Lodge 2006; Stroud 2011). Possible consequences of polarization include lack of understanding, tolerance, and/or empathy toward one's political opponents. An increase in attacks over acclaims is a possible consequence of polarization.

Second, since Bill Clinton's reelection campaign in 1996 when the Clinton team used a strategy designed by Dick Morris that involved airing televised advertising nearly a year and a half before the general election

(Edsall 1999: A4), the campaign "season" extends beyond the boundaries of one year prior to a general election. Howard Dean declared himself an official candidate for the Democratic nomination one and a half years before the 2004 general election took place and was "campaigning for more than a year" prior to that announcement (National Public Radio 2003). The introduction of 2008 Democratic candidate and then-Senator Barack Obama to the public was effectively the 2004 Democratic National Convention. Consequently, the primary season—previously thought to begin right before the Iowa caucuses and New Hampshire primary—is no longer the candidates' introduction to potential voters. Candidates must be well known nationally in advance of the year that party nominations and the presidential election take place in order to be considered serious nomination contenders. Considering that negative information is remembered better than positive information (Pratto and John 1991) and negative information about candidate attributes in media transfers more readily to the public (Wu and Coleman 2009) and that lengthening the campaign process means additional money has to be raised and spent to run a viable campaign, it may not be tenable for candidates to keep up with positive image cultivation over sustained periods of time. Consequently, the preprimary and primary phases that previously focused on acclaims are likely to include increased attacks by candidates. This may be further compounded when considering that open presidential primaries, such as that of 2016, are generally more competitive than incumbent–challenger races (Mayhew 2008), and the sheer size of the 2016 primary field was large (Catanese 2015).

Third, social media have changed the speed with which news stories are delivered to the public from the 24-hour broadcast news cycle to hourly cable news programs to minute-by-minute exchanges of information. With the increase in volume and speed of information delivery, candidates need to offer messages that stand out. Attacks tend to get noticed, and perhaps most importantly, repeated by news media that tend to focus on the negative more heavily than the positive as a norm (Lengauer, Esser, and Berganza 2011; Bennett 2012). These factors also suggest that attacks may have been higher in 2016 than they were in previous elections. If attacks were present, they will be evident in candidates' social media presence. Specifically, if candidates felt compelled to attack the opposing party and/or its candidates, we expect to see their names and group affiliations mentioned in candidate messaging.

The current study investigates the 2016 surfacing phase and primary campaign tweets of the major party nomination candidates to gauge the extent to which the candidates focused on intraparty or interparty themes as part of their marketing on social media. The surfacing phase, also known as the invisible primary or the preprimary period, is an understudied phase of the presidential campaign politics, but it is increasingly important as presidential campaigns stretch on for longer periods of time.

CANDIDATES AND SOCIAL MEDIA

Candidates use social media as integral parts of their campaign packages (Golbeck, Grimes, and Rogers 2010; Grant, Moon, and Grant 2010; Johnson and Perlmutter 2010; Towner and Dulio 2012; Adams and McCorkindale 2013; Conway, Kenski, and Wang 2013; Graham et al. 2013). Between 2005 and 2013, social media use by U.S. adults increased from 8 percent to 72 percent (Brenner and Smith 2013). With 62 percent of citizens reporting that they get political news from social media (Gottfried and Shearer 2016), such media now play key roles in campaign messaging.

Research has examined politicians' uses of the Twittersphere during election campaigns with content analyses (see Jungherr 2016) and the relationship between the Twitter agenda and that of traditional news media as it relates to politics (Metzgar and Maruggi 2009; Groshek and Groshek 2010; Sayre et al. 2010; Jungherr 2014; Conway, Kenski, and Wang 2015; Jang and Pasek 2015). Gueorguieva (2008) observes that social networking sites benefit political campaigns because of their low cost, fundraising potential, enhanced recruitment ability for campaign volunteers, and increased possibilities for candidate exposure. In 2016, they may have also served as a means of setting the national news agenda (Conway-Silva, Filer, Kenski, and Tsetsi 2017; Wells et al. 2016). While social media have different affordances than do traditional media, current research suggests that there is significant overlap between the issue priorities that presidential candidates put on Twitter and display in television campaign ads (Kenski, Conway, and Filer 2015). Consequently, social media can be used as an indicant of campaign themes.

RESEARCH QUESTIONS AND HYPOTHESIS

Studying political identity from the perspective of social identity theory (Tajfel and Turner 1979; Greene 2004; Pacilli, Roccato, Pagliaro, and Russo 2016) and reference dependence in political primaries (Bendle 2014), we investigated the themes in the 2016 Democratic and Republican presidential preprimary and primary candidate tweets to test the extent to which candidates defined themselves by focusing their messages on the opposing party and/or their ingroup opponents in comparison to more established party candidates.

Based on social identity theory's contention that group members may enhance their self-image by attacking an outgroup, we anticipated that primary candidates would use party and ideological labels to demonstrate that they are strong group members. Specifically, we anticipated that candidate messages would be used to attack the opposing party and its ideological orientation. Research suggests that, at least in 2004 and 2008, frontrunners leveled more interparty attacks than did other candidates (Ridout and

Holland, 2010). While taking this into account, we also suspected that candidates who did not have a long or deep history with their party, through official membership with the party or as a holder of elected office representing that party, would need to use party and ideological labels to locate and highlight their identity for citizens. We also surmised that they would need to define themselves by differentiating themselves from the other side's party and candidates in comparison to more established candidates with whom party members were already familiar. That would suggest that Lincoln Chafee, Lawrence Lessig, and Bernie Sanders should have tweeted more party and ideological labels than did Democratic front-runner Hillary Clinton and that Ben Carson, Mark Everson, Carly Fiorina, and Donald Trump should have tweeted more party and ideological labels than did their established Republican competitors.

The potential challenges to these assertions lie in historical precedent. While the communication environment changed dramatically over the past several years, other than 2012 when primary candidates attacked as much as they advocated for themselves (Benoit and Compton 2014), primary campaigns have been typically used for self-advocacy more than not (Benoit 2007). It is possible that social identity theory's contribution to understanding campaign behaviors should be relegated to general elections and is not as useful when there are multiple outgroups at play in highly competitive preprimary and primary phases (e.g., various factions within a party). That attacks on the opposition are notable among frontrunners as they prepare for the general election supports this notion (Ridout and Holland 2010). Consequently, we ask two questions. First, how frequently did primary candidates use party and ideological labels in their preprimary and primary tweets? Second, did outsider status affect the extent to which primary candidates used party and ideological labels in their preprimary and primary tweets?

Reference dependence theory does not suggest how candidates should use party labels, but it does suggest that within a party's nomination competition, moderate or well-known candidates tend to mention other ingroup candidates, specifically the extreme or outsider candidates, as a point of comparison for voters. We therefore anticipated that candidates such as Chafee, Lessig, Sanders, Carson, Everson, Fiorina, and Trump would be mentioned by the other candidates in their respective races as points of comparison for the moderate and/or more well-known candidates (H1).

METHODS

This study examined party and ideological labels and candidate emphasis within Twitter feeds of U.S. presidential preprimary and primary candidates and their campaigns. We examined the presence of labels in the preprimary and primary campaigns by candidates and outsider/insider status. We conducted a computer-assisted content analysis employing a dictionary approach.

Data Set

We collected all tweets on verified major party candidate Twitter feeds and candidate campaign feeds from March 5, 2015, through June 7, 2016 ($N = 94,310$). Although many eventual candidates posted frequently to Twitter prior to the start date of this time period, March 5, 2015 marks the date when Republican Mark Everson became the first official entrant in the presidential race. The state primaries and caucuses ended on June 7, 2016. The collection of candidate tweets included six Democrats (Lincoln Chafee, Hillary Clinton, Lawrence Lessig, Martin O'Malley, Bernie Sanders, and Jim Webb) and 18 Republicans (Jeb Bush, Ben Carson, Chris Christie, Ted Cruz, Mark Everson, Carly Fiorina, Jim Gilmore, Lindsey Graham, Mike Huckabee, Bobby Jindal, John Kasich, George Pataki, Rand Paul, Rick Perry, Marco Rubio, Rick Santorum, Donald Trump, and Scott Walker). The frequencies of the candidate/campaign tweets are in Table 1. When candidates dropped out of the race, their tweet collection was discontinued.

Tweets were downloaded using the "twitteR" package in R and Twitter's REST API. Twitter data for each tweet consist of the user who posted the tweet, the date and time it was posted, and the tweet's content.[2]

Coding

QDA Miner and WordStat were used to code and analyze party, ideology, and candidate mention frequencies across tweets. QDA Miner is a computer-assisted qualitative coding program capable of handling a variety of media for human coding. WordStat is its quantitative component that allows researchers to search for words, word strings, and complex word combinations. We used this text-mining software to compose custom party, ideology, and candidate dictionaries to examine the included tweets. Similar to Jang and Pasek (2015), we argue that such keywords have strong face validity in identifying the presence of themes.

Dictionaries were created for party labels, ideological labels, and candidate names. Party labels were identified by words such as Democrat, Dem, DNC, GOP, Rep, Republican, RNC, plural forms of such words, and other derivations. Ideological labels included words such as liberal, liberalism, progressive, conservative, and conservatism. The candidates were identified by their names, Twitter handles, and popular hashtags associated with their names. A validation check was conducted to ensure that there was face validity to the results of the dictionary coding approach.

TABLE 1 Tweet Frequency by Campaign Phase

Candidates	Handle	Party outsider	Preprimary tweet frequency	Primary tweet frequency	Campaign stop date
			Democrats		
Lincoln Chafee	@LincolnChafee	Yes*	421	—	10/23/15
Hillary Clinton	@HillaryClinton	No	4,203	4,564	
	@TheBriefing2016				
	@HFA				
Lawrence Lessig	@lessig	Yes	3,549	—	11/2/15
	@Lessig2016				
Martin O'Malley	@MartinOMalley	No	2,312	193	2/1/16
Bernie Sanders	@BernieSanders	Yes*	5,949	4,594	6/7/16
	@SenSanders				
Jim Webb	@JimWebbUSA	No	1,443	—	10/20/15

70

Name	Twitter handle		Republicans		Date
Jeb Bush	@JebBush	No	2,080	742	2/20/16
Ben Carson	@RealBenCarson	Yes	1,438	647	3/4/16
Chris Christie	@ChrisChristie	No	2,371	722	2/10/16
	@GovChristie				
Ted Cruz	@SenTedCruz	No	5,377	4,783	5/3/16
	@tedcruz				
	@TeamTedCruz				
Mark Everson	@MarkForAmerica	Yes*	1,100	—	11/5/15
Carly Fiorina	@CarlyFiorina	Yes	1,302	192	2/10/16
Jim Gilmore	@gov_gilmore	No	971	389	2/12/16
Lindsey Graham	@GrahamBlog	No	3,203	—	12/21/15
	@LindseyGrahamSC				
Mike Huckabee	@GovMikeHuckabee	No	1,778	360	2/1/16
Bobby Jindal	@BobbyJindal	No	1,371	—	11/17/15
John Kasich	@JohnKasich	No	1,929	3,234	5/4/16
	@TeamJohnKasich				
George Pataki	@GovernorPataki	No	1,678	—	12/29/15
Rand Paul	@RandPaul	No	4,674	1,248	2/3/16
Rick Perry	@Governor Perry	No	1,571	—	9/11/15
	@TeamRickPerry				
Marco Rubio	@marcorubio	No	5,171	3,036	3/15/16
	@TeamMarco				
Rick Santorum	@RickSantorum	No	3,439	1,012	2/3/16
	@TeamSantorum				
Donald Trump	@realDonaldTrump	Yes	6,778	2,131	
Scott Walker	@ScottWalker	No	2,355	—	9/21/15
	@GovWalker				

Note. *Chafee and Sanders were elected officials but did not have long histories with their party. Mark Everson was an administration insider but had not served in an elective capacity.

We categorized Democrats Lincoln Chafee, Lawrence Lessig, and Bernie Sanders and Republicans Ben Carson, Mark Everson, Carly Fiorina, and Donald Trump as outsiders. While Chafee and Sanders were elected officials, both also did not have long histories with the Democratic Party. Sanders served in the Senate as an Independent until 2015, while Chafee was a Republican, then an Independent, and finally a Democrat in 2013. Mark Everson served as deputy director for management at the Office of Management and Budget but did not have elective experience. The other candidates considered outsiders did not have elective experience nor extensive government experience.

Analysis

Tweets were analyzed for their content by candidates/campaigns and preprimary versus primary phase of the campaigns. There were 66,463 tweets during the invisible primary (March 5 to December 31, 2015) and 27,847 tweets during the primary (January 1 to June 7, 2016). Because the data set contained the entirety of the candidate and campaign tweets during the time periods under investigation, inferential statistics were not generated, as such statistics are only useful for making inferences about a population. As Gorard (2013) explains, "Significance tests are relevant only to making a judgement about sampling variation produced by the random selection of cases for a sample ... and whether this variation is a good explanation of any manifested difference between the groups" (54). Here, no inference needed to be made about the population as the entire population was captured; any observed differences are the real differences.

RESULTS

The research questions asked about the extent to which party and ideological labels were used and whether these frequencies were affected by outsider candidate status. Our party and ideological label dictionaries identified 4,035 (4.4 percent) candidate tweets that contained Republican identification labels, 1,231 (1.3 percent) tweets that contained Democratic identification labels, 1,067 (1.1 percent) tweets that contained conservative labels, and 297 candidate (0.3 percent) tweets that contained liberal labels over the preprimary and primary campaigns.

As shown in Table 2, party labels were used by candidates more than were ideological labels, and they were used slightly more in the preprimary than in the primary campaign. Six Republican candidates and one Democrat (Clinton) used "Republican" labels in more than 5 percent of their preprimary tweets; three Republicans and one Democrat used the Republican label in more than 5 percent of their primary tweets. By contrast, three Democrats and no Republicans used "Democratic" words in more than 5 percent of their

TABLE 2 Percentage of Tweets Mentioning Party and Ideology Categories

Candidate	Republican (%)		Conservative (%)		Democrat (%)		Liberal (%)	
	Pre	Prim	Pre	Prim	Pre	Prim	Pre	Prim
			Democrats					
Chafee	3.1	—	0.0	—	**12.1**	—	0.5	—
Clinton	**10.0**	**5.4**	0.1	0.1	1.1	1.6	0.4	0.6
Lessig	1.3	—	0.2	—	**5.9**	—	0.2	—
O'Malley	1.3	1.6	0.0	0.0	4.2	1.6	0.8	0.0
Sanders	3.6	2.1	0.1	0.2	2.1	2.5	0.3	0.8
Webb	1.7	—	0.1	—	**8.6**	—	0.1	—
			Republicans					
Bush	1.2	1.1	2.4	**5.7**	0.8	0.3	0.4	1.1
Carson	**5.6**	1.5	0.1	0.2	0.1	0.0	0.1	0.6
Christie	2.7	1.1	0.1	0.1	0.6	0.8	0.3	0.0
Cruz	3.8	3.8	3.8	3.6	0.5	0.8	0.2	0.4
Everson	**33.9**	—	0.8	—	1.7	—	0.2	—
Fiorina	3.4	2.6	1.7	0.5	0.5	0.5	0.4	1.0
Gilmore	**8.9**	**9.5**	1.1	1.3	0.8	0.3	0.2	0.3
Graham	2.8	—	0.2	—	0.2	—	0.0	—
Huckabee	3.0	1.1	1.0	0.6	0.4	0.6	0.5	0.3
Jindal	**5.4**	—	4.1	—	1.7	—	0.9	—
Kasich	4.4	**5.0**	0.8	0.7	0.2	0.3	0.1	0.0
Pataki	**10.3**	—	0.6	—	0.4	—	0.1	—
Paul	4.5	3.8	1.1	0.8	0.7	0.6	0.4	0.2
Perry	3.4	—	1.5	—	0.3	—	0.1	—
Rubio	2.6	1.9	0.8	2.9	0.6	0.3	0.3	0.1
Santorum	**8.3**	**5.8**	2.4	1.5	0.3	0.5	0.1	0.0
Trump	4.0	4.2	0.3	0.2	0.8	1.0	0.2	0.1
Walker	2.5	—	2.0	—	0.3	—	0.4	—

Note. Pre = preprimary phase; Prim = primary phase. Bolded percentages are greater than 5 percent.

preprimary tweets; none of the candidates used such words in more than 5 percent of their primary tweets. Ideological labels were used sparingly. One Republican in the primary used the conservative label in more than 5 percent of his tweets (Bush), and no Republicans mentioned the word "liberal" in more than 5 percent of their tweets. None of the Democrats used the labels "conservative" or "liberal" in their preprimary or primary tweets more than 5 percent of the time.

Outsider candidates did not appear to use party and ideological labels consistent with their party much more than did their insider peers. Democratic insider Jim Webb and outsider Lincoln Chafee used Democratic words the most out of the Democratic candidates at 8.6 percent and 12.1 percent, respectively, during the surfacing phase. Liberal ideological terms were not used widely. While outsider Mark Everson used Republican words the most out of the GOP candidates at 33.9 percent, far outpacing his intraparty competitors, outsider candidate Donald Trump was among the least likely to use such labeling, at 4 percent. The Republican candidates were on the low end of conservative ideological labeling, and outsider status did not make a difference.

When it came to using opposition party labels, the Democrat who used Republican words the most was Hillary Clinton, party insider and front-runner. Ten percent of Clinton's tweets in the surfacing phase and 5.4 percent of her tweets in the primary phase used Republican words. Republicans did not use Democratic words frequently.

H1 maintained that moderate/insider candidates would mention outsider candidates more to establish their appeal to the mainstream in the general election. Republican candidate names were mentioned in 34,981 (37.1 percent) candidate tweets during the preprimary and primary season, while Democratic candidate names were mentioned in 14,399 (15.3 percent) of candidate tweets, as shown in Table 3. There is some slight indication that insider candidates did mention outsider candidates more, but the mixed

TABLE 3 Percentage of Candidate Tweets Mentioning Democratic Candidates and Obama

Sources	Chafee (%)		Clinton (%)		Lessig (%)		O'Malley (%)		Sanders (%)		Webb (%)		Obama (%)	
	Pre	Prim	Pre	Prim	Pre	Prim	Pre	Prim	Pre	Prim	Pre	Prim	Pre	Prim
						Democrats								
Chafee	**54.9**	—	2.1	—	0.0	—	1.4	—	0.7	—	0.7	—	4.3	—
Clinton	0.0	0.0	**51.0**	**43.1**	0.0	0.0	0.0	0.0	0.4	**6.9**	0.0	0.0	1.0	3.0
Lessig	0.7	—	1.5	—	**57.3**	—	0.2	—	3.6	—	0.7	—	0.7	—
O'Malley	0.0	0.0	1.0	0.0	0.0	0.0	**39.1**	**28.0**	0.3	0.5	0.0	0.0	1.1	**8.3**
Sanders	0.0	0.0	1.2	4.3	0.0	0.0	0.1	0.1	**35.6**	**24.7**	0.0	0.0	0.5	0.6
Webb	0.8	—	2.1	—	0.0	—	0.8	—	1.7	—	**66.7**	—	2.2	—
						Republicans								
Bush	0.0	0.0	**7.5**	**8.1**	0.0	0.0	0.0	0.0	0.1	0.1	0.0	0.0	**7.9**	**9.3**
Carson	0.0	0.0	1.7	1.2	0.0	0.0	0.0	0.0	0.3	0.0	0.1	0.0	0.6	3.9
Christie	0.0	0.0	4.1	3.0	0.0	0.0	0.0	0.0	0.2	0.3	0.0	0.0	2.6	2.1
Cruz	0.0	0.0	0.9	2.0	0.0	0.0	0.0	0.0	0.0	0.2	0.0	0.0	3.8	2.5
Everson	0.0	—	0.7	—	0.0	—	0.1	—	0.0	—	0.0	—	**8.1**	—
Fiorina	0.0	0.0	**5.1**	**8.3**	0.0	0.0	0.0	0.0	0.0	0.5	0.0	0.0	1.2	3.6
Gilmore	0.0	0.0	3.3	0.8	0.0	0.0	0.1	0.0	0.4	0.3	0.0	0.0	2.5	1.5
Graham	0.0	—	2.6	—	0.0	—	0.0	—	0.3	—	0.1	—	**7.9**	—
Huckabee	0.0	0.0	4.6	4.2	0.0	0.0	0.0	0.0	0.7	0.3	0.0	0.0	**8.1**	**10.8**
Jindal	0.0	—	**5.9**	—	0.0	—	0.0	—	0.5	—	0.0	—	**5.5**	—
Kasich	0.0	0.0	1.5	4.4	0.0	0.0	0.0	0.0	0.0	0.5	0.0	0.0	0.2	0.7
Pataki	0.0	—	**6.0**	—	0.0	—	0.0	—	0.2	—	0.0	—	3.7	—
Paul	0.0	0.0	3.7	1.8	0.0	0.0	0.0	0.3	0.3	3.2	0.0	0.0	1.8	1.0
Perry	0.0	—	4.2	—	0.0	—	0.0	—	0.0	—	0.0	—	**5.7**	—
Rubio	0.0	0.0	2.4	3.6	0.0	0.0	0.0	0.0	0.0	0.1	0.0	0.0	2.1	2.0
Santorum	0.0	0.0	2.0	1.1	0.0	0.0	0.0	0.0	0.1	0.3	0.0	0.0	3.2	4.5
Trump	0.0	0.0	2.9	**7.4**	0.0	0.0	0.0	0.0	0.3	1.5	0.0	0.0	2.7	1.8
Walker	0.0	—	**6.8**	—	0.0	—	0.0	—	0.2	—	0.0	—	**5.2**	—

Note. Pre = preprimary phase; Prim = primary phase. Bolded percentages are greater than 5 percent.

TABLE 4 Percentage of Candidate Tweets Mentioning Republican Candidates

Sources	Bush (%) Pre	Bush (%) Prim	Carson (%) Pre	Carson (%) Prim	Christie (%) Pre	Christie (%) Prim	Cruz (%) Pre	Cruz (%) Prim	Everson (%) Pre	Everson (%) Prim	Fiorina (%) Pre	Fiorina (%) Prim	Gilmore (%) Pre	Gilmore (%) Prim	Graham (%) Pre	Graham (%) Prim	Huckabee (%) Pre	Huckabee (%) Prim
Democrats																		
Chafee	1.0	—	0.2	—	0.0	—	0.2	—	0.0	—	0.0	—	0.0	—	0.0	—	0.0	—
Clinton	1.7	0.1	0.1	0.0	0.2	0.0	0.5	0.5	0.0	0.0	0.4	0.0	0.0	0.0	0.1	0.1	0.0	0.0
Lessig	0.3	—	0.0	—	0.1	—	0.1	—	0.0	—	0.1	—	0.0	—	0.1	—	0.1	—
O'Malley	0.3	0.0	0.3	1.0	0.0	0.0	0.1	0.5	0.0	0.0	0.1	0.0	0.0	0.0	0.0	0.0	0.1	0.0
Sanders	0.5	0.1	0.1	0.0	0.0	0.0	0.0	0.1	0.0	0.0	0.0	0.0	0.0	0.0	0.0	0.0	0.0	0.0
Webb	0.1	—	0.2	—	0.0	—	0.1	—	0.0	—	0.0	—	0.0	—	0.0	—	0.1	—
Republicans																		
Bush	**7.5**	**14.4**	0.0	0.1	0.0	0.1	0.0	0.3	0.0	0.0	0.0	0.0	0.0	0.0	0.2	2.0	0.0	0.0
Carson	0.6	0.0	**44.7**	**28.6**	0.0	0.0	0.4	0.9	0.0	0.0	0.9	0.0	0.0	0.0	0.2	0.0	0.1	0.0
Christie	0.2	1.7	0.0	0.3	**34.2**	**42.1**	0.2	0.4	0.0	0.0	0.2	0.0	0.0	0.0	0.1	0.0	0.0	0.3
Cruz	0.1	0.3	0.2	0.3	0.1	0.1	**41.1**	**58.2**	0.0	0.0	0.0	2.6	0.0	0.0	0.0	0.1	0.1	0.0
Everson	0.6	—	0.3	—	0.3	—	1.1	—	**27.3**	—	0.7	—	1.2	—	0.5	—	0.5	—
Fiorina	0.0	0.0	0.2	0.0	0.0	0.0	0.0	1.0	0.0	0.0	**50.0**	**26.6**	0.0	0.0	0.0	0.0	0.0	0.0
Gilmore	0.7	0.3	0.8	1.0	0.7	0.5	0.4	0.5	0.2	0.0	1.2	2.8	**35.0**	**45.5**	1.4	0.3	0.1	0.0
Graham	0.5	—	0.2	—	0.1	—	0.1	—	0.0	—	0.1	—	0.0	—	**27.4**	—	0.0	—
Huckabee	0.1	0.3	0.1	0.6	0.1	0.0	0.1	0.3	0.0	0.0	0.2	0.0	0.0	0.0	0.2	0.0	**21.4**	**25.8**
Jindal	0.7	—	0.1	—	0.1	—	0.7	—	0.0	—	0.1	—	0.0	—	0.1	—	0.0	—
Kasich	0.7	1.8	0.2	0.1	0.0	0.5	0.2	4.0	0.0	0.0	0.2	0.1	0.0	0.0	0.2	0.0	0.2	0.0
Pataki	2.3	—	0.7	—	0.8	—	1.0	—	0.0	—	0.8	—	0.2	—	1.8	—	0.4	—
Paul	0.6	0.8	0.1	0.3	0.6	0.6	0.5	2.8	0.0	0.0	0.2	0.1	0.0	0.0	0.1	0.0	0.0	0.1
Perry	0.5	—	0.1	—	0.1	—	0.1	—	0.0	—	0.3	—	0.0	—	0.2	—	0.0	—
Rubio	0.7	0.7	0.2	0.4	0.0	0.4	0.4	2.7	0.0	0.0	0.1	0.0	0.0	0.0	0.0	0.0	0.0	0.1
Santorum	0.3	0.2	0.3	0.5	0.3	0.1	1.0	2.0	0.0	0.0	0.3	0.8	0.0	0.0	0.2	0.1	0.0	0.0
Trump	3.6	3.3	1.0	0.9	0.3	0.3	0.9	**10.2**	0.0	0.0	0.4	0.1	0.0	0.0	0.4	0.8	0.3	0.3
Walker	0.1	—	0.2	—	0.0	—	0.0	—	0.0	—	0.1	—	0.0	—	0.0	—	0.1	—

(Continued)

TABLE 4 Continued

Sources	Jindal (%)		Kasich (%)		Pataki (%)		Paul (%)		Perry (%)		Rubio (%)		Santorum (%)		Trump (%)		Walker (%)	
	Pre	Prim	Pre	Prim	Pre	Prim	Pre	Prim	Pre	Prim	Pre	Prim	Pre	Prim	Pre	Prim	Pre	Prim
Democrats																		
Chafee	0.0	—	0.0	—	0.0	—	0.5	—	0.0	0.0	0.0	—	0.0	—	0.5	—	0.2	—
Clinton	0.0	0.0	0.2	0.2	0.0	0.0	0.1	0.1	0.0	0.0	0.9	0.2	0.0	0.0	2.1	**12.6**	0.5	0.1
Lessig	0.0	—	0.0	—	0.1	—	0.3	—	0.0	—	0.2	—	0.0	—	1.5	—	0.0	—
O'Malley	0.0	0.0	0.0	0.5	0.0	0.0	0.0	0.0	0.0	0.0	0.1	0.0	0.0	0.0	1.3	1.6	0.0	0.0
Sanders	0.0	0.0	0.1	0.0	0.0	0.0	0.1	0.1	0.0	0.0	0.1	0.1	0.0	0.0	0.9	1.6	0.1	0.2
Webb	0.0	—	0.0	—	0.0	—	0.1	—	0.0	—	0.1	—	0.1	—	1.5	—	0.0	—
Republicans																		
Bush	0.0	0.0	0.0	0.7	0.0	0.0	0.3	0.0	0.1	0.0	0.0	1.1	0.0	0.0	3.8	**9.6**	0.1	0.0
Carson	0.1	0.0	0.1	0.0	0.0	0.0	0.1	0.2	0.0	0.0	0.7	0.0	0.0	0.0	3.5	0.3	0.2	0.0
Christie	0.0	0.0	0.0	0.4	0.0	0.0	0.1	0.7	0.0	0.0	0.3	4.6	0.0	0.0	1.0	2.5	0.1	0.0
Cruz	0.1	0.0	0.0	0.6	0.0	0.0	0.3	0.1	0.1	0.4	0.4	1.5	0.0	0.0	0.4	**11.0**	0.2	0.8
Everson	0.1	—	0.6	—	0.3	—	0.2	—	0.2	—	0.1	—	0.1	—	0.6	—	0.0	—
Fiorina	0.0	—	0.0	0.0	0.0	0.0	0.2	0.0	0.0	0.0	0.0	0.5	0.0	0.5	0.3	2.1	0.0	0.0
Gilmore	0.0	0.0	0.5	0.3	0.6	0.0	1.1	0.5	0.4	0.0	0.3	0.3	0.3	0.8	**6.5**	3.6	1.2	0.0
Graham	0.1	—	0.2	—	0.0	—	0.4	—	0.0	—	0.1	—	0.0	—	2.5	—	0.2	—
Huckabee	0.2	0.0	0.1	0.0	0.0	0.0	0.2	0.0	0.1	0.0	0.1	0.0	0.0	0.0	0.4	0.8	0.1	0.0
Jindal	**10.1**	—	0.0	—	0.0	—	0.4	—	0.0	—	0.1	—	0.0	—	**6.8**	—	0.8	—
Kasich	0.1	0.0	**54.9**	**70.4**	0.1	0.3	0.2	0.1	0.0	0.0	0.2	1.9	0.0	0.0	3.3	**6.2**	0.2	0.0
Pataki	0.6	—	0.7	—	**49.4**	—	1.0	—	0.0	—	1.0	—	1.1	—	**9.9**	—	1.3	—
Paul	0.0	0.0	0.1	0.3	0.0	0.0	**49.0**	**55.8**	0.0	0.0	1.9	1.4	0.0	0.1	1.7	2.3	0.1	0.0
Perry	0.4	—	0.2	—	0.3	—	0.0	—	**35.0**	—	0.1	—	0.3	—	4.9	—	0.4	—
Rubio	0.0	0.2	0.1	0.5	0.0	0.1	0.1	0.1	0.0	0.0	**56.6**	**66.3**	0.0	0.2	0.4	**6.8**	0.2	0.0
Santorum	0.4	0.0	0.1	0.1	0.1	0.0	0.2	0.2	0.1	0.0	0.5	0.0	**68.9**	**89.6**	0.5	2.4	0.2	0.0
Trump	0.1	0.0	0.4	1.8	0.1	0.0	0.4	0.4	0.1	0.0	1.5	4.3	0.0	0.0	**58.2**	**35.7**	0.4	0.0
Walker	0.0	—	0.0	—	0.0	—	0.1	—	0.0	—	0.2	—	0.0	—	0.5	—	**36.4**	—

Note. Pre = preprimary phase; Prim = primary phase. Bolded percentages are greater than 5 percent.

nature of the findings suggest that it was not necessarily to improve their electability.

At their cores, both social identity theory and reference dependence purport that social comparison is an important tool for forging identification. Yet, Tables 3 and 4 show that tweets were used for self-advocacy more than comparison. As shown in Table 4, on the Republican side, Ben Carson, Mark Everson, and Carly Fiorina were outsiders, and the only candidates to mention them more than 5 percent of the time were themselves. Trump, who became the frontrunner and eventual nominee, was mentioned by three Republican insider candidates more than 5 percent of the time in the preprimary (6.5 to 9.9 percent) and by four insider Republican candidates (6.2 to 11.0 percent) plus Clinton 12.6 percent of the time during the primary. Trump was the only outsider candidate who was mentioned by other candidates consistently. It is not clear that the insider Republicans mentioned him to provide a contrast demonstrating their electability. Rather, Republican insider candidates may have mentioned Trump because he was the dark horse who took over the race.

Across the board, candidates overwhelmingly mentioned their own name more than anyone else's. This suggests that during the surfacing phase and primary campaigns, the candidates focus more on self-advocacy rather than define themselves by attacking others directly or using others to explain who they are. The most frequent "other" mentioned in Republican candidate tweets was President Obama. He received much more attention than did frontrunner Hillary Clinton. During the surfacing phase, Obama was mentioned in more than 5 percent of the tweets made by seven Republican candidates during the preprimary phase and two Republicans during the primary. Clinton was the object of more than 5 percent of tweets made by Jeb Bush, Carly Fiorina, Bobby Jindal, George Pataki, and Scott Walker during the preprimary phase and by Bush, Fiorina, and Donald Trump in the primary.

DISCUSSION

The findings of this study indicate that outsider candidates were not more likely than insider candidates to market themselves to voters through a heightened use of party or ideological labels in their social media presence during the surfacing phase and primary campaigns. Despite Benoit and Compton's (2014) finding that there was parity between acclaim and attack in 2012, the current study shows that advocating for oneself was used far more than focusing on intraparty or interparty opponents on the social media platform Twitter. Opponents were not mentioned with much frequency in comparison to self-references in both the preprimary and primary phases of the campaigns.

On the Democratic side, Jim Webb, who was not an outsider but did not receive as much attention from the media and public as did intraparty rivals Sanders and Clinton, used Democratic party labels more so than the other candidates. Webb was at an exposure disadvantage to the frontrunners and may have been using party labels to better situate himself within the Democratic Party. Clinton was not inclined to use Democratic Party labels in her tweets, but she used Republican labels more than the other Democratic candidates did. Her use of Republican labels ranged between 5.4 percent and 10 percent and was a reminder to constituents that defeating the Republicans was the ultimate goal.

That Clinton referenced Republicans to a greater extent than other Democratic candidates supports previous findings on frontrunners (Ridout and Holland 2010) and suggests that even in the preprimary phase, Clinton was already orienting herself to the general election fight, rather than setting out to win the Democratic Party's nomination. Yet the findings on Trump suggest that attacking the opposition should not be considered frontrunner-specific.

The eventual Republican winner Donald Trump did not use party or ideological labels frequently. He occasionally mentioned his intraparty opponents, but not more so than they mentioned him. Having never served in the military or elective office, Trump embraced his outsider status and did not seem compelled to go out of his way to demonstrate that he was a "real" Republican or conservative through party and ideological labels. As the front-runner for most of the surfacing phase and primary campaign, Trump did not give his opponents much of his limelight. He mentioned Democrat Hillary Clinton in 2.9 percent of his preprimary tweets and 7.4 percent of his primary tweets. While Trump spent some time attacking Clinton, she was not the focus of his posts as much as he was of hers in the primary. Clinton mentioned Trump in more than 12 percent of her primary tweets with posts such as, "It's time to judge Donald Trump by his words and his deeds. And they make him unfit to be president of the United States." (June 4, 2016) and. "As @POTUS spoke powerfully on protecting kids from gun violence, @realDonaldTrump said end gun free school zones. We deserve better. –H" (January 8, 2016). When Trump tweeted, he often focused on her fitness to be president. For example, he tweeted, "The new e-mail release is a disaster for Hillary Clinton. At a minimum, how can someone with such bad judge-ment be our next president?" (January 29, 2016) and. "Hillary Clinton is unfit to be president. She has bad judgement, poor leadership skills and a very bad and destructive track record. Change!" (June 5, 2016).

Particularly noteworthy is the amount of attention Trump received from other candidates, in addition to that from Clinton. Although our results suggest that candidates focused on themselves during early campaigning, likely in an effort to increase name recognition and build a positive image, they also devoted messages to critiquing Trump. Some of these attacks did suggest Trump was an unworthy Republican nominee because of questionable ideology. For instance, @TedCruz tweeted, "This race is simple. Donald Trump and Hillary Clinton are both big government liberals" (April 27, 2016). Others critiqued his character, such as @JebBush on February 17, 2016, who tweeted, "Honored to have the support of Green Beret Michael Waltz. Watch him expose Trump as unfit to be Commander-in-Chief. https://t.co/cHdaE5eO30." The frequent attention paid to Trump likely implied to the public that the other presidential candidates viewed him as a legitimate threat for the nomination. Rather than conveying a contrast that established their credibility and hence electability, the focus may have backfired and added to the perception that Trump was a viable, and electable Republican candidate for the presidency.

The data in this study were comprehensive, but not without limitations. We chose to focus on manifest content about party and ideological labels and candidate names. Important latent themes may have been missed with the dictionary approach to the analysis. The data, moreover, were collected during a specific campaign and within a specific period of that campaign, which naturally circumscribes the generalizations that should be made from them. Although our findings do not support social identity theory expectations in the social media preprimary/primary context, it is possible that the theory contributes to our understanding of partisan labeling when the ingroups and outgroups are more transparent (e.g., general election).

Although much research focuses on negative tactics during presidential elections, it appears that self-references outweigh attacks on social media in the initial stages of the presidential campaigns. This finding was true of both Democratic and Republican candidates. Mentioning other candidates was simply not as frequent as mentioning oneself in the 2016 presidential preprimary and primary campaigns. The analyses in this study suggest that it does appear that, rather than attacking the opposition party as social identity theory would predict, candidates chose to use social media to focus on themselves. In the surfacing and primary phases of the campaign when the candidates are trying to boost name recognition, mentioning oneself is the primary theme on Twitter. Social media provide affordances for diffusion. Candidates may feel particularly compelled to reference themselves in social media posts in anticipation that their tweets will be retweeted and/or picked up in mainstream news. A single tweet is not guaranteed coverage, but Twitter overall permits relatively quick and inexpensive access to opportunities for coverage within one's network of followers and beyond. Self-reference in social media assures that one's name is passed along with one's ideas if and when the messages are spread. Future research should continue to explore such trends and compare self-references and attacks in new media messaging to other campaign modalities and in the general election to determine the scope and nature of social media affordances in presidential campaigns.

NOTES

1. Ridout and Holland's (2010) analysis of campaign advertising found that rather than attacking ideologically similar candidates, "candidates are more apt to engage in intraparty attacks against ideologically distinct opponents than those who are ideologically similar" (628). Such an analysis does not equate with the insider–outsider dynamics explored here but does add credence to our assertions.

2. Original tweets contain 140 characters. Retweets (RTs) contained 140 characters in the scraping but that included the identification of the source of the RT, resulting in a few words at the very end of the material retweeted occasionally cut off to make room for the source's handle.

ORCID

Christine R. Filer ⓘ http://orcid.org/0000-0001-9969-8928

REFERENCES

Abramowitz, A. I. 2015. "Partisan Nation: The Rise of Affective Partisanship in the American Electorate." In *The State of the Parties: The Changing Role of Contemporary American Parties*, 7th ed., edited by J. C. Green, D. J. Coffey, and D. B. Cohen, 21–36. New York: Rowman and Littlefield.

Adams, A., and T. McCorkindale. 2013. "Dialogue and Transparency: A Content Analysis of How the 2012 Presidential Candidates Used Twitter." *Public Relations Review* 39 (4):357–59. doi:10.1016/j.pubrev.2013.07.016

Allport, G. W. 1954. *The Nature of Prejudice*. Cambridge, MA: Addison-Wesley.

Bafumi, J., and R. Y. Shapiro. 2009. "A New Partisan Voter." *Journal of Politics* 7 (1): 1–24.

Bendle, N. T. 2014. "Reference Dependence in Political Primaries." *Journal of Political Marketing* 13:307–33. doi:10.1080/15377857.2012.721738

Bennett, W. L. 2012. *News: The Politics of Illusion*. 9th ed. New York: Longman.

Benoit, W. L. 2007. *Communication in Political Campaigns*. New York, NY: Peter Lang.

Benoit, W. L. 2017. "The Functional Theory of Political Campaign Communication." In *The Oxford Handbook of Communication*, edited by K. Kenski and K. H. Jamieson, 195–204. New York: Oxford University Press.

Benoit, W. L., and J. L. Compton. 2014. "A Functional Analysis of 2012 Republican Primary TV Spots." *American Behavioral Scientist* 58:497–509. doi:10.1177/0002764213506209

Brenner, J., and A. Smith. 2013. "72% of Online Adults Are Social Networking Site Users." Pew Research Center. August 5. Accessed September 1, 2016. http://www.pewinternet.org/2013/08/05/72-of-online-adults-are-social-networking-site-users/

Brewer, M. B. 1999. "The Psychology of Prejudice: Ingroup Love and Outgroup Hate?" *Journal of Social Issues* 55 (3):429–44. doi:10.1111/0022-4537.00126

Catanese, D. 2015. "The Biggest Republican Primary in 100 Years." U.S. News & World Report. July 2. Accessed May 4, 2017. www.usnews.com/news/blogs/run-2016/2015/07/02/the-biggest-republican-primary-in-100-years

Conway-Silva, B. A., C. R. Filer, K. Kenski, and E. Tsetsi. 2017. "Reassessing Twitter's Agenda-Building Power: An Analysis of Intermedia Agenda-Setting Effects During the 2016 Presidential Primary Season." *Social Science Computer Review.*

Conway, B. A., K. Kenski, and D. Wang. 2013. "Twitter Use by Presidential Primary Candidates During the 2012 Campaign." *American Behavioral Scientist* 57 (11):1596–610. doi:10.1177/0002764213489014

Conway, B. A., K. Kenski, and D. Wang. 2015. "The Rise of Twitter in the Political Campaign: Searching for Intermedia Agenda-setting Effects in the Presidential Primary." *Journal of Computer Mediated Communication* 20 (4):363–80. doi:10.1111/jcc4.12124

Edsall, T. B. 1999. "Study Disputes Clinton 1996 Campaign Strategy." The Washington Post. May 22. A4.

Fiorina, M. P., S. J. Abrams, and J. Pope. 2006. *Culture War? The Myth of a Polarized America.* 2nd ed. New York: Pearson.

Golbeck, J., J. M. Grimes, and A. Rogers. 2010. "Twitter use by the U.S. Congress." *Journal of the American Society for Information Science and Technology* 61 (8):1612–621.

Gorard, S. 2013. *Research Design: Creating Robust Approaches for the Social Sciences.* Los Angeles: Sage.

Gottfried, J., and E. Shearer. 2016. "News use Across Social Media Platforms 2016." Pew Research Center. Accessed September 1, 2016. http://www.journalism. org/2016/05/26/news-use-across-social-media-platforms-2016/

Graham, T., M. Broersma, K. Hazelhoff, and G. van't Haar. 2013. "Between Broadcasting Political Messages and Interacting with Voters: The Use of Twitter During the 2010 UK General Election Campaign." *Information, Communication & Society* 16 (5):692–16. doi:10.1080/1369118x.2013.785581

Grant, W. J., B. Moon, and J. B. Grant. 2010. "Digital Dialogue? Australian Politicians' Use of the Social Network Tool Twitter." *Australian Journal of Political Science* 45 (4):579–604. doi:10.1080/10361146.2010.517176

Greene, S. 2004. "Social Identity Theory and Party Identification." *Social Science Quarterly* 85 (1):136–53. doi:10.1111/j.0038-4941.2004.08501010.x

Groshek, J., and M. C. Groshek. 2010. "Agenda Trending: Reciprocity and the Predictive Capacity of Social Networking Sites in Intermedia Agenda Setting Across Topics over Time." *Media and Communication* 1 (1):15–27.

Gueorguieva, V. 2008. "Voters, MySpace, and YouTube: The Impact of Alternative Communication Channels on the 2006 Election Cycle and Beyond." *Social Science Computer Review* 26 (3):288–300.

Herrera, R. (1996–1997). "Understanding the Language of Politics: A Study of Elites and Masses." *Political Science Quarterly* 111 (4):619–37.

Iyengar, S., G. Sood, and Y. Lelkes. 2012. "Affect, Not Ideology: A Social Identity Perspective on Polarization." *Public Opinion Quarterly* 76 (3):405–31.

Jamieson, K. H. 1992. *Dirty Politics: Deception, Distraction, and Democracy.* New York: Oxford University Press.

Jamieson, K. H. 1996. *Packaging the Presidency: A History and Criticism of Presidential Campaign Advertising.* 3rd ed. New York: Oxford University Press.

Jang, S. M., and J. Pasek. 2015. "Assessing the Carrying Capacity of Twitter and Online News." *Mass Communication and Society* 18 (5):577–98. doi:10.1080/15205436.2015.1035397

Jarvis, S. E. 2005. *The Talk of the Party: Political Labels, Symbolic Capital, & American Life*. Lanham, MD: Rowman & Littlefield.

Jarvis, S. E. 2017. "Political Messages and Partisanship." In *The Oxford Handbook of Communication*, edited by K. Kenski and K. H. Jamieson, 133–146. New York: Oxford University Press.

Jarvis, S. E., and E. B. Jones. 2005. "Party Labels in Presidential Acceptance Addresses: 1948–2000." In *In the Public Domain: Presidents and the Challenge of Public Leadership*, edited by L. C. Han and D. J. Heith, 29–48. Albany, NY: State University of New York Press.

Johnson, T. J., and D. D. Perlmutter. 2010. "Introduction: The Facebook Election." *Mass Communication and Society* 13 (5):554–59.

Jungherr, A. 2014. "The Logic of Political Coverage on Twitter: Temporal Dynamics and Content." *Journal of Communication* 64 (2):239–59. doi:10.1111/jcom.12087

Jungherr, A. 2016. "Twitter Use in Election Campaigns: A Systematic Literature Review." *Journal of Information Technology & Politics* 13 (1):72–91.

Kenski, K. M., B. A. Conway, and C. R. Filer. 2015. *Campaign Media Congruence: Issues in 2012 Presidential Election Tweets and Ads*. CA: Paper presented at the American Political Science Association in San Francisco, September 3–6, 2015.

Lengauer, G., F. Esser, and R. Berganza. 2011. "Negativity in Political News: A Review of Concepts, Operationalizations, and Key Findings." *Journalism* 13 (2):179–202.

Mayhew, D. R. 2008. *Parties and Policies: How the American Government Works*. New Haven, CT: Yale University Press.

Metzgar, E., and A. Maruggi. 2009. "Social Media and the 2008 U.S. Presidential Election." *Journal of New Communications Research* 4 (1):141–65.

National Public Radio. 2003. "Former Vermont Gov. Howard Dean." July 2. Accessed April 30, 2017. http://www.npr.org/programs/specials/democrats2004/dean.html

Pacilli, M. G., M. Roccato, S. Pagliaro, and S. Russo. 2016. "From Political Opponents to Enemies? The Role of Perceived Moral Distance in the Animalistic Dehumanization of the Political Outgroup." *Group Processes & Intergroup Relations* 19:360–73.

Pew Research Center. 2014. "Political Polarization in the American Public." June 12. Accessed May 1, 2017. http://www.people-press.org/2014/06/12/political-polarization-in-the-american-public/

Pfau, M., and H. C. Kenski. 1990. *Attack Politics: Strategy and Defense*. New York: Praeger.

Pratto, F., and O. P. John. 1991. "Automatic Vigilance: The Attention-Grabbing Power of Negative Social Information." *Journal of Personality and Social Psychology* 61 (3):380–91.

Ridout, T. N., and J. L. Holland. 2010. "Candidate Strategies in the Presidential Nomination Campaign." *Presidential Studies Quarterly* 40 (4):611–30. doi:10.1111/j.1741-5705.2010.03803.x

Sayre, B., L. Bode, D. Shah, D. Wilcox, and C. Shah. 2010. "Agenda Setting in a Digital Age: Tracking attention to California proposition 8 in social media, Online News, and Conventional News." *Policy & Internet* 2 (2):7–32. doi:10.2202/1944-2866.1040

Stroud, N. J. 2011. *Niche News: The Politics of News Choice*. New York: Oxford University Press.

Taber, C. S., and M. Lodge. 2006. "Motivated Skepticism in the Evaluation of Political Beliefs." *American Journal of Political Science* 50:755–69. doi:10.1111/j.1540-5907.2006.00214.x

Tajfel, H., and J. Turner. 1979. "An Integrative Theory of Intergroup Conflict." In *The Social Psychology of Intergroup Relations*, edited by W. G. Austin and S. Worchel, 33–47. Monterey, CA: Brooks/Cole.

Towner, T. L., and D. A. Dulio. 2012. "New Media and Political Marketing in the United States: 2012 and Beyond." *Journal of Political Marketing* 11 (1–2): 95–119. doi:10.1080/15377857.2012.642748

Webb, P. H., and M. L. Ray. 1979. "Effects of TV Clutter." *Journal of Advertising Research* (June):7–14.

Wells, C., D. V. Shah, J. C. Pevehouse, J. Yang, A. Pelled, F. Boehm, J. Lukito, S. Ghosh, and J. L. Schmidt. 2016. "How Trump Drove Coverage to the Nomination: Hybrid Media Campaigning." *Political Communication* 33 (4):669–76. doi:10.1080/10584609.2016.1224416

Wu, H. D., and R. Coleman. 2009. "Advanced Agenda-Setting Theory: The Comparative Strength and New Contingent Conditions of the Two Levels of Agenda-Setting Effects." *Journalism and Mass Communication Quarterly* 86 (4):775–89. doi:10.1177/107769900908600404

The Image is the Message: Instagram Marketing and the 2016 Presidential Primary Season

CAROLINE LEGO MUÑOZ

TERRI L. TOWNER

The 2016 presidential primary candidates expanded their social media marketing campaigns to include the image- and video-centered social network platform Instagram. To explore the role that images play in framing political character development and to identify which images received higher levels of engagement, content analyses were performed on the top seven primary candidates' Instagram accounts. Results indicate that candidates most frequently employ the ideal candidate frame in their images, which also garnered the highest number of user likes and comments. Results also reveal that among Instagram image attributes, candidates frequently and successfully used text within their images, but filters were inconsistently applied across the candidates.

INTRODUCTION

The 2008 Obama presidential campaign demonstrated the profound impact of social media platforms. In the eight years following, social media marketing has continued to evolve, incorporating sophisticated data-mining techniques, geolocation services, and mobile technologies to increase candidate communication with constituents. Previous campaigns relied on social media communication that was often text-based; as such, most of the research conducted on social media has been on its textual content (Highfield and Leaver 2015). Yet, social media platforms are increasingly shifting away from text to visual communication (Gupta 2013). Image- and video-centered social media platforms, such as YouTube, Instagram, Tumblr, Pinterest, and Snapchat, have had quick consumer adoption rates. These visual-centric social media platforms provide new avenues of self-presentation and image management. This shift to more visual social media platforms is notable and signals the potential of increasingly persuasive political social media messages. It is therefore prudent that scholars seek to understand the role that images play in political campaigning.

To explore images' role in presidential political marketing and framing political character development, this study examines Instagram. Released in 2010, the photo- and video-sharing social networking platform Instagram allows users to communicate by posting, sharing, and liking images. User engagement is significantly higher on Instagram when compared to Facebook and Twitter (Elliott 2015a). In December 2016, Instagram reached 600 million users—a user base that is approximately double the size of Twitter (Instagram 2016; Twitter 2016). Regarding demographics, Instagram users are more likely to be female, nonwhite, and between the ages of 18 and 29, with 28 percent of adult Internet users using the platform (Duggan 2015). Instagram's growing popularity and potential constituent reach made it an ideal political marketing platform. Each of the 2016 presidential primary candidates embraced Instagram as visually rich self-presentation platform, offering behind-the-scenes looks, family photographs, issue messages, thank you messages, and pictures of rallies.

While political researchers have begun to address the effects of Facebook and Twitter (Towner 2013; Bode and Dalrymple 2016; Towner and Muñoz 2016), we know very little of how politicians use Instagram images in their self-presentation, what types of images will illicit the most engagement, and the images' attitudinal and behavioral impact on voters. Industry research, coupled with literature in the computer science discipline, offer some guidelines to increase Instagram engagement (Bakhshi, Shamma, and Gilbert 2014; Hu, Manikonda, and Kambhampati 2014a; Zarella 2014; Manikonda, Meduri, and Kambhampati 2016; Jaakonmaki, Muller, and vom Brocke 2017), but does this advice apply to political candidates' Instagram accounts? To address this gap, we apply Grabe and Bucy's (2009) visual analysis framework used in examining traditional, offline political television news coverage to the 2016 presidential primary candidate's Instagram feed. In addition, we seek to identify which frames and image attributes contribute to higher levels of engagement (i.e., most liked and commented on images).

Visual Communication

"A picture is worth a thousand words" is not a cliché phrase. Previous research demonstrates that images can be more memorable, garner more attention, and illicit more emotive responses than text in traditional, offline advertising (Childers and Houston 1984; Graber 1996; Pieters and Wedel 2004; Brader 2005; Bucher and Schumacher 2006). In psychology research, this phenomenon has been called "the picture superiority effect" (Paivio, Rogers, and Smythe 1968; Stenberg 2006), which, when applied to political campaigning, asserts that the power of even a single photograph has the ability to affect a voter's judgments on a variety of candidate character traits (Rosenberg et al. 1986). Despite the persuasive potential of images, they have often been overlooked in recent political research (Grabe and Bucy 2009; Schill 2012). In particular, we know little on how political actors utilize images in "self-presentation" on social media sites, such as Twitter and Instagram. Self-presentation, or impression management, acknowledges an individual's attempts to influence the impression of others in an effort to achieve their own goals (Goffman 1974). Political research on traditional media and new media has explored self-presentation (Schutz 1995; Stanyer 2008; Cmeciu 2014; Lee 2016), but our research focuses on the one self-presentation strategy that political candidates can control: how their visual images are framed on social media.

Visual Framing

Framing theory, originated by Goffman's (1974) work, examines how communication is presented to individuals, acknowledging its ability to influence how they process this information, thus swaying their perceptions of what is depicted. Frames provide a "schemata of interpretation" or story lines that enable individuals to make sense of what they read or see by drawing upon their previous experiences (Goffman 1974: 10; see also Entman 1993). Traditionally, framing studies have been used to examine text (Berger 1991); however, visual framing has been utilized to explore a number of wide-ranging topics (Hardin et al. 2002; Fahmy 2005; Borah 2009), including the portrayal of political actors in traditional television coverage (Grabe and Bucy 2009).

Grabe and Bucy's (2009) visual framing analysis of television coverage of the 1992 through 2004 presidential campaigns is central to our research, as we build on their master character frames found in newscasts: *the ideal candidate, the populist campaigner*, and *the sure loser*. To briefly summarize, Grabe and Bucy's findings reveal that Democratic candidates were more commonly depicted in the news as a populist campaigner, whereas Republican candidates were shown as the ideal candidate. They also note a disconnect between the character traits that the campaign organizers wanted to communicate versus what was ultimately covered in the news. While Grabe and Bucy (2009) analyzed news coverage, other scholars have also applied their visual framing framework on candidates' visual self-presentation strategies on online media. For example, Lee's (2016) cross-cultural comparison of presidential website photos of President Obama and President Lee Myung-bak (South Korea) reveals that the ideal candidate subdimension of statesmanship was the most commonly emphasized charac-ter frame for the South Korean's president, whereas Obama emphasized populist frames, such as compassion and mass appeal, more frequently (Lee 2016).

Moving beyond presidential candidate websites to newer forms of online media, Goodnow (2013) applied Grabe and Bucy's (2009) framework in a semiotic analysis of Barack Obama and Mitt Romney's Facebook timeline photos during the 2012 general election. Specifically, the visual analysis revealed that both Obama and Romney's Facebook timeline photos depicted the ideal candidate and populist campaigner master frames, although each candidate employed them using different subdimensions (statesmanship vs. compassion) on Facebook. However, mass appeal, a subdimension of the populist master frame, was applied in similar ways between the candidates. Also applying Grabe and Bucy's (2009) visual frames in the 2014 European Parliament elections, Cmeciu's (2014) content analysis of the Facebook images of Romanian candidates reveals that candidates pri-marily used the ideal candidate master frame focusing on statesmanship. Images within statesmanship were commonly elected officials and other influentials and identifiable entourage. Within the compassion subdimen-sion, Cmeciu (2014: 424) notes that female candidates posted images interacting with children and "represented themselves as the prototype of a protective mother," whereas the male candidates did not. Romanian candidates only infrequently posted photos of their families.

The previous research indicates that candidates strategically employ visual frames in traditional and online media to fulfill certain campaign func-tions. While some research exists regarding visual political communication within social media, less is known on how politicians incorporate Instagram into their marketing strategies. Our purpose is to apply Grabe and Bucy's (2009) framing typology to examine the visual frames employed on Instagram by the 2016 presidential primary candidates. The research goes further by examining which visual frames garner the most engagement from Instagram users.

Instagram

Previous work addressing Instagram's role in politics examines how voters, political candidates, and parties communicate on the platform as well has how candidates present themselves on Instagram (Mahoney et al. 2016;

Russmann and Svensson 2017). Research conducted on the Scottish electorate examined voters' "everyday social political talk." Mahoney et al.'s (2016) qualitative analysis of Instagram images, using the hashtags #IndyRef and #GE2015, uncovered visual themes, such as propaganda and persuasion, voting process, portrayal of self, portrayal of others, and established symbolism. Other studies have also examined how political candidates and parties have employed Instagram in their political marketing communications. In the 2014 Swedish national elections, Russmann and Svensson (2017) found that political parties rarely used Instagram to directly communicate with their followers and the quality of these interactions—when they occur—was not substantial. Filimonov, Russman, and Svennsoon (2016) reveal that Swedish parties employed Instagram primarily to broadcast information, not to mobilize voters. Approximately half of the Instagram posts depicted other campaign instruments (e.g., depictions of other new media sources and traditional media) in what the authors called a "hybridity" strategy. Another study, addressing Bahraini candidates on Instagram, notes that candidates utilized mobilization strategies by offering an "invitation into their campaign tents," and the platform served as means to personally connect with their voters (Eldin 2016).

More recently, scholars have begun to explore how parties and politicians manage their images on Instagram. To our knowledge, only two studies have addressed politicians' and parties' impression management strategies on Instagram. This limited research has found that Instagram was used as a "virtual billboard" for Swedish political parties, often providing personalized yet professional postings of the parties' top candidates. Personal lives of candidates, such as images depicting their families and hobbies, were rarely provided (Filimonov, Russman, and Svennsoon 2016). Instagram political communication addressing image management has also been examined utilizing a visual framing perspective to compare how the Syrian presidency communicated to English and Arabic audiences (Holiday, Lewis, and LaBaugh 2015). Holiday et al. (2015) found that some themes (e.g., youth, societal support, and religion) were shown equally between these two groups, whereas nationalism and patriotism where communicated more readily to the English audiences.

In the context of the U.S. presidential primary election, applying the Grabe and Bucy (2009) framing typology we ask: (RQ1A) How did each candidate market himself or herself through self-framing strategies via image Instagram posts?

Instagram Engagement and Image Attributes

To determine the success of social media campaigns, marketers turn to a number of engagement metrics. In general, these metrics allow marketers to determine how often consumers interact with content, which may signal the posted material's popularity. The number of account followers, "likes" or "favorited" content, comments, and shares are some of the primary means to determine whether a campaign has achieved its objectives. Within Instagram, engagement is primarily evaluated through number of likes and comments. However, it is important to note that all forms of social media engagement are not the same (Li 2010). For example, the one-click activity of "liking" a post is less involved than writing a comment. Writing a comment involves more time and effort and allows a consumer to personalize their involvement. In both cases, a post with a large number of "likes" and comments signals its value to other viewers. Yet, what types of content drive engagement on Instagram? Unfortunately, there is little work done in this area.

Hu, Manikonda, and Kambhampati (2014) identified eight categories of image content posted on Instagram: friends, food, gadgets, captioned photos, pets, activities, selfies, and fashion. However, they did not find a significant relationship between a user's photo content and their number of followers (Hu, Manikonda, and Kambhampati 2014b). Another study examining Instagram posts found that Instagram users were more likely to post positive "lighthearted happy personal" updates and less likely to share negative content (Manikonda, Meduri, and Kambhampati 2016). To understand what types of content drive political communication, we ask: (RQ2B) What is the relationship between self-framing themes and Instagram engagement?

Outside of image content, scholars have also examined how specific image attributes, such as filter use and text applied to pictures, can influence engagement. In relationship to filters, Instagram has provided additional technology affordances. Affordance theory originated as a relational construct focusing on the possibility of actions in an environment (Gibson 1979). Later research by Norman (1988) extended affordance theory to the "properties of things." It addresses both the real and perceived properties of an item. It emphasizes that items are designed to promote specific behaviors, but users must perceive the potential benefit(s) it can offer (Norman 1988). The design functions of Instagram filters encourage users to alter their images. It is also apparent that some users do perceive that filters afford them an opportunity to present their best "self" online. Specifically, filters can correct perceived problems, improve the overall aesthetic, and add creativity to images. Motivations to use filters can also include changing the color, highlighting an item in the photo, and creating nostalgic effects (Bakhsi, Shamma, Kennedy and Gilbert 2014). These filter affordances should also benefit political campaign marketing.

A relationship between filter use and engagement has been found, although the results are somewhat mixed. On Instagram, the Clarendon filter is the most popular filter applied to photos. It is described as "an all-purpose filter that brightens, highlights, and intensifies shadows for color that pops." It is also the default filter after the "normal" option (Canva 2016). One study analyzing Instagram found that when the Clarendon filter was used, a post would receive 79 more likes and comments (Jaakonmaki, Muller, and vom Brocke 2017). In contrast, an Instagram study found that photos with "no filter" generated the highest number of likes per follower (Zarella 2014).

Utilizing captioned photos on Instagram has become a common practice for both marketers and users (Hu, Manikonda, and Kambhampati 2014). Text is either placed on top of an image or is presented on a block of color. Although there is limited research on this topic, one study found that pictures containing text increased the number of likes and comments (Jaakonmaki, Muller, and vom Brocke 2017). In addition, text quotes have been demonstrated to increase engagement (i.e., retweets) on Twitter (Zarella 2013; Rogers 2014). While Instagram research has explored image attributes used and their influence on engagement for consumers, we do not have an understanding of the specific image attributes used by political actors or their effectiveness in driving engagement. We, therefore, propose the following research questions: (RQ1B) Which image attributes (text and filters) did the presidential primary candidates utilize in their Instagram feed? (RQ2B) Which image attributes (text and filters) are found in the most engaged Instagram posts?

METHODOLOGY

This research analyzed the Instagram postings of the Democratic, Republican, and Independent party's top seven presidential primary candidates over the 2016 presidential primary period: Hillary Clinton, Ted Cruz, Gary Johnson,[1] John Kasich, Marco Rubio, Bernie Sanders, and Donald Trump. Instagram data were obtained through the Beautifeye (www.beautifeye.co) visual intelligence software platform. Beautifeye was contracted to scan images and collect corresponding image data: direct URL link to the posted image, date of image posted, number of likes, number of comments, image captions, and type of image filter used.

The Instagram data for the content analysis were drawn and analyzed throughout the 2016 presidential primary period from January 1, 2016, to June 30, 2016. The starting date represents a one-month period prior to the Iowa Caucuses held on February 1. Whereas the end point date represents two weeks after the last presidential primary (i.e., the District of Columbia primary held on June 14, 2016). The number of Instagram posts from the seven candidates' verified Instagram accounts varied depending primarily on the length of their presidential primary run and their social media proficiency: hillaryclinton ($n = 307$), sentedcruz ($n = 16$) and cruzforpresident ($n = 110$),[2] govgaryjohnson ($n = 107$), johnkasich ($n = 155$), marcorubiofla ($n = 122$), berniesanders ($n = 286$), and realdonaldtrump ($n = 449$). Each image and, when applicable, corresponding data (e.g., type of filter) served as the unit of analysis. Instagram posts that included videos were not included in the content analyses.[3]

Content Analyses

SELF-FRAMING

To explore how each candidate presented themselves via Instagram, a deductive qualitative content analyses was performed by the authors. The initial coding sheet was derived from Grabe and Bucy's (2009) systemic coding of the visual framing of presidential candidates in news coverage. The sure loser master frame projects the candidate in a negative light, highlighting campaign mistakes and the visual loss of support. Given that self-presentation strategies will not highlight negative candidate depictions, the sure loser category is not discussed further in this research. This is consistent with previous studies examining visual framing within social media (Goodnow 2013; Cmeciu 2014). The following discussion briefly summarizes the ideal candidate and populist campaigner themes and their related dimensions and subdimensions.

The ideal candidate theme is portrayed through two broad dimensions: statesmanship and compassion. Statesmanship was visually communicated through images of "power, control, and active leadership" (Grabe and Bucy 2009, p. 102). Images containing elected officials and influentials, patriotic symbols, symbols of progress (e.g., manufacturing plants), identifiable entourage (e.g., reporters, aides), campaign paraphernalia, political hoopla (e.g., streamers), and candidates in formal attire were consistent with this dimension. Compassion is depicted through images conveying warmth and kindness: children, family associations, admiring women, religious symbols, affinity gestures (e.g., thumbs up), interaction with individuals, and physical embraces. The populist theme builds upon the idea that "ordinary people, a noble troupe, stand in opposition to an aristocratic and self-serving elite" (p. 105). Populism is visually communicated through mass appeal and ordinariness dimensions. Mass appeal draws upon the notion that the candidate has achieved popular approval. Images depicting celebrities, large audiences, approving audiences, and interaction with crowds demonstrate various forms of popularity. Ordinariness depicts candidates wearing informal attire, casual dress, or athletic clothing, interacting with ordinary people and participating in physical activity.

Each Instagram image was coded for a primary and, if relevant, a secondary frame.[4] While the coding criteria employed was similar to Grabe and Bucy's (2009) original coding, several changes were made when we applied it to Instagram.[5] Any changes to the coding sheet were made in the initial interrater preliminary coding session of randomly selected images done prior to the content analyses. Theme determination was made by looking at the posted image's content, which included examining the foreground and background, not the accompanying caption. The primary frame was determined when the majority of the image's focus was directed toward that theme. In some cases, a secondary frame was present in the image. When a theme could not be determined, the image caption was read to provide context; however, this occurred for only 8 percent (thirteen images) of the images in the self-framing random sample. A random sample of 10 percent of Instagram posts was drawn from each of the candidate's verified Instagram accounts ($n = 157$). Interrater agreement of the primary frame in the self-framing sample ranged from 100 to 94.93 percent agreement.

ENGAGEMENT

To explore which frames elicited the highest levels of engagement, the top ten engaged photos for each of the seven presidential candidates for both number of likes and number of comments were analyzed ($N = 140$).[6] Using the same self-framing coding sheet, a separate content analysis was conducted to determine which specific frames garnered the most engagement. Engagement was determined by the number of likes and number of comments that each image obtained during the primary period. Similar to the previous self-framing content analysis, theme determination was made by examining the posted image, not the accompanying caption. When a theme could not be determined, the image caption was read to provide context. The latter occurred for only 3 percent (four images) of the images in the engagement sample. Interrater agreement of the primary frame for the most liked and most commented on images ranged from 100 to 91.42 percent agreement.

In addition to the qualitative content analysis, a descriptive quantitative analysis of candidate images was conducted to determine the popular practices of incorporating text and filters in the Instagram images. A combined sample, which included all posts from each of the seven presidential candidates' Instagram feeds, was used in the filter analysis (filter $N = 1552$).

RESULTS

The presidential candidate's use of Instagram varied dramatically between the candidates. Trump was the most frequent user ($n = 449$), followed by Clinton ($n = 307$) and Sanders ($n = 286$). The remaining Republican and Independent candidates had relatively similar use patterns (Cruz $n = 126$; Johnson $n = 107$; Kasich $n = 155$; Rubio $n = 122$). As discussed in the section below, we sought to answer how each candidate marketed themselves through self-framing strategies via image Instagram posts (RQ1).

Research Question 1: Self-Framing Results

The presidential candidates relied more heavily on the ideal candidate master frame, opposed to the populist campaigner (see Table 1). In particular, more

TABLE 1 Frame Totals From Self-Framing Random Sample

Master theme	Dimension	Subdimension	Primary frame	Secondary frame
Ideal candidate				
	Statesmanship			
		Elected Official/ influential	11	1
		Patriotic symbols	23	16
		Progress	7	1
		Identifiable Entourage	5	4
		Campaign Paraphernalia	14	2
		Formal attire	1	1
	Statesmanship total		**61**	**25**
	Compassion			
		Children	4	3
		Family Associations	10	0
		Admiring Individuals	2	1
		Religious	1	2
		Affinity gestures	10	13
		Interaction with individuals	5	3
		Physical embraces	8	3
	Compassion total		**40**	**25**
Ideal candidate total			**101**	**50**
Populist campaigner				
	Mass appeal			
		Celebrities	6	2
		Large audiences	34	13
		Approving Audiences	5	4
		Interaction with crowds	1	1
	Mass appeal total		**46**	**20**
	Ordinariness			
		Informal attire	1	0
		Casual dress	0	3
		Ordinary people	9	7
	Ordinariness total		**10**	**10**
Populist campaigner total			**56**	**30**

Note. The following subdimensions were not present in sampled images: Political hoopla, athletic clothing, and physical activity.

images incorporated the statesmanship dimensions with patriotic symbols (six candidates), campaign paraphernalia (seven candidates), and elected officials/influentials (five candidates). The dimension of compassion was executed primarily through posting photos of one's family as well as offering a number of different types of affinity gestures. Some candidates, particularly Kasich, Cruz, and Trump, offered current family photos, whereas Clinton used historical family photos. Affinity gestures were readily demonstrated by having the candidate raise their hands to a crowd or offering a thumbs-up gesture (i.e., a common gesture for Trump). The populist campaigner master theme was seen most readily in the mass appeal dimension. Each candidate, with the exception of Johnson, had multiple large audience images. Ordinariness was infrequently utilized (see Table 2 for specific examples of all dimensions).

While there were many commonalities in self-framing across the candidates, there were also notable differences in how each candidate framed themselves via Instagram. Candidate differences were determined by calculating the percentage of the frames in a category from their overall sample size. Each candidate had a majority of their sampled images fall within the ideal candidate master theme with the exception of Kasich. Kasich was the only candidate to have a slight majority of images sampled fall under the populist master frame. Johnson had the highest percentage of ideal candidate images in the primary frame relative to the other candidates. Rubio and Johnson also applied the statesmanship theme in a majority of their images, whereas the other candidates had approximately a third of their Instagram posts contain that dimension. In particular, Rubio frequently used elected officials in his images. Most of the sampled candidate images contained patriotic symbols, but Trump was a more frequent user of patriotic symbols in both primary and secondary image frames. Within the compassion dimension, Clinton and Cruz implemented it most frequently. Specifically, Clinton's images included more family photographs relative to the other candidates, whereas Cruz posted images depicting physical contact with his supporters (e.g., arm around a supporter). The use of affinity gestures also differed between candidates. Sanders and Trump frequently posted images that depicted them gesturing with their hands. Sanders typically was seen with outstretched arms to a crowd, whereas Trump gave a thumbs-up gesture in photos. This was most often a secondary frame to the image. Within the populist campaigner master frame, Trump, Sanders, and Kasich had the largest percentage of mass appeal images. Trump and Kasich relied heavily on large crowd images, whereas Sanders used more celebrities in his Instagram posts. Ordinariness was used only by four of the candidates (i.e., Clinton, Sanders, Rubio, and Kasich).

RESEARCH QUESTION 1B: FILTER

Most of the candidate Instagram posts did not use a filter. Of the 1552 images analyzed, only 274 (17.7 percent) applied a filter. Relative to the overall number of posts to their Instagram account, Sanders, Kasich, and Cruz were the heaviest users of filters, whereas Clinton and Rubio used either no filters or practically none (see Table 3). Twenty-five different filters were used among the candidates. Clarendon ($n = 74$) was the most popular filter type, used by five of the seven candidates, followed by Lark ($n = 33$), Juno ($n = 29$), Gingham ($n = 24$), and Ludwig ($n = 17$).

TABLE 2 Primary Framing Examples on Instagram Sample

Master theme	Dimension subdimension	Selected Instagram examples
Ideal candidate	**Statesmanship**	
	Elected official/influential	• Republican candidates at podiums during debate • Photo collage of Trump with Rudy Giuliani
	Patriotic symbols	• American and state flags as backdrops to candidate speeches • White House as backdrop • Statue of Liberty • Posing with military and police
	Progress	• Clinton headshot with quote, "If we can blast 50 women into space we will someday launch a woman into the White House." • Photo collage of industrial buildings, a bridge, and seafront
	Identifiable entourage	• Announcement and image of Heidi Cruz appearing on *The Kelly File* • Johnson being interviewed on CNN's *New Day* • Clinton staffers at a meeting
	Campaign paraphernalia	• Highlighted campaign signs • Candidates posing with prominent campaign signage • Picture of campaign bus (i.e., back of Ted Cruz bus; campaign supporters posing by Kasich bus) • Campaign merchandise (e.g., Rubio's calendar, Johnson T-shirts)
	Formal attire	• Johnson shown wearing a suit and tie
	Compassion	
	Children	• Photo collage highlighting baby wearing a costume, Trump holding baby

(*Continued*)

TABLE 2 Continued

Master theme	Dimension subdimension	Selected Instagram examples
	Family associations	• Kasich family photo taken in a photography studio • Rubio's son standing next to father at debate prep • Clinton sitting with President Clinton holding newborn grandchild
	Admiring individuals	• Two women looking on/admiring Clinton as she embraces one woman
	Religious	• Picture of concentration camp with words "Never Forget–Never Again" • Sanders arm outstretched over his head • "Thank you South Carolina" text placed over Clinton headshot
	Affinity gestures	• Kasich speaking with three women over a restaurant table
	Interaction with individuals	
	Physical embraces	• Cruz and supporter posing for a photo, with arm around supporter
Populist campaigner	**Mass appeal**	
	Celebrities	• Rosario Dawson speaking from podium supporting Sanders • Clinton speaking with Jessie Jackson and Al Sharpton
	Large audiences	• Large aerial crowd images • Images taken from the back of a room showing the crowd • Images taken from behind the candidate, illustrating the audience size from their perspective
	Approving audiences	• Audience members clapping with Sanders in the background
	Interaction with crowds	• Johnson with a group of supporters in a restaurant
	Ordinariness	
	Informal attire	• Rubio without a suit jacket holding a Twix candy bar in a private jet
	Ordinary people	• Kasich supporters sitting at a sign-in table • Sanders posing with a group of Native Americans wearing traditional clothing

TABLE 3 Instagram Filter Usage

Candidate	No filter	Filter	Percentage	Image total
Clinton	305	2	0.7%	307
Sanders	182	104	36.4%	286
Trump	412	37	8.2%	449
Rubio	122	0	0%	122
Cruz	91	35	27.8%	126
Kasich	67	88	56.8%	155
Johnson	99	8	7.5%	107
Total	1278	274	100%	1552

TEXT

The candidates frequently used text-integrated images in their Instagram feed. Forty-five out of the one hundred fifty-seven images sampled included text. Clinton, Sanders, and Trump were the most frequent users of text images, whereas Kasich and Johnson's samples included only one image. Text was applied in numerous ways across the candidates' feeds. Quotes, thank you messages, branding elements, campaign success illustrations, selling merchandise, issue presentation, tweets, and personal communication were the various types of text-integrated images that candidates posted on Instagram (see Table 4 for text typology and Examples).

Research Question 2: Engagement Results

To address the relationship between self-framing themes and Instagram engagement (RQ2), we sought to explore what thematic image content contributed to higher levels of image engagement, which was determined by the number of Instagram likes and number of comments. An initial combined numeric count of master themes and dimensions was conducted of the top ten images among all seven candidates.[7] Both primary and secondary theme findings are reported in Table 5. In comparing the top ten most liked images with the top ten most commented image posts, Clinton and Trump saw no repetition in images between their top ten most liked and most commented on Instagram. However, the remainder of the candidates saw the same image posts receive high engagement numbers in both number of likes and comments: Sanders (three images), Johnson, (seven images), Rubio (five images), Kasich (four images), and Cruz (six images).

NUMBER OF "LIKES"

As shown in Table 5, images that included the highest number of likes were prominently part of the ideal candidate master frame, with the statesmanship dimension driving more engagement. These types of images included a variety of subdimension content within the images. Instagram users liked

TABLE 4 Common Types of Text-Integrated Images

Type	Selected examples
Politician's or influential's image + quote	Sanders: Sanders speaking at a podium and a quote next to him reading: "It is beyond my comprehension that in the year 2016 in the United States of America, we are poisoning our children."
Solid block of color + quote	Clinton: "We are on the brink of a historic moment, but we still have work to do." Hillary Clinton June 6, 2016: white lettering over blue background
Thank you message to supporter groups	Cruz: "National Police Week 2016 Thank You"—over a picture of an officer and police car
	Trump: "Armed Forces Day May 21, 2016 [image of military seals]. Thank you to all ... "
Thank you message to cities and states	Trump: "THANK YOU CLINTON, IOWA! 1/30/2016" overlapping an image of the event
Campaign branding elements	Sanders: Picture of a big "B" with "A Future to Believe In" underneath
Documenting campaign successes	Clinton: Image of a newspaper front page revealing a strong voter reception
	Trump: Image stating "Indiana Trump 49%; Cruz 34%; Kasich 13%" [poll results]
Selling merchandise	Johnson: Selling "LiveFree" T-shirts; offering examples of different shirts
	Rubio: Selling 2016 calendar
Mobilizing	Sanders: "Caucus for Bernie" title with specific details on the event
	Rubio: Image of simulated text message stating "Got a friend in Florida? Tell them to vote for Marco Rubio."
Issue presentation	Clinton: "Equal pay for women impacts everyone"
Tweets	Clinton: Posting a tweet from the Associated Press that states she "clinch[es] the Demographic nomination for president"
Personal communication	Sanders: Handwritten note from supporter praising Sanders
	Clinton: Handwritten note from Clinton thanking her supporters

having elected officials/influentials highlighted. The most popular elected officials/influentials images depicted the candidate with other elected officials, including influentials as the sole focus of the image (e.g., vintage image of Ronald and Nancy Reagan); patriotic symbols were also popular statesmanship dimensions. Identifiable entourage received more likes when the candidate posed next to reporters or being interviewed. Last, campaign paraphernalia was realized through text-based images containing campaign branding elements and pictures of the candidate with prominent campaign signage. Notably, not all of the campaign signage was in support of the candidate directly (e.g., Rubio posting a text-based image of the hashtag #NeverTrump). The compassion dimension was most commonly applied by depicting the candidate's family, which readily included their children and grandchildren.

The most popular populist campaigner frame contained primarily mass appeal images focusing on either celebrities or large audiences. Large

TABLE 5 Candidate Frames for Engagement (Number of Likes and Number of Comments)

Master theme	Dimension	Subdimension	No. of likes		No. of comments	
			Primary frame	Secondary frame	Primary frame	Secondary frame
Ideal candidate	Statesmanship	Elected official/influential	8	0	7	1
		Patriotic symbols	6	2	8	5
		Progress	0	0	0	1
		Identifiable Entourage	7	2	4	0
		Campaign paraphernalia	6	1	6	1
		Political hoopla	1	0	0	0
		Formal attire	3	0	7	0
	Statesmanship total		**31**	**5**	**32**	**8**
	Compassion	Children	2	6	2	1
		Family Associations	9	0	1	0
		Admiring Individuals	0	1	0	0
		Affinity gestures	8	5	4	5
		Physical embraces	3	4	1	3
	Compassion total		**22**	**16**	**8**	**9**

(Continued)

TABLE 5 Continued

Master theme	Dimension	Subdimension	No. of likes		No. of comments	
			Primary frame	Secondary frame	Primary frame	Secondary frame
Ideal candidate total			**53**	**21**	**40**	**17**
Populist campaigner						
	Mass appeal					
		Celebrities	4	0	3	0
		Large audiences	5	0	17	1
		Approving Audiences	2	1	3	0
		Interaction with crowds	0	0	0	1
	Mass appeal total		**11**	**1**	**23**	**2**
	Ordinariness					
		Informal attire	1	0	1	0
		Casual dress	0	4	1	0
		Ordinary people	5	0	5	0
	Ordinariness total		**6**	**4**	**7**	**0**
Populist campaigner total			**17**	**5**	**30**	**2**

Note. The following number of likes subdimensions were not present: symbols of progress, admiring individuals, interaction with individuals, casual dress, athletic clothing, and physical activity.
The following number of comments subdimensions were not present for primary frame: progress, political hoopla, formal attire, family, religious, interaction, celebrities, interaction with crowds, informal attire, athletic clothing, ordinary people, and physical activity.

audiences were shown at candidate rallies and speeches but also through a screenshot of Johnson's Twitter account, which focused on his follower count. Celebrities were shown either with the candidate or by themselves. The most liked ordinariness dimension images contained ordinary people and/or everyday actions (e.g., Kasich eating a messy sandwich in a Bronx store) and casual dress as a secondary frame. Casual dress was seen with candidates not wearing their suit and tie/formal dress (see Table 6 for selected examples of the most engaged Instagram images).

In looking at individual candidates' primary frames of the most liked posts, all of the candidates had more engagement for content consistent with the ideal candidate theme. The most popular overall statesmanship subdimensions were images including elected officials/influentials ($n = 8$ across four candidates), identifiable entourage ($n = 7$ across three candidates), and patriotic symbols ($n = 6$ across three candidates). Yet, there were notable differences between the parties and candidates in which themes generated the highest number of likes. Republican candidates more readily received higher likes on images that contained elected officials/influentials (Cruz $n = 4$; Rubio $n = 2$; Trump $n = 1$) and patriotic symbols (Kasich $n = 3$; Cruz $n = 2$; Trump $n = 1$). In fact, Rubio's most liked image had him walking arm in arm with Nancy Reagan. Only one of Clinton's top ten liked photos contained the primary theme of elected officials/influentials. Johnson relied heavily on the identifiable entourage content ($n = 5$), more than any other candidate. These photos consisted primarily of him posing with and interviewed by reporters. Rubio also garnered engagement with his textual campaign paraphernalia images ($n = 4$).

Across all candidates, the most popular compassion subdimensions were family ($n = 9$ between four candidates) and affinity gestures ($n = 8$ across four candidates). Of all the subdimensions, images that included family, many of which included children and grandchildren, garnered the most likes for candidates. In particular, Trump and Clinton received the most likes with this strategy. In fact, Clinton's top two liked images were those that included her family and her new grandchild. Affinity gestures were the primary frames in the most liked images by four candidates. Sanders had four out of his top ten images highlight affinity through illustrating his raised fist to the audience and thanking his voters. His most popular Instagram post was a vintage black-and-white photo of him walking out of a door to an approving, clapping audience.

None of the candidates had much "like" engagement with the populist theme. Only one to three posts for each candidate contained any of the mass appeal subdimensions. A notable finding is that Kasich's most liked image was him posing with Will Smith. Within the ordinariness dimension, candidates had fewer most liked images. However, some of the ordinary frames did receive some of the highest "liked" images for the candidates. In particular, Trump's most liked image depicted him eating McDonald's food

TABLE 6 Primary Framing Examples of the Most Engaged Instagram Images

Master theme	Dimension subdimension	Selected Instagram examples
Ideal candidate	**Statesmanship**	
	Elected official/influential	• Rubio walking arm and arm with Nancy Reagan (like) • Clinton walking with President Obama waving to crowd (like) • Rubio and Trump at Republican debate (like and comments)
	Patriotic symbols	• Kasich speaking with a large American flag filling the background (like) • Trump posing with four police officers, American flag in background (like) • Historical photo of Hillary Clinton and President Clinton in front of the White House with a sign "Happy Easter 1994" (comments)
	Identifiable entourage	• Trump posing with Megyn Kelly (like) • Johnson being interviewed on *Meet the Press* (like and comments) • Rubio with a staffer in a plane looking at a computer (comments)
	Campaign paraphernalia	• Sides of brick building that were painted "Welcome Home Bernie" (with Bernie logo) and another wall that had the outline of Bernie's hairline and glasses and a get-out-the-vote message (like)
	Political hoopla	• Rubio's face on a blue T-shirt with the T-shirt text "RU(BAE)O" (comments) • Clinton headshot with her looking up and the text, "June 7, 2016, History made" (like)
	Formal attire	• Rubio wearing suit and a blue tie with the text, "I'm rooting for Marco Rubio" next to him (like and comments) • Sanders wearing suit and tie behind a podium (like and comments)
	Compassion	
	Children	• Clinton watching a toddler walk down the hallway (like) • Clinton and a toddler being held by her mother; toddler is playing with Clinton's necklace (comments)
	Family associations	• Ivanka Trump in hospital bed holding newborn baby (like) • Cruz posing with his two daughters (like and comments)
	Affinity gestures	• Black and white historical photo of Sanders, arm outstretched over his head with people clapping (like)

Populist campaigner	Physical embraces	• Image of Cruz and "Thank you: Committed delegates since March 23rd; Cruz: 102; Trump: 7" (comments) • Collage of Johnson photos; 3 out of 5 images have him embracing the person next to him (like)
	Mass appeal	
	Celebrities	• Danny DeVito at a podium with Sanders signage around him (like and comments) • Will Smith with an arm around Kasich (like and comments)
	Large audiences	• Kasich at a rally with large crowd around him (like and comments) • Sanders speaking behind a podium his back to the camera facing a large audience (comments)
	Approving audiences	• Sanders with crowd in the background waving signs with the text headline, "The Political Revolution Wins in Indiana" [more text followed] (comments)
	Ordinariness	
	Informal attire	• Trump wearing jacket, no tie, and a baseball game with the text, "I don't have time for political correctness and neither does this country" (like)
	Casual dress	• Clinton leaning against a wall with a sweater over her shoulders wearing sunglasses (comments)
	Ordinary people	• Sanders appearing to order at the In-N-Out Burger counter (like) • Johnson speaking to a supporter on a street sidewalk (like and comment)

(albeit on a private jet), Johnson's most liked image depicted him talking to a supporter on the street, and Sanders second most liked image depicted him in what appears to be an In-N-Out Burger fast food restaurant.

COMMENTS

The master theme of the ideal candidate also garnered high engagement, which was determined by number of comments that each candidate received (see Table 5). Forty of the primary themes and seventeen of the secondary themes were categorized as either part of the statesmanship or compassion dimensions. Similar to the themes found for the most liked images, statesmanship provided to be a more successful theme. In particular, posts framed in the patriotic symbol subdimension had the most comments, followed by elected officials/influentials, formal attire, and campaign paraphernalia. Notably, Clinton, Cruz, Rubio, and Trump incorporated their opposing candidates in a variety of ways to drive comments. To illustrate, Trump used the "Liar Liar" movie poster and replaced Jim Carrey's face with Cruz's, whereas Cruz used another Jim Carrey movie poster (e.g., "Me, Myself & Irene") and replaced the word Irene with "Don" and posted a headshot of Trump (to replace Jim Carrey's face). Compassion dimensions were lower when compared to the "like" analysis in their ability to drive comments. Affinity gestures, children and family association, and physical embraces were the subdimensions utilized. Children and family drove far fewer amounts of engagement for comments compared to "likes." Affinity gestures were either text-related "thank you" messages to voters, supporting a cause, or a physical, affirming gesture to a crowd. The master frame of the populist campaigner drove comments primarily through the mass appeal dimension and large audience subdimension. Large audience frames were considerably more popular in driving comments opposed to Instagram likes.

RESEARCH QUESTION 2B: FILTER

The most engaged Instagram posts, for the most part, did not use a filter. Only ten of the top most liked posts and fourteen of the most commented on images incorporated a filter. Clinton and Rubio had no filters used in their top engaged photos and Cruz and Trump only had one filtered post in their top ten most liked and most commented on Instagram posts. Sanders and Kasich were the only candidates with high engagement on Instagram filter posts (Sanders used four for "most liked" and three for most commented on; Kasich had four for "most liked" and nine for most commented on). The most popular filter used was Clarendon, which was used in ten of the twenty-four filters applied on the most engaged images across candidates. To understand whether the use of filters impacted engagement, an independent samples t-test was run on each of the candidates' Instagram feed that used filters during the primary period. With the exception of Cruz's "like" engagement numbers (filter applied ($M = 1612.3$, $SD = 1025.7$) and not applied ($M = 2596.7$, $SD = 1800.5$); $t(106) = 3.841$, $p = .000$), there was no significant difference across candidates in either the number of likes or comments when a filter was applied.

TEXT

Twenty-two of the seventy most liked images and nineteen of the top seventy most commented on images contained text-integrated images. Each candidate had at least one image that included text in their top ten liked images and, with the exception of Kasich, this also occurred for the most commented on images. The most popular application across candidates was the use of quotes (like = 6 quotes; most commented = 4 quotes). Candidates posted their own quotes ("You have millions of allies who will always have your back. I am one of them": Clinton) and other elected officials' quotes ("The people are the only legitimate fountain of power": James Madison quote on Cruz's account). Three of Cruz's top ten most liked images included quotes. Other successful applications of popular text posts included campaign logos, thanking states for their support, announcing state wins, screenshots of tweets and account information, declaring campaign milestones, hashtag prompts (#NeverTrump; #petsfortrump), and comedic movie trailer posters. Candidates saw differing levels of engagement in their use of text-integrated images. Rubio ($n = 6$), Cruz ($n = 5$), and Clinton ($n = 4$) had text included for the most liked images and Rubio ($n = 5$), Cruz ($n = 5$), Clinton ($n = 3$), and Trump ($n = 3$) for the most commented on images.

DISCUSSION

Overall, the presidential primary candidates sought to visually present themselves as the ideal candidate on Instagram. Specifically, this was demonstrated primarily through the dimension of statesmanship. These findings are consistent with previous content analyses of candidate campaign websites (Davis 1999, 2005; Bimber and Davis 2003; Postelnicu, Martin, and Landreville 2006) as well as similar work examining candidates' framing in the context of Facebook (Goodnow 2013; Cmeciu 2014). Presidential primary candidates readily employed patriotic symbols, campaign paraphernalia, and elected officials/influentials in their images. Within the compassion subdimension, family associations, affinity gestures, and physical embraces were most commonly used. In general, the candidates used the populist campaigner frame less frequently. Yet the mass appeal dimension depicting large audiences was the most frequently used subdimension. This may have been utilized as a persuasion tactic to demonstrate "social proof" of the candidate's popularity to potential voters (Cialdini 2006). The dependence that candidates had on a smaller subset of Grabe and Bucy's (2009) framing depictions speaks to either lost opportunity in not fully exploring other subdimensions (e.g., religious symbols, political hoopla, interaction with crowds) or signals the need to create a new framing structure for Instagram.

Similar to previous findings (Filimonov, Russman, and Svennsoon 2016), candidates did use Instagram as a "virtual billboard." However, unlike previous studies there were efforts to mobilize candidates through textual images that included voting location information or simply get-out-the-vote messages. In general, Clinton, Trump, and Sanders demonstrated a more sophisticated use of Instagram marketing. The diversity of communicated frame types, their ample use of images that included text, and their frequency of Instagram posts illustrated a higher level of social media proficiency. This may also be attributed to these candidates having a larger campaign staff and marketing budget than the other primary candidates (Levinthal, Beckel, and Levine 2016). As a proportion of images sampled for each candidate, Trump relied on patriotic symbols and large audiences more than other candidates, whereas Clinton had more focus on family and children associations. This finding is consistent with work that found that female Romanian candidates included more compassionately framed images in their Facebook timeline compared to male candidates (Cmeciu 2014). Sanders more frequently included celebrities. Given that Sanders and Trump both were described as "populist" candidates by the mainstream media (Kazin 2016), there appears to be disconnect between media depictions and their self-presentation on Instagram as the ideal candidate. Furthermore, one may have expected to see more religious framing in conservative candidates such as Cruz. Last, the content of the candidate's Instagram account mirrored many aspects found in previous research on voter's everyday political talk on Instagram (Mahoney et al. 2016).

Image content that received the highest engagement rates (number of likes and number of comments) across all candidates were from the ideal candidate master frame, with an emphasis on statesmanship. Yet the populist campaigner master frame also performed well for images with a high number of comments. Elected officials/influentials and patriotic symbols were popular for both number of likes and number of comments. The success of the elected officials/influentials as well as the celebrity subdimension found within the populist campaigner may be explained through the "halo effect," whereby the positive associations attached to a political actor or celebrity are transferred to the political candidate they are endorsing. The ample use and success of patriotic symbols by candidates demonstrate, as Goodnow (2013) notes, that candidates "borrowed" credibility from venerated symbols. This practice is also consistent with symbolic self-completion theory, where individuals utilize and communicate symbols that serve to complete, in this case, the identity of a potential president (Wicklund and Gollwitzer 1982).

There were notable differences between image content that received a high number of likes versus a high number of comments. In particular, consumers were much more likely to "like" an image with family and children association than comment on it. In addition, images with large audiences had high engagement for number of comments but lacked a high number of "likes." This finding suggests that specific types of content posted on social media lend themselves to different levels of consumer involvement and that candidates would be well served to continue to post pictures of family (both present and nostalgic) and crowds. Consistent with Manikonda, Meduri, and Kambhampati (2016), it is worth noting that many of the most liked images and, to a lesser extent, most commented on images were positive and some were rather "lighthearted" in nature.

It was apparent that the candidates readily adjusted their image attributes to the Instagram platform. Approximately a third of the sampled images and a third of the most engaged images contained text. Candidates incorporated text in a variety of ways; however, a common application of text was through candidate quotes and quotes taken from other elected officials/influentials. Filters were not consistently used across candidates. Applying no filter was by far the most common option and Clarendon was the most used. This is consistent with consumer usage patterns (Canva 2016). Most of the candidates' most engaged images did not incorporate filters. It is possible that the campaigns did not perceive real technology affordances offered by the filter option and therefore did not use them in a meaningful way.

We acknowledge that the number of likes and number of comments were not weighted for time posted. In other words, pictures posted earlier in the primary period had more opportunity to be liked and commented on. However, many of the top ten posts for both liked and commented on photos were from the last month or two of the campaign for each candidate. In addition, industry research on sponsored posts has shown that half a post's engagement on Instagram occurs within 1.2 hours of it being posted (Takumi 2015). Therefore, not weighting for time should not have a detrimental effect.

CONCLUSION

This study serves as an important first step in our understanding of how presidential candidates are using Instagram to visually construct and manage their political selves. In addition, it identifies which specific types of themes and image attributes provide the most consumer engagement. Similar to previous researchers (Goodnow 2013; Cmeciu 2014; Lee 2016), this work extends Grabe and Bucy's (2009) visual framing analysis on traditional media to new media and it is the first to apply the framework to Instagram. Our research describes how political campaigns are utilizing visual communication in the marketing and self-presentation of their candidates and offers insights as to which strategies are the most successful in garnering higher rates of engagement. Previous politically oriented Instagram research has examined voters' political conversations (Mahoney et al. 2016), Swedish and Bahraini candidates' political marketing communication (Filimonov, Russman, and Svennsoon 2016; Russmann and Svensson 2017), and impression management strategies on Instagram (Holiday, Lewis, and LaBaugh 2015; Filimonov, Russman, and Svennsoon 2016). However, our study is the first to examine U.S. presidential candidates' self-presentation frames and how they were implemented on Instagram. The findings provided should offer political marketers guidance and serve as an idea generator for future political campaigns.

It is our hope that this research provides the foundation for later studies that will examine the relationship between highly engaged images on Instagram and candidate likability and political participation. Indeed, our study has several notable limitations, particularly that our small sample size of Instagram posts limits our ability to generalize to the larger universe of candidate Instagram images. In addition, we are constrained to making inferences to the presidential primary campaign period rather than the general election. However, we offer a baseline of how political candidates visually present themselves in the digital era. In future research, we seek to determine whether exposure to highly engaged images on Instagram will have an effect on candidate likability and voter political participation. We will also experimentally address the relationship between specific frames and engagement. In addition, the increasing integration of videos within Instagram requires that we further explore their potential role in political marketing. In conclusion, as presidential candidates embrace more visual social media in campaigning, the image becomes the message. It is now time to explore not only what these images are saying but also what consumers are hearing.

NOTES

1. Governor Gary Johnson entered the presidential primary on January 6, 2016.

2. Senator Ted Cruz had two separate verified accounts: SenTedCruz and CruzforPresident. Data from both accounts were combined and used in the analysis.

3. We sought to limit the scope of this study to one type of visual communication modality and examine the attributes of fixed and still images that did not include sound and movement. The researchers did video detection manually for the content analyses. The Beautifeye software does not distinguish whether an Instagram post is a video or image and therefore analyzes the static, frozen image of a video that individuals see when within the Instagram feed. Therefore, videos were included the quantitative analysis of filters.

4. Unlike Grabe and Bucy (2009), who coded only for the presence of a subdimension frame, we assess the strength of a frame by determining the primary frame and, if relevant, a secondary frame.

5. Given the reliance on text graphics, it was noted whether text was a dominant feature. Then the text's meaning was used to determine its coding classification. For example, "thank you" images were included in the compassion/affinity gestures category. Second, police officers and firefighters were incorporated into statesmanship/patriotic symbols category. Third, the ordinary people subdimension was also expanded to include "ordinary" candidate-related activities, such as eating, exercising, or playing

basketball. Fourth, the compassion subdimension category of admiring women was also expanded to include admiring men (i.e., admiring individuals). Fifth, adjustments were also made for collages, which consisted of two to five images incorporated into one Instagram image. Each image in the collage was analyzed and the most dominant themes from across the images were used for the primary and secondary frames.

6. Johnson removed one of the top ten most liked images and three of the top ten most commented on images between the time the data were downloaded and when we analyzed the images. These images were replaced with the next most highly engaged image.

7. Two videos were part of the original top ten most liked Instagram posts for Kasich, whereas nine videos were included as part of the top seventy most commented on Instagram posts among Sanders, Clinton, Kasich, Rubio, and Trump. These videos were removed from the analysis and replaced with the next highest engaged image posted.

REFERENCES

Bakhshi, S., D. Shamma, and E. Gilbert. 2014. "Faces Engage us: Photos with Faces Attract More Likes and Comments on Instagram." CHI'14 Proceedings of the SIGHI Conference on Human Factors in Computing Systems. Toronto, Ontario, Canada, April 26–May 01, 2014, 965–74.

Bakhshi, S., D. Shamma, L. Kennedy, and E. Gilbert. 2015. "Why We Filter Our Photos and How It Impacts Engagement." International AAAI Conference on Human Factors in Computing Systems, 12–22. Oxford, UK. http://comp.social. gatech.edu/papers/icwsm15.why.bakhshi.pdf.

Berger, A. 1991. *Media Analysis Techniques*. Newbury Park, CA: Sage Publications.

Bimber, B., and R. Davis. 2003. *Campaigning Online: The Internet in U.S. Elections*. New York: Oxford University Press.

Bode, L., and K. Dalrymple. 2016. "Politics in 140 Characters or Less: Campaign Communication, Network Interaction, and Political Participation in Twitter." *Journal of Political Marketing* 15 (4):311–32. doi:10.1080/15377857.2014.959686

Borah, P. 2009. "Comparing Visual Framing in Newspapers: Hurricane Katrina versus Tsunami." *Newspaper Research Journal* 30 (1):50–57. doi:10.1177/07395329090 3000106

Brader, T. 2005. "Striking a Responsive Chord: How Political Ads Motivate and Persuade Voters by Appealing to Emotions." *American Journal of Political Science* 49 (2):388–405. doi:10.2307/3647684

Bucher, H., and P. Schumacher. 2006. "The Relevance of Attention for Selecting News Content. An Eye-tracking Study on Attention Patterns in the Reception of Print and Online Media." *Communications: The European Journal of Communication Research* 31:347–68. doi:10.1515/commun.2006.022

Canva. 2016. "Study: The Most Popular Instagram Filters From Around the World." (Blog), Accessed February 10, 2016. https://designschool.canva.com/blog/popular-instagram-filters/.

Childers, T., and M. Houston. 1984. "Conditions for a Picture-Superiority Effect on Consumer Memory." *Journal of Consumer Research* 11:643–53. doi:10.1086/209001

Cialdini, R. 2006. *Influence: The Psychology of Persuasion*. New York: Harper Business.

Cmeciu, C. 2014. "Beyond the Online Faces of Romanian Candidates for the 2014 European Parliament Elections - A Visual Framing Analysis of Facebook Photographic Images." In *Ten Years of Facebook: Proceedings from the Third International Conference on Argumentation and Rhetoric*, edited by G. Horvath, R. K. Bako, and E. Biro-Kaszas, 405–34. Nagyvarard, Romania: Partium Press. https://argumentor.files.wordpress.com/2015/01/argumentor-2014_horvath_bako_biro-kaszas_en.pdf.

Davis, R. 1999. *The Web of Politics: The Internet's Impact on the American Political System*. New York: Oxford University Press.

Davis, S. 2005. Presidential Campaigns Fine-time Online Strategies. *Journalism Studies* 6 (2):241–244. doi:10.1080/14616700500057452

Duggan, M. 2015. "The Demographics of Social Media Users." Pew Research. http://www.pewinternet.org/2015/08/19/the-demographics-of-social-media-users/.

Eldin, A. 2016. "Instagram Role in Influencing Youth Opinion in 2015 Election Campaign in Bahrain." *European Scientific Journal* 12 (2):245–57. doi:10.19044/esj.2016.v12n2p245

Elliott, N. 2015a. "How Does Your Brand Stack Up on Facebook, Twitter and Instagram?" (blog), Forrester. http://blogs.forrester.com/nate_elliott/15-09-15-how_does_your_brand_stack_up_on_facebook_twitter_and_instagram.

Entman, R. M. 1993. "Framing: Toward Clarification of a Fractured Paradigm." *Journal of Communication* 43 (4):51–58.

Fahmy, S. 2005. "Photojournalists' and Photo-editors' Attitudes and Perceptions: The Visual Coverage of 9/11 and the Afghan War." *Visual Communication Quarterly* 12 (3–4):146–63. doi:10.1207/s15551407vcq1203&4_4

Filimonov, K., U. Russman, and J. Svennsoon. 2016. "Picturing the Party: Instagram and Party Campaigning in the 2014 Swedish Elections." *Social Media and Society* 2:1–11. doi:10.1177/2056305116662179

Gibson, J. 1979. *The Ecological Approach to Visual Perception*. Boston, MA: Houghton Mifflin.

Goffman, E. 1974. *Frame Analysis: An Essay on the Organization of Experience*. Cambridge: Harvard, University Press.

Goodnow, T. 2013. "Facing Off: A Comparative Analysis of Obama and Romney Facebook Timeline Photographs." *American Behavioral Scientist* 57 (11): 1584–95.

Grabe, M., and E. Bucy. 2009. *Image Bite Politics: News and the Visual Framing of Elections*. New York: Oxford University Press.

Graber, D. 1996. "Say It with Pictures." *Annals of the American Academy of Political and Social Science* 546:85–96. doi:10.1177/0002716296546001008

Gupta, A. 2013. "The Shift from Words to Pictures and Implications for Digital Marketers." Forbes. http://www.forbes.com/sites/onmarketing/2013/07/02/the-shift-from-words-to-pictures-and-implications-for-digital-marketers/#586b936c2549.

Hardin, M., S. Lynn, K. Walsdorf, and B. Hardin. 2002. "The Framing of Sexual Difference in SI for Kids Editorial Photos." *Mass Communication & Society* 5 (3):341–59. doi:10.1207/s15327825mcs0503_6

Highfield, T., and T. Leaver. 2015. "A Methodology for Mapping Instagram Hashtags." *First Monday* 20 (1). doi:10.5210/fm.v20i1.5563.

Holiday, S., M. Lewis, and J. LaBaugh. 2015. "Are You Talking to Me? The Socio-Political Visual Rhetoric of the Syrian Presidency's Instagram Account." *Southwestern Mass Communication Journal* 30 (2):1–27.

Hu, Y., L. Manikonda, and S. Kambhampati. 2014. "What We Instagram: A First Analysis of Instagram Photo Content and User Types." In *Proceedings of International AAAI Conference on Weblogs and Social Media*, 595–98. Ann Arbor, MI.

Instagram. 2016. "Press News." www.instagram.com/press/?hl=en.

Jaakonmaki, R., O. Muller, and J. vom Brocke. 2017. "The Impact of Content, Context, and Creator on User Engagement in Social Media Marketing." Proceedings of the 50th Hawaii International Conference on System Science, 1152–60. Waikoloa, HI. http://scholarspace.manoa.hawaii.edu/bitstream/10125/41289/1/paper0140.pdf.

Kazin, M. 2016. "How Can Donald Trump and Bernie Sanders Both Be 'Populist'?" *The New York Times*. www.nytimes.com/2016/03/27/magazine/how-can-donald-trump-and-bernie-sanders-both-be-populist.html.

Lee, J. 2016. "President's Visual Presentation in Their Official Photos: A Cross-Cultural Analysis of the US and South Korea." *Cogent Arts & Humanities* 3 (1):1–14. doi:10.1080/23311983.2016.1201967

Levinthal, D., M. Beckel, and C. Levine. 2016. "$1 Billion Spent in 2016 Presidential Race - and Other Numbers to Know." *The Center for Public Integrity*. www.publicintegrity.org/2016/04/21/19580/1-billion-spent-2016-presidential-race-and-other-numbers-know.

Li, C. 2010. *Open Leadership: How Social Technology Can Transform the Way You Lead*. New York: John Wiley & Sons, Inc.

Mahoney, J., T. Feltwell, O. Ajuruchi, and S. Lawson. 2016. "Constructing the Visual Online Political Self: An Analysis of Instagram Use by the Scottish Electorate." CHI'16 Proceedings of the 2016 CHI Conference, San Jose, CA, 3339–51, May 7–12, 2016.

Manikonda, L., V. Meduri, and S. Kambhampati. 2016. "Tweeting the Mind and Instagramming the Heart: Exploring Differentiated Content Sharing on Social Media." In *International AAAI Conference on Web and Social Media*, 639–42. Cologne, Germany. https://arxiv.org/pdf/1603.02718.pdf.

Norman, D. 1988. *The Psychology of Everyday Things*. New York: Basic Books.

Paivio, A., T. B. Rogers, and P. Smythe. 1968. Why Are Pictures Easier to Recall Than Words? *Psychonomic Science* 11 (4):137–38. doi:10.3758/bf03331011

Pieters, R., and M. Wedel. 2004. Attention Capture and Transfer in Adverting: Brand, Pictorial, and Text-size Effects. *Journal of Marketing* 68 (2):36–50. doi:10.1509/jmkg.68.2.36.27794

Postelnicu, M., J. D. Martin, and K. D. Landreville. 2006. "The Role of Campaign Web Sites in Promoting Candidates and Attracting Campaign Resources." *The Internet Election*, edited by A. P. Williams and J. C. Tedesco. 99–109. New York: Rowman & Littlefield Publishers.

Rogers, S. 2014. "What Fuels a Tweet's Engagement." Twitter Blog. https://blog.twitter.com/2014/what-fuels-a-tweets-engagement.

Rosenberg, S., L. Bohan, P. McCafferty, and K. Harris. 1986. "The Image and the Vote: The Effect of Candidate Presentation on Voter Preference." *American Journal of Political Science* 30 (2):108–27. doi:10.2307/2111296

Russmann, U., and J. Svensson. 2017. "Interaction on Instagram? Glimpses from the 2014 Swedish Elections." *International Journal of E-Politics* 8 (1):50–65. doi:10.4018/ijep.2017010104

Schill, D. 2012. The Visual Image and the Political Image: A Review of Visual Communication Research in the Field of Political Communication. *Review of Communication* 12 (2):118–42. doi:10.1080/15358593.2011.653504

Schutz, A. 1995. "Entertainers, Experts, or Public Servants? Politicians' Self-Presentation on Television Talk Shows." *Political Communication* 12 (2):211–21. doi:10.1080/10584609.1995.9963066

Stanyer, J. 2008. "Elected Representatives, Online Self-presentation and the Personal Vote: Party, Personality and Webstyles in the United States and United Kingdom." *Information, Communication and Society* 11 (3):414–32. doi:10.1080/13691180802025681

Stenberg, G. 2006. "Conceptual and Perceptual Factors in the Picture Superiority Effect." *European Journal of Cognitive Psychology* 18 (6):813–47. doi:10.1080/09541440500412361

Takumi. 2015. "The Half-life of Instagram Posts." (blog) August 30, 2015. https://blog.takumi.com/the-half-life-of-instagram-posts-3db61fb1db75#.u4m1byjpw.

Towner, T. 2013. "All Political Participation Is Socially Networked? New Media and the 2012 Election." *Social Science Computer Review* 31 (5):527–41. doi:10.1177/0894439313489656

Towner, T., and C. Muñoz. 2016. "Baby Boom or Bust? The New Media Effect on Political Participation." *Journal of Political Marketing* 1–30. doi:10.1080/15377857.2016.1153561

Twitter. 2016. "Company". https://about.twitter.com/company.

Wicklund, R., and P. Gollwitzer. 1982. *Symbolic Self-completion*. Hillsdale, NJ: Erlbaum.

Zarella, D. 2013. "Use Quotes and #Hashtags to Get More Retweets." Dan Zarrella. http://danzarrella.com/new-data-use-quotes-and-hastags-to-get-more-retweets.

Zarella, D. 2014. "The Science of Instagram." Dan Zarrella. http://danzarrella.com/infographic-the-science-of-instagram/.

Appeals to the Hispanic Demographic: Targeting through Facebook Autoplay Videos by the Clinton Campaign during the 2015/2016 Presidential Primaries

EDWARD ELDER and JUSTIN B. PHILLIPS

By looking at the autoplay videos posted and shared on Hillary Clinton's Facebook account during the 2015/2016 primary election season, this article offers much needed insight into the communication aspect of campaign targeting. Using data analysis extracted from the leading social media platform, the article examines what groups of Hispanic Facebook users were attracted to Clinton's targeted autoplay videos, what elements within these videos best enticed these people into liking the videos, and if the Clinton campaign appeared to learn what types of autoplay videos were most effective over the course of the primary season.

INTRODUCTION

The use of social media by the public, and consequently by political actors, has grown substantially over the past 12 plus years. Only 5% of American adults used at least one social media platform in early 2005. That number had grown to 69% by late 2016 (Pew Research Center 2017). With this widespread adoption, nearly one quarter of eligible voters are looking to social media to keep them informed (Shearer 2016). Social media's importance in the relationship between political elites, political information, and the public is ever growing. However, not all social media is equal. Only one platform manages to capture a broad sample of the American public: Facebook. Approximately 68% of American adults have an account with the social media giant. Its nearest competitor, Instagram, holds accounts for only 28% of American adults (Pew Research Center 2017).

In December 2013, Facebook introduced autoplay videos to American Facebook users' feeds. As the name suggests, these videos play automatically, without sound, when a Facebook user scrolls through their feed. Within a year, Facebook saw video views grow by 94% in USA, to over a billion views a day, with 76% of users in the country saying they tend to find videos through the platform (Griffin 2015).

The impact of this technology is not limited to casual Facebook users. While political elites and a significant portion of the general voting public have adapted to this new platform, this emerging tool has clear implications for political marketing both in practice and theory. Facebook's algorithm scans, ranks, and posts items on a user's feed from friends, people they follow, pages they like, and groups they belong to—based on what Facebook believes the user will find most interesting (Oremus 2016). This allows political candidates to target communication to chosen demographics relatively easily on the platform. The 2015/2016 US primary election season was the first presidential primary season to see autoplay videos utilized en masse by presidential candidates to appeal to target demographics that could be converted into potential voters. One of the most coveted target demographics in recent presidential elections has been Hispanic voters. With 73% of all American Hispanic adults having a Facebook account, targeting this demographic through Facebook's autoplay video feature was understandably a part of Democratic Party primary candidate Hillary Clinton's Facebook communication strategy.

Due to its modernity, a more comprehensive academic understanding of this method of targeted political communication in action is missing. Our paper advances knowledge in this relatively underdeveloped area by exploring active participation on Clinton's Facebook autoplay video posts targeting the Hispanic demographic during the 2015/2016 primaries. Using the data collected from these posts, this article examines how the Clinton campaign attracted new support from Hispanic Facebook users, and how effective they were in doing so, through the measurement of first time "likes" of a Clinton post on an autoplay video. We expose basic visual messaging techniques which proved effective in attracting new Hispanic support to Clinton's campaign. However, our findings also suggest that the Clinton campaign was potentially unaware of such data, or instead was fixated on another metric for success, as successful targeting strategies were stopped in the latter half of the primary season in favor of less successful ones.

REVIEW OF PREVIOUS LITERATURE

Given the recent introduction and rapid rise in popularity of autoplay videos on Facebook, it is not surprising research around how to strategically utilize the format is yet to be published in the field of political marketing. While the study of internet use for political purposes has been explored for over 20 years now (for example see, Margolis, Resnick, and Tu 1997; Jackson 2006; Kreiss 2012), social media's impact on the world of politics is still a relatively young field. Most academic literature in this area has been published since the Obama for America campaign utilized the platform successfully in 2008 (Sanson 2008; Germany 2009; Harfoush 2009; Johnson and Perlmutter 2011; Gibson 2012). Since then, research on the topic has expanded in many directions. This has included research on social media's growing political utilization by down ballot candidates (Miller 2013), in elections beyond USA (Cameron, Barrett, and Stewardson 2016), and by political movements (Turcotte and Raynauld 2014; Kharroub and Bas 2016). Research has also expanded into areas around how new media platforms can be utilized in a variety of areas of political marketing, including as a platform for government communication of decisions and agendas (Lieber and Golan 2011) and as an additional tool for relationship marketing (Small 2012; Williams and Gulati 2013). In doing so, research has looked more specifically at how individual platforms such as Twitter (Larsson and Moe 2012; Conway, Kenski, and Wang 2013) and Instagram (Filimonov, Russman, and Svennsoon 2016) are utilized by political outfits.

From a normative perspective, studies have explored social media's influence from societal and democratic perspectives (Baumgartner and Morris 2010; Zhang et al. 2010). However, the investigation of these platforms in the field of political marketing has generally focused on the practical application of particular campaign strategies to reach current and potential supporters through this new communication medium (see for example Williams and Gulati 2013; Bayraktutan et al. 2014; Borah 2014). While these two broad approaches to examining new media's impact on the political world differ greatly, both overwhelmingly agree that it has an influence on political behavior—although this is not entirely uncontested (see Hong and Nadler 2012).

As research in this area grows, so too does social media's popularity and use—both in terms of the number of people using social media and the amount of time they use them (Pew Research Center 2017), suggesting the medium's theorized effects on the political sphere may be ever growing. Many Americans have started using platforms such as Facebook as their primary method of consuming and distributing political views and information (Goodnow 2013: 1584–1585; Pew Research Center 2016). Political elites are aware of this, and have started relying more heavily on social media to organize and communicate with supporters and the public at large—to the point that some research suggests politicians have detrimentally relied on social media as a substitute for—rather than a complement to—more traditional campaign tactics (Miller 2013). Beyond mere reliance, however, campaigns have begun to focus their strategic social media campaign efforts more specifically on coveted demographics, often described as targeting.

In USA, for example, the Hispanic demographic has become one of the most coveted voting blocks for political candidates. This is true even though voter turnout among this segment of the US population is relatively low (Abrajano and Panagopoulos 2011). The demographic represents the largest ethnic minority group in USA, making up 17% of the population (United States Census Bureau 2015). Thus, the Hispanic demographic has increasingly become a focus for targeted campaign messaging, especially by Presidential candidates (Barreto, Merolla, and Defrancesco Soto 2011).

The research on targeting potential Hispanic voters through traditional paid media channels, such as television advertising, highlights several trends in these targeting efforts. In terms of resource allocation, Hispanic targeting is often—but certainly not exclusively—focused geographically in swing states with relatively high ratios of Hispanic people, such as Florida and Nevada (see United States Hispanic Chamber of Commerce 2012). Also in terms of resource allocation, the use of Spanish media outlets such as Univision and Telemundo are seen as strategically wise (Subervi-Velez and Connaughton 2008).

Concurrently, there is a perception that one of the keys to targeting this demographic is communicating in Spanish (Panagopoulos and Green 2011). Yet growing evidence suggests that appeals in English are more broadly effective, as it is more attractive to Hispanic US-born and naturalized citizens who are accustomed to the US political and social environment (Oberfield and Segal 2008; Lewis-Beck and Stegmaier 2016; also see Lopez and Gonzalez-Barrera 2013).[1] It is therefore unsurprising that research has shown that a vast majority of issues covered in Hispanic-targeted television advertising has not been around issues such as immigration, but around issues more broadly seen as important such as the economy, health care, and education—from a Hispanic perspective (Connaughton, Nekrassova, and Lever 2008). This is often done through visual representations of Hispanic people communicating the campaign message as well as having prominent Hispanic people and leaders endorse candidates (Knuckey and Lees-Marshment 2005: 46; Oberfield and Segal 2008).

However, in terms of gaining new support among potential Hispanic voters, such research does not measure how effective these methods are directly. While Oberfield and Segal (2008), for example, compare money spent by the two 2004 Presidential candidates compared to their percentage of the Hispanic vote, they do not look at the types of advertising that increased support among potential Hispanic voters.

Indeed, broadly speaking, research on targeting has predominately focused on the methods campaigns use to gain knowledge of individuals and demographics so they can calculate who to target, and through what methods of communication to do so, to best utilize their resources (see Hillygus and Shields 2008; Burton 2012; Issenberg 2012; Bimber 2014; Nickerson and Rogers 2014; Spiller and Bergner 2014). In other words, without detailed access to campaigns, or large data sets involving electioneering communications and voter influence, the research has been predominately fixated on the groups that are targeted and where these messages are deployed (TV, radio, internet, for example). This can be seen in the fact that targeted communication is often a small aspect of studies into targeting and strategy more broadly (see McGough, 2005; Busby 2009; Lees-Marshment 2010; Johnson 2013; Nteta and Schaffner 2013; Ridout 2014). Certain studies do look closer at the techniques used and the effectiveness, or indeed the potential detrimental implications, of targeted communication on targeted and nontargeted audiences (see for example Harmer and Wring 2013; Hersh and Schaffner 2013). Most studies in political marketing that are conducted in this fashion assume effects take place, but they focus less explicitly on how campaigns attempt to persuade potential voters through specific communication techniques—particularly on social media.

By exploring the effectiveness of certain targeting techniques online, we might be able to identify their varied persuasiveness. Some work has attempted to do this in certain areas of online communication. Notably, research has looked at how campaigns use language to target known supporters in fundraising as well as personnel and issue mobilization efforts through specific e-mail messaging (Cogburn and Espinoza-Vasquez 2011; Marland 2012; Johnson 2013). However, such research almost exclusively focuses on written online communication rather than visual communication (Goodnow 2013: 1585) and, again, focuses on more on the usefulness of the data used to contact these supporters and the trial-and-error process of refining messages than the actual message itself.[2] Social media offers a host of different methods of communication (video, still images, audio as well as text). Online video communication, in particular, is important for campaigns. This field would benefit from more research on the actual messages from these campaigns, especially visual communication.

Research suggests that visual communication is generally more easily absorbed and retained than text-based communication (Paivio 1991; Barrett and Barrington 2005). Beyond just the hierarchy of imagery over textual communication, though, the specific imagery presented is also important. After all, not all images are equal, or equally effective. One of the great advantages for political candidates of new media platforms is that they make dispersing a variety of such communication to millions of people quick, easy, relatively cheap, and without the time, spatial, and geographical limitations of traditional paid media (Gueorguieva 2008; Nelson-Field, Riebe, and

Newstead 2013; Vesnic-Alujevic and Van Bauwel 2014). As campaigns seek to capitalize on reaching new voters with visual communication, it is their response to the different communications presented that is likely to result in the overall effectiveness of the communication itself (Stenberg 2006). Research considering how politicians are visually presented through new media communication is available (Miller 2013). However, the presentation of candidates is not the only way to appeal to target voters through imagery on social media. Furthermore, a lot of this has been around still images rather than video (Goodnow 2013).

Political communication through video messages is not a new phenomenon. Much research in political communication has looked at the role and effectiveness they have on perceptions of candidates (Graber 1996), linking its importance to the growth in televised politics as well as the decline in strong partisanship (Rosenberg, Kahn, and Tran 1991; Schill 2012). Marketing research does highlight the growing importance of such media in companies' efforts to reach out to customers. It notes that, while social media has become an important part of a company's marketing strategy (Andzulis, Panagopoulos, and Rapp 2012; Funk 2013), the richness of video content increases the likelihood social media users will engage with the content (Sabate et al. 2014). It is therefore considered a valuable addition to marketing through traditional sources (Parsons 2013).

Yet investigation into the strategic effectiveness of video, especially Facebook autoplay videos, on these platforms in politics has not been as deeply explored. Political communication on YouTube is one area of recent investigation. Such research has looked at areas like candidate adoption of the platform (Gulati and Williams 2010) and the comparative success of candidates to get video views and the potential virality of political video content (Miller 2013). The results also suggest that while it has the potential to reach a larger audience, the self-selective nature of the YouTube platform restricts this outreach to political active like-minded individuals (Towner and Dulio 2011). But many of these findings are related to specific aspects of the platform. For example, since Facebook autoplay videos play automatically (although without sound), they do not have the same self-selection barriers in attempting to reach target audiences. Therefore, this field would benefit from more research on the actual messages from these campaigns, especially visual communication through the popular Facebook autoplay video format.

As Hersh and Schaffner (2013) note, academics or practitioners both know relatively little about how well targeting works at persuading voters. While there is little research in political marketing so far that looks at the kind of strategies that are most commonly used by politicians on these relatively new platforms (Borah 2014: 210), there is even less that looks at what visual cues are most effective for targeting. Therefore, what is missing in the existing political marketing academic literature is research that looks explicitly at how to effectively target certain demographics through the Facebook autoplay feature, that is, what this research is designed to address.

METHODOLOGY

This research addresses this topic by exploring active participation on Clinton's Facebook autoplay video posts targeting the Hispanic demographic during the 2015/2016 primaries. Without access to internal campaign data, it is nearly impossible to identify the varied demographics targeted by campaigns through Facebook with great certainty. Targeting potential Hispanic voters, however, is one clear exception. Spanish language videos are clearly targeted to consumers fluent in that language. While all viewers may not necessarily be Hispanic, it is fair to assume that Spanish language posts signify one attempt—likely out of many—by a campaign to reach Hispanic voters. Given the ideological preference of many within this demographic (see Dinan 2013), and her status as the front-runner in the Democratic primary campaign (Agiesta 2015; Skelley 2015), it is reasonable to assume that Democratic primary candidates like Clinton would, and indeed did, reach out to this demographic through this method. Given the potency of visual over textual communication and the explosion in video outreach since the introduction of Facebook's autoplay feature, we have focused on this method of communication by the Clinton campaign. In line with most research in political marketing (see Lilleker and Lees-Marshment 2005; Lees-Marshment, Stromback, and Rudd 2010), case study analysis was utilized, as it provides an insight into a topic where little is known (Leppäniemi et al. 2010: 22).

The campaign could have defined the success of autoplay videos by total views, or likes, reactions, shares, or variety of other metrics. Ultimately, the goal of any social media post is to bring new followers into the fold, because it potentially increases your total level of support in the electorate. On social media platforms like Facebook, there is also a viral effect, as more supporters also increase your total outreach. For example, when a Facebook user likes, reacts, shares, or comments on a video, that video is displayed on the news feeds of their friends. A large amount of these various interactions from users disseminates the video to potentially millions of new viewers. Likes, however, are the predominant method of interaction. Therefore, this study focuses on this action.

"New likes," which can be defined as "likes" from Facebook users who have not liked any previous Clinton campaign posts, are particularly valuable. They too represent a potential increase in support and permit the candidate to potentially reach new audiences through the news feed of their friends. We define successful Clinton posts as those that capture new supporters from the Hispanic demographic during her participation in the

Democratic primary season. Therefore, this research looked at the data from Facebook posts that were posted by Clinton from the date she announced her run for President, on 12 April 2015, to the date of the last Democratic primary election, on 14 June 2016—while the data set represents Facebook user interactions with the posts up to 22 August 2016.[3]

Collection of the data utilized Facebook's Graph Application Programming Interface Explorer (API). This API is a publicly available tool which has been used in academic research in a wide array of fields, such as statistics (Giglietto, Rossi, and Bennato 2012), in social science fields such as psychology (Davalos and Merchant 2015) and Gender Studies (Bivens 2015) as well as in wider fields like Medicine (Smith et al. 2017). Using this API, we extracted the data from all of Hillary Clinton's Facebook posts during the 2016 presidential primary season. Further, Graph API calls extracted the full names of Facebook users who "liked" these posts. Thus, a database of over 200 million politically active users was created.

Given our study derives the success of Clinton's campaign videos by how well it secured new "likes" from the targeted demographic, we needed to identify all the potential Hispanic people among the 200 million Facebook users extracted. Over the past half-century, the US Census Bureau, and various other medical institutions have conducted surname analysis to identify Hispanic people in USA (Fiscella and Fremont 2006). Indeed, this method has more recently been adopted by consultants both in politics and in marketing (Abrahamse, Morrison, and Bolton 1994; Lee and Sutton 2002). While this approach may produce false positives, such as married non-Hispanic people taking the name of their spouse, the institutions above have found this type of analysis to be largely successful.

Assessing the content of these videos, and how they attempt to persuade new Hispanic people to support the Clinton campaign, is of critical importance here. Facebook's internal research suggests that only 3 s of user attention is necessary to create some type of ad recall and brand awareness. From a commercial perspective, they claim that intent to purchase can be prompted during this brief time as well (Facebook 2015). Given the nature of Facebook's autoplay feature—without audio—engagement is almost certainly precipitated by a user's brief assessment of the initial visual stimuli of the autoplay video, as the above suggests. We have therefore examined the first 5 s of visual content of Clinton's Spanish language videos to better understand what potentially drew new Hispanic Facebook users into liking the content.

Within this first 5 s, we coded for several potentially influential variables, including the presence of presidential candidates (Clinton, Sanders, Trump, other Republican candidates, etc.) as well as Hispanic people.[4] The videos were also categorized for their production quality. Unedited footage of live events, sometimes utilizing handheld devices, were coded as such, with the remaining being defined as produced videos. Two coders were used to identify the presence or absence of the above variables, and variables were only recorded as present if both coders agreed (a double positive).

Ultimately, of the 3,301 Clinton posts extracted during the primary, only 39 autoplay videos were identified as specifically targeted to Hispanic voters through Spanish language in the text above the video post or the subtitles of the first five seconds of the video. To be an effective expenditure of limited campaign resources, these Hispanic targeted videos were expected to perform better at attracting new Hispanics (through likes) than all other nontargeted videos. The following details the relative success of these posts in attracting new Hispanic support and the various effective visual cues used in these videos.

CASE STUDY: CLINTON AND HISPANICS IN THE PRIMARIES

The tables and figures that follow explore three aspects of Clinton's Hispanic-targeted autoplay video posts: First, we seek to more clearly identify the political leanings and affiliations of new Hispanic voters. Subsequently, we expose effective and ineffective techniques utilized by the campaign in attempting to attract these potential supporters. Finally, we evaluate whether the campaign itself was aware of these trends and, if so, we explore how adept they were at targeting a demographic with shifting interests.

Potential Hispanic Support for Targeted Facebook Autoplay Videos

We selected Hillary Clinton as our case study because, as noted in the previous section, we assumed she would attract the most Hispanic support, given her outreach and status as the front-runner in the Democratic primary campaign. The results in Table 1 confirm this assumption. The Clinton campaign was indeed able to secure a majority of Hispanic support in the Democratic presidential primary campaign, and the Democratic Party amassed a majority of the share of Hispanic support on Facebook. The ratio between the parties in the primaries is not too dissimilar to the final general election result, as approximately 58% of Hispanic people identified in the data set supported Democrats during the primaries—while exit polls suggest

TABLE 1 Hispanic Users' Party and Candidate Affiliation

Total Hispanic affiliation of the 2016 presidential primaries		
Democrat only	Republican only	Both
1,370,566	1,009,529	111,242
Total Hispanic affiliation of the 2016 democratic primaries		
Clinton only	Sanders only	Both
804,786	485,060	80,720

that under two-thirds supported Clinton on November 8, 2016 (Huang et al. 2016).

Support among the candidates in 2016 was not entirely static, however. Around 100,000 Hispanic Facebook users liked both Democratic and Republican posts during the primary. This means that roughly 5% of Hispanic users were willing to switch their support between or within the two parties in 2016. Given the relatively small size of this party switcher electorate on Facebook, Clinton's most effective targeted messages to Hispanics likely avoided attempting to convert supporters of other candidates.

Table 2 establishes the metric for a successful Hispanic-targeted post. If targeted posts can solicit a greater number of likes from new Hispanics than an average nontargeted post (n > 21), then it signifies a successful use of resources. Hispanic-targeted videos, as Table 2 shows, were indeed far more successful at attracting new Hispanic users—again, defined as those users who had not previously liked a Clinton post—than all other videos from the campaign. While targeted videos attracted almost twice as many likes from Hispanic users who had already liked a Clinton post than other Clinton videos, these videos brought in over 10 times more new Hispanics than other Clinton videos. Put another way, Hispanic-targeted videos, or at least those that utilize Spanish in text above the video or in the video itself, do seem to be an effective tool in gaining new support among this community online, for the reasons we note in the previous section.

Effective and Ineffective Techniques to Attract New Hispanic Support

Table 3 suggests that all videos displaying a presidential candidate met our metric of success, as the median number of new Hispanic likes under every category where evidence was found is higher than the baseline. However, evidence of certain candidates was more effective than others. For example, videos that displayed GOP presidential primary candidates, other than Donald Trump, performed only slightly better than nontargeted videos at enticing new likes from Hispanic users, while videos presenting Trump or Clinton were more effective. Indeed, videos of Clinton outperformed the baseline by a ratio of over 14:1. Curiously, while videos containing images

TABLE 2 Likes for Videos from Hillary Clinton in 2016

	Median number of likes per Clinton video	
	Hispanic-targeted videos ($n = 39$)	All other videos ($n = 704$)
New Hispanic likes	213	21
Total Hispanic likes	1796	926

TABLE 3 Median New Hispanic Likes by Presidential Candidate Presence

	Median likes of new Hispanics
All other Clinton videos (nontargeted)	21
All Hispanic-targeted videos	213
Displays Hillary Clinton	299
Displays Donald Trump	100
Displays of other GOP candidates	25
Displays of Bernie Sanders	–

of Donald Trump outperformed the baseline, they performed worse than the average for Hispanic-targeted videos. Theoretically, we might explain the relatively poor performance of Trump and other GOP videos by utilizing research on negative political advertising, which suggests that voters do not reward candidates for this method of communication (see Lau, Sigelman, and Rovner 2007).[5] Indeed, recent research suggests that Democratic candidates are particularly vulnerable to this phenomenon (Blackwell 2013), and that positive campaign messages are the more effective method of communication (Malloy and Pearson-Merkowitz 2016).

Recent research does suggest that targeted demographics respond better to imagery of those of apparent similar descent (see Harmer and Wring 2013). Table 4 explores whether this is the case for Clinton. The apparent presence of Hispanic individuals in targeted videos performed against the baseline as well as all videos that included the presence of a presidential candidate. This seems to fall in with theory, but a more detailed examination of these posts with and without Clinton reveals another interesting trend: videos of Hispanic people without Clinton present were far more popular than when the two were paired. What this suggests is that voters did not necessarily respond as well to potentially more blatant attempts to pander to their demographic (Hersh and Schaffner 2013). Nevertheless, Clinton still benefitted more from videos that included both herself and Hispanic individuals, based on new Hispanic likes compared to the baseline.

As Table 5 shows, there appears to be a clear preference from potential new Hispanic supporters between "live" and "produced" videos. Some of the most effective videos at garnering new Hispanic likes were those that we would not describe as traditional advertising. Rather, the videos that looked

TABLE 4 Median New Hispanic Likes by Hispanic Presence

	Median likes of new Hispanics
Displays Hispanic person(s)	357
Median new Hispanic likes by Hispanic and Clinton presence	
Displays Hispanic person(s) without Clinton	455.5
Displays Hispanic person(s) with Clinton	292
Displays Clinton without Hispanic Person(s)	260

TABLE 5 "Live" vs. Produced Content and New Hispanic Likes

Category	Median number
Edited/Produced	123
"Live"	334

less professional—in other words, showed footage of one event or situation seamlessly (as if it were a live feed)—were more effective at attracting new support. One possible reason for this may be that voters are averse to traditional televised advertising techniques and respond accordingly when confronted with it on social media platforms such as Facebook. Indeed, research does suggest that noncommercial online videos typically gain more user interaction (measured by shares) than commercial videos that elicit similar emotional responses, potentially as they are seen as less filtered and thus more credible (Towner and Dulio 2011; Nelson-Field, Riebe, and Newstead 2013).

Theory aside, the embodiment of these ideas in specific videos is perhaps more instructive. Take, for example, an autoplay video of the "union of peasants" posted on March 7, 2016 (Clinton 2016)—which got 833 new Hispanic likes. Here, a free (handheld) camera records a moment in which a mother with her young daughter speaks to a group of Hispanic people about her excitement to be present at a Clinton event. This type of autoplay video capitalizes on two of Clinton's most effective targeting techniques: Hispanic presence and the perception of a "live" event. The element of unpredictability, and by association, authenticity, associated with live television is something that a great deal of literature in media circles has explored as far back as the development of modern local TV news itself (Allen 2005). Interestingly, the popularity of live video utilized in this setting appears to adhere to this philosophy despite the fact it occurs in a completely different medium. The live element of these videos is, in fact, so popular that many of Clinton's top posts at attracting new Hispanics were merely short clips of political rallies or, in some extreme cases, clips of her giving a speech without any editing. Of all the targeting techniques explored, creating the perception of a live, unedited, event appears to be the most effective, particularly when paired with imagery of the desired demographic.

Campaign's Self-Awareness and of What was Effective and Ineffective

Figure 1 above, curiously, suggests that the campaign may not have been aware of this, as more professional developed videos were deployed in the final months of the primary season. The two distinct spikes in Figure 1 highlight the success the campaign had at gaining new Hispanic likes with "live" Hispanic-targeted videos. The first and most extreme spike represents

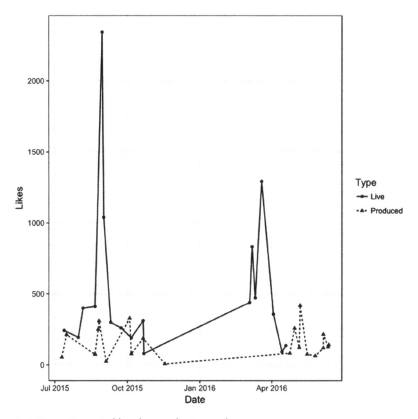

FIGURE 1 New Hispanic likes by production value.

new Hispanic likes from two posts that included short snippets from Clinton's speech at the same live event, the Democratic National Committee Summer Meeting in late August 2015. While these videos did not include visual representations of Hispanic people, they were the first "live" Hispanic-targeted videos posted after Univision's Jorge Ramos was forcibly removed from a Trump press conference on August 25 (see Schleifer 2016),[6] suggesting external events may have played some role in this dramatic increase in activity. The second noticeable outlier, addressed more explicitly around Figure 2 below, involves five "live" videos[7] posted after an extended period without the campaign posting Hispanic-targeted videos and in the run up to primaries where Hispanic support was an important deciding factor.

Despite the success of "live" videos at attracting new Hispanic likes, Figure 1 also shows that "live" Hispanic-targeted videos were not released after mid-April 2016. This came in the midst of a host of Sanders victories (seven straight primary contests) including a state which would prove vital in the presidential election: Wisconsin. Instead, the campaign began relying entirely on more heavily produced videos—many of which were simply nontargeted videos re-edited with Spanish subtitles and text—as a method

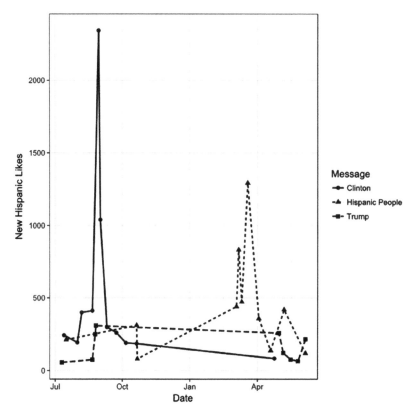

FIGURE 2 New Hispanic likes by message.

of attracting potential new Hispanic support in the run up to the presidential election. The findings above suggest this may not have been a wise strategy.

Figure 2 above suggests the campaign was also not particularly mindful of the practical effect of the targeting techniques noted earlier. The second major spike seen in Figure 1 is again present in Figure 2. This significant increase in new Hispanic engagement comes from five "live" Hispanic-targeted videos that, importantly, also included visual representations of Hispanic people in the first 5 s. These were posted in the lead up to the primaries including Florida and Arizona which, while important primary states in their own right, are also ones that required large proportions of Hispanic support to secure victory.

Despite the success of videos with visual representations of Hispanic people at attracting new likes from this demographic, the campaign appears to have adhered to a more traditional primary strategy. This included defining the candidate early in the process, linking the candidate to issues that the demographic cares about, and then focusing on the opponent as the presidential election approached. Had the campaign focused on the effect of the videos rather than the process, they may have found that Trump-focused autoplay videos did not bring in new Hispanic support as effectively. Again, this is a curious result, because this type of analysis was readily available to a campaign with a vast array of resources. It is entirely possible that another explanation exists, such as the fact that all the videos with visual evidence of Trump were also more heavily produced. However, given the clear results above, it is indeed possible that the campaign simply was not aware of the effectiveness of their Hispanic-targeted autoplay video posts.

CONCLUSION

Targeted political communication through social media platforms like Facebook allows us to measure their strategic effectiveness through attainable data about user interactions. What is interesting, however, is that our findings suggest that the Clinton campaign did not learn from what type of Hispanic-targeted autoplay videos were effective and ineffective at garnering new likes from Hispanic Facebook users. This is particularly curious given such data are publicly available. Also, given the vast resources at the campaign's disposal, it is likely they had access to more detailed material. Instead, the campaign focused on what we deem to be an ineffective message for attracting new Hispanic supporters: Donald Trump. While we cannot tell how well that worked overall, other strategies were more effective at garnering new Hispanic likes during the primary season. The preproduced quality seen in many of Clinton's autoplay video posts may have played into the brand of her as a candidate overly manufactured and focus grouped. This may have been why the live element of certain videos helped so much in gaining new support from Hispanic Facebook users.

While the findings do highlight certain effective and ineffective visual elements at garnering new support through candidates' targeted Facebook autoplay videos, there are limitations that need to be acknowledged. First, the visual content analyzed was almost strictly coded on the criteria of who was presented. It did not look deeper into how they were presented, such as facial expressions, hand gestures, or body stance. While there is literature that looks at such visual cues, these studies normally focus solely on candidates. At this stage, we were more focused on looking at the various people who were visually presented, and what potential impact that had on the effectiveness of the targeted communication (although we did look at cinematography to a degree). Second, while we argue for the importance of likes for buy-in in the methodology section, there are other metrics—such as video views—that could be used. However, scraping views from Facebook pages is in violation of the platforms' terms and service. While we could have manually taken the views from our smaller sample once we finally identified them, at that later stage that number would not correlate with the number of views as they were during the primaries, or with the results we already had, due to the timing of their extraction. Third, we did not look at variables such as the impact of the autoplay videos' lengths which, due to time commitment, could play a role in users' willingness to engage with them. However, because we were only looking at the first 5 s of videos, we did not look at this. Finally, our research only looks at the results for Facebook autoplay videos around one target demographic and one candidate. Other candidates, such as Trump, may have had success with different kinds of autoplay videos or, indeed, posts. After all, Trump was a very different type of candidate than Clinton, targeting a very different market.

Thankfully, the methodology and data set of this article provides ample room for future investigation. We extracted the data from all of Hillary Clinton's Facebook posts during the 2016 presidential primary season, we did so for seven other presidential primary candidates during this period as well.[8] Therefore, the methodology could be used to see if the findings are candidate specific or more universally applicable. The methodology could be used to explore if the findings here are universal across cultures, or strictly applicable to the Hispanic demographic's engagement with autoplay videos. It could also potentially reveal the interactions of users who like posts by gender (Liu and Ruths 2013) or age (Silver and McCann 2014). Using the database, future research could look deeper into what is seen in these autoplay videos in their entirety as well as the nuances of how the people visually presented in them are portrayed and likely decoded by viewers through semiotic analysis. Finally, the database also reveals a complex ecosystem of user participation on Facebook between political candidates, cable news organizations (including cable news hosts), various other key political and media actors as well as the most prominent religious pages on Facebook. In doing so, future research could offer a unique insight into the followers these primary candidates develop: what they like, who they follow, and when they change their allegiances.

Despite its limitations, this research still provides insight that helps us back up and builds on current research. Broadly, as the study of targeting in political marketing has tended to treat the actual communication of targeted efforts as secondary, this research highlights a process to more directly look at the potential strategic advantage of certain visual cues in targeted appeals through one of the newest and important avenues of online communication. Indeed, while there is existing research that suggests targeted communication could result in lost support, this research adds to the bulk of literature that champions the benefits of targeted communication— and does so with numerical evidence. In doing so, it also builds on current theory by highlighting how much more effective such appeals are at gaining new support from targeted groups, compared to just maintaining existing support from them—likely due to the autoplay format having less self-selection barriers as other online video formats.

In terms of research around online video virality, the findings of this article further suggest that less produced online videos are likely to elicit more user engagement, potentially because they are less filtered and thus perceived as more credible. Finally, this research backs up and builds on existing theory around targeted political advertising more generally. Importantly, it backs up the argument that voters do not reward candidates for utilizing negative advertising as well as the argument that utilizing visual representations of the target audience will be rewarded. While currently research highlights how advertising covering important nontarget-specific issues from a target audience's perspective is effective, this article builds on this by suggesting that simply re-editing general purpose adverts with subtitles in ethnic minorities' particular languages is not as effective.

The findings therefore provide insight that could be utilized in practical application. It suggests that, to fit in with the surrounding content, campaigns should focus on mimicking the less professionally edited visual cues of user-generated content. This way, the content simulates the interactions target audiences have with their actual Facebook friends and may help in somewhat replicating that bond. This could also be achieved by focusing the visual content of such videos on people who look like the target audience. The findings also suggest practitioners should focus their content away from opposition candidates, especially those from other parties. Also, the results suggest that campaigns need to create original content to effectively target demographics, as re-editing more generalized videos is not as effective at gaining support. Most importantly, however, the findings suggest that campaigns need to utilize such data to find out what is effective at reaching and appealing to the audience they are targeting and alter their autoplay video outputs accordingly.

NOTES

1. On the other hand, appeals in Spanish have been found to be more effective among newer arrivals to America, who are low-propensity voters and Hispanics whose primary language was Spanish (Abrajano and Panagopoulos 2011).

2. Also, known supporters are a broad and different type of demographic than the Hispanic demographic we are looking at in this research.

3. The closer the data are collected to the time of the primaries the better. While not perfectly in line, it more closely represents user interaction with the content during the primaries.

4. These were coded for the presence or absence of each variables, so areas of overlap—like a video which displayed both Clinton and Sanders in the first five seconds, for example—are not distinguished in the tables and graphs below unless explicitly stated. Instead, they are treated individually as a video that shows Clinton, and another video that shows Sanders. Overlap is only accounted for when explicitly stated, such as in Table 4, where we show that the presence of two variables—Clinton and a Hispanic person—brings in new Hispanic supporters in greater numbers than just the presence of Hillary Clinton alone.

5. This requires us to accept a limited definition of negative political advertising as one that contains an attack on the opponent—not entirely uncontested itself (see Geer 2006)—nonetheless, this might reasonably explain why these attacks do not effectively pull in new support.

6. Both videos were posted with Spanish text above the video, while the second clip was also about immigration.

7. However, there are two pairs of near duplicates. The difference being that each pair had one version with English subtitles and the other had Spanish subtitles.

8. The other candidates' data extracted being Bernie Sanders, Jeb Bush, Ben Carson, Ted Cruz, John Kasich, Marco Rubio, and Donald Trump.

REFERENCES

Abrahamse, A. F., P. A. Morrison, and N. M. Bolton. 1994. "Surname Analysis for Estimating Local Concentration of Hispanic and Asians." *Population Research and Policy Review* 13:383–98. doi:10.1007/bf01084115

Abrajano, M., and C. Panagopoulos. 2011. "Does Language Matter? The Impact of Spanish versus English-Language GOTV Efforts on Latino Turnout." *American Politics Research* 39 (4):643–63. doi:10.1177/1532673x10397000

Agiesta, J. 2015. "CNN/ORC Poll: In Democratic Race, Clinton Solidifies Lead. CNN." Article Retrieved 29 April 2017. http://edition.cnn.com/2015/12/04/politics/cnn-orc-poll-democrats-hillary-clinton-2016-election-democratic-primary/

Allen, C. 2005. "Discovering "Joe Six Pack" Content in Television News: The Hidden History of Audience Research, News Consultants, and the Warner Class Model." *Journal of Broadcasting & Electronic Media* 49 (4):363–82. doi:10.1207/s15506878jobem4904_1

Andzulis, J. M., N. G. Panagopoulos, and A. Rapp. 2012. "A Review of Social Media and Implications for the Sales Process." *Journal of Personal Selling & Sales Management* 32 (3):305–16. doi:10.2753/pss0885-3134320302

Barreto, M. A., J. Merolla, and V. Defrancesco Soto. 2011. "Multiple Dimensions of Mobilization: The Effect of Direct Contact and Political Ads on Latino Turnout in the 2000 Presidential Election." *Journal of Political Marketing* 10 (4):303–27. doi:10.1080/15377857.2011.614548

Barrett, A. W., and L. W. Barrington. 2005. "Is a Picture Worth a Thousand Words? Newspaper Photographs and Voter Evaluations of Political Candidates." *Press/Politics* 10 (4):98–113. doi:10.1177/1081180x05281392

Baumgartner, J. C., and J. S. Morris. 2010. "MyFaceTube Politics: Social Networking Web Sites and Political Engagement of Young Adults." *Social Science Computer Review* 28 (1):24–44. doi:10.1177/0894439309334325

Bayraktutan, G., M. Binack, T. Comu, B. Dogu, G. Islamogu, and A. Aydemir. 2014. "The Use of Facebook by Political Parties and Leaders in the 2011 Turkish General Elections in Bogdan Pătruţ and Monica Pătruţ." In *Social Media in Politics: Case Studies on the Political Power of Social Media*, edited by Bogdan Pătruţ and Monica Pătruţ 165–99. Cham: Springer.

Bimber, B. 2014. "Digital Media in the Obama Campaigns of 2008 and 2012: Adaptation to the Personalized Political Communication Environment." *Journal of Information Technology & Politics* 11 (2):130–50. doi:10.1080/19331681.2014.895691

Bivens, R. 2015. "The Gender Binary will not be Deprogrammed: Ten Years of Coding Gender on Facebook." *New Media & Society* 19:880–98. doi:10.1177/1461444815621527

Blackwell, M. 2013. "A Framework for Dynamic Causal Inference in Political Science." *American Journal of Political Science* 57 (2):504–20. doi:10.1111/j.1540-5907.2012.00626.x

Borah, P. 2014. "Facebook Use in the 2012 USA Presidential Campaign." In *Social Media in Politics: Case Studies on the Political Power of Social Media*, edited by B. Pătruţ and M. Pătruţ, 201–11. Cham: Springer.

Burton, M. J. 2012. "Strategic Voter Selection." In *Routledge Handbook of Political Marketing*, edited by J. Lees-Marshment, 34–47. New York: Routledge.

Busby, R. 2009. *Marketing the Populist Politician: The Demotic Democrat*, 34–47. Basingstoke; New York: Palgrave Macmillan.

Cameron, M., P. Barrett, and B. Stewardson. 2016. "Can Social Media Predict Election Results? Evidence from New Zealand." *Journal of Political Marketing* 15 (4): 416–32. doi:10.1080/15377857.2014.959690

Clinton, H. 2016. "A Special Moment during a Meeting with the Union of Peasants. Yes You Can! Watch the Video. Facebook Status Update." Retrieved 20 November 2016. https://www.facebook.com/hillaryclinton/posts/1090969694292892

Cogburn, D. L., and F. K. Espinoza-Vasquez. 2011. "From Networked Nominee to Networked Nation: Examining the Impact of Web 2.0 and Social Media on Political Participation and Civic Engagement in the 2008 Obama Campaign." *Journal of Political Marketing* 10 (1–2):189–213. doi:10.1080/15377857.2011.540224

Connaughton, S. L., D. Nekrassova, and K. Lever. 2008. "Talk about Issues: Policy Consideration in the 2004 Latino-oriented Spots." In *The Mass Media and Latino Politics*, edited by F. A. Subervi-Velez, 309–22. New York: Routledge.

Conway, B. A., K. Kenski, and D. Wang. 2013. "Twitter use by Presidential Primary Candidates during the 2012 Campaign." *American Behavioral Scientist* 57 (11):1596–610. doi:10.1177/0002764213489014

Davalos, S., and A. Merchant. 2015. "Using Big Data to Study Psychological Constructs: Nostalgia on Facebook." *Journal of Psychology & Psychotherapy* 5: 1–3. doi:10.4172/2161-0487.1000221

Dinan, S. 2013. "Hispanics Favor Democrats more than 2-to-1: Gallup." *The Washington Times*. Article retrieved 26 April 2017. http://www.washingtontimes.com/news/2013/aug/8/gallup-hispanics-favor-democrats-more-2-to-1/

Facebook. 2015. "The Value of Video for Brands." Webpage Accessed 28 April 2017. https://www.facebook.com/business/news/value-of-video

Filimonov, K., U. Russman, and J. Svennsoon. 2016. "Picturing the Party: Instagram and Party Campaigning in the 2014 Swedish Elections." *Social Media and Society* 2:1–11. doi:10.1177/2056305116662179

Fiscella, K., and A. M. Fremont. 2006. "Use of Geocoding and Surname Analysis to Estimate Race and Ethnicity." *Health Services Research* 41 (4 Pt 1):1482–500.

Funk, T. 2013. *Advanced Social Media Marketing: How to Lead, Launch, and Manage a Successful Social Media Program*. New York: Apress.

Geer, J. G. 2006. *In Defense of Negativity: Attack Ads in Presidential Campaigns*. Chicago, IL: University of Chicago Press.

Germany, J. B. 2009. "The Online Revolution." In *Campaigning for President 2008: Strategy and Tactics, New Voices and New Techniques*, edited by D. W. Johnson, 147–60. New York: Routledge.

Gibson, R. 2012. "From Brochureware to "MyBo": An Overview of Online Elections and Campaigning." *Politics* 32 (2):77–84. doi:10.1111/j.1467-9256.2012.01429.x

Giglietto, F., L. Rossi, and D. Bennato. 2012. "The Open Laboratory: Limits and Possibilities of Using Facebook, Twitter, and YouTube as a Research Data

Source." *Journal of Technology in Human Services* 30 (3/4):145–59. doi:10.1080/15228835.2012.743797

Goodnow, T. 2013. "Facing Off: A Comparative Analysis of Obama and Romney Facebook Timeline Photographs." *American Behavioral Scientist* 57 (11): 1584–95. doi:10.1177/0002764213489013

Graber, D. 1996. "Say It with Pictures." *The Annals of the American Academy* 546: 85–96. doi:10.1177/0002716296546001008

Griffin, A. 2015. "Facebook is Planning to become New YouTube as Video Growth Surges. Independent." Article Retrieved 24 February 2016. http://www.independent.co.uk/life-style/gadgets-and-tech/news/facebook-is-planning-to-become-new-youtube-as-video-growth-surges-9964840.html

Gueorguieva, V. 2008. "Voters, MySpace, and YouTube: The Impact of Alternative Communication Channels on the 2006 Election Cycle and Beyond." *Social Science Computer Review* 26 (3):288–300.

Gulati, G. J., and C. B. Williams. 2010. "Congressional Candidates' use of YouTube in 2008: Its Frequency and Rationale." *Journal of Information Technology and Politics* 7 (2–3):93–109. doi:10.1080/19331681003748958

Harmer, E., and D. Wring. 2013. "Julie and the Cybermums: Marketing and Women Voters in the UK 2010 General Election." *Journal of Political Marketing* 12 (2/3):262–73. doi:10.1080/15377857.2013.781472

Harfoush, R. 2009. *Yes We Did; An Inside Look at How Social Media Built the Obama Brand.* Berkeley: New Riders.

Hersh, E. D., and B. F. Schaffner. 2013. "Targeted Campaign Appeals and the Value of Ambiguity." *Journal of Politics* 75 (2):520–1534. doi:10.1017/s0022381613000182

Hillygus, D. S., and T. G. Shields. 2008. *The Persuadable Voter: Wedge Issues in Presidential Campaigns.* Princeton, NJ: Princeton University Press.

Hong, S., and Nadler, D. 2012. "Which Candidates Do the Public Discuss Online in an Election Campaign? The Use of Social Media by 2012 Presidential Candidates and its Impact on Candidate Salience." *Government Information Quarterly.* 29 (4):455–61.

Huang, J., S. Jacoby, M. Strickland, and K. K. Rebecca Lai. 2016. "Election 2016: Exit Polls." *New York Times.* Article Accessed 30 April 2017. https://www.nytimes.com/interactive/2016/11/08/us/politics/election-exit-polls.html

Issenberg, S. 2012. *The Victory Lab: The Secret Science of Winning Campaigns.* New York: Crown.

Jackson, N. 2006. "Banking Online: The use of the Internet by Political Parties to Build Relationships with Voters." In *The Marketing of Political Parties*, edited by D. G. Lilleker, N. Jackson, and R. Scullion, 157–84. Manchester: Manchester University Press.

Johnson, D. W. 2013. "The Election 2012." In *Campaigning for President 2012: Strategy and Tactics*, edited by D. W. Johnson, 1–22. New York: Routledge.

Johnson, T., and D. D. Perlmutter. 2011. *New Media, Campaigning and the 2008 Facebook Election.* London, UK: Routledge.

Kharroub, T., and O. Bas. 2016. "Social Media and Protests: An Examination of Twitter Images of the 2011 Egyptian Revolution." *New Media & Society* 18 (9): 1973–92. doi:10.1177/1461444815571914

Knuckey, J., and J. Lees-Marshment. 2005. "American Political Marketing: George W. Bush and the Republican Party." In *Political Marketing: A Comparative Perspective*, edited by D. G. Lilleker and J. Lees-Marshment, 39–58. Manchester: Manchester University Press.

Kreiss, D. 2012. *Taking Our Country Back: The Crafting of Networked Politics from Howard Dean to Barack Obama*. New York: Oxford University Press.

Larsson, A. O., and H. Moe. 2012. "Studying Political Micro-blogging: Twitter users in the 2010 Swedish Election Campaign." *New Media & Society* 14 (5):729–47. doi:10.1177/1461444811422894

Lau, R. R., L. Sigelman, and I. B. Rovner. 2007. "The Effects of Negative Political Campaigns: A Meta-analytic Reassessment. *Journal of Politics* 69 (4):1176–209. doi:10.1111/j.1468-2508.2007.00618.x

Lee, R., and D. Sutton. 2002. "Better Ethnic Targeting: New Methodology Enhances Voter Files." *Campaigns and Elections*. Article accessed 27 April 2017. https://www.highbeam.com/doc/1G1-89973718.html

Lees-Marshment, J. 2010. New Zealand Political Marketing: Marketing Communication Rather than the Product. In *Global Political Marketing*, edited by J. Lees-Marshment, J. Stromback, and C. Rudd, 65–81. Abingdon: Rutledge.

Lees-Marshment, J., J. Stromback, and C. Rudd. 2010. *Global Political Marketing*. Abingdon: Rutledge.

Leppäniemi, M., H. Karjaluoto, H. Lehto, and A. Goman. 2010. "Targeting Young Voters in a Political Campaign: Empirical Insights into an Interactive Digital Marketing Campaign in the 2007 Finnish General Election." *Journal of Nonprofit & Public Sector Marketing* 22 (1):14–37. doi:10.1080/10495140903190374

Lewis-Beck, M. S., and M. Stegmaier. 2016. "The Hispanic Immigrant Voter and the Classic American Voter: Presidential Support in the 2012 Election." *The Russell Sage Foundation Journal of the Social Sciences* 2 (3):165–81.

Lieber, P. S., and G. J. Golan. 2011. "Political Public Relations, News Management, and Agenda Indexing." In *Political Public Relations: Principles and Applications*, edited by J. Stromback and S. Kiousis, 54–74. New York: Routledge.

Lilleker, D. G., and J. Lees-Marshment. 2005. *Political Marketing: A Comparative Perspective*. Manchester, NY: Manchester University Press.

Liu, W., and D. Ruths. 2013. "What's in a Name? Using First Names as Features for Gender Inference in Twitter." *AAAI Spring Symposium: Analyzing Microtext* 13 (1):10–16.

Lopez, M. H., and A. Gonzalez-Barrera. 2013. "A Growing Share of Latinos Get Their New in English." *Pew Research Center*. Article retrieved 26 April 2017. http://www.pewhispanic.org/2013/07/23/a-growing-share-of-latinos-get-their-news-in-english/

Malloy, L. C., and S. Pearson-Merkowitz. 2016. "Going Positive: The Effects of Negative and Positive Advertising on Candidate Success and Voter Turnout." *Research & Politics* 3 (1):1–15.

Margolis, M., D. Resnick, and C. Tu. 1997. Campaigning on the Internet: Parties and candidates on the World Wide Web in the 1996 primary season. *The Harvard International Journal of Press/Politics* 2 (1):59–78. doi:10.1177/1081180x 97002001006

Marland, A. 2012. "Yes We Can (Fundraise): The Ethics of Ethics in Political Fundraising." In *The Routlegde Handbook of Political Marketing*, edited by J. Lees-Marshment, 190–202. London and New York: Routledge.

McGough, S. 2005. "Political Marketing in Irish Politics: The Case of Sinn Fein." In *Political Marketing: A Comparative Perspective*, edited by D. G. Lilleker and J. Lees-Marshment, 97–113. Manchester: Manchester University Press.

Miller, W. J. 2013. "We Can't All Be Obama: The Use of New Media in Modern Political Campaigns." *Journal of Political Marketing* 12 (4):326–47. doi:10.1080/15377857.2013.837312

Nelson-Field, K., E. Riebe, and K. Newstead. 2013. "The Emotions that Drive Viral Video." *Australasian Marketing Journal* 21 (4):205–11. doi:10.1016/j.ausmj.2013.07.003

Nickerson, D. W., and T. Rogers. 2014. "Political Campaigns and Big Data." *The Journal of Economic Perspectives* 28 (2):51–73.

Nteta, T., and B. Schaffner. 2013. "Substance and Symbolism: Race, Ethnicity, and Campaign Appeals in the United States." *Political Communication* 30 (2):232–53. doi:10.1080/10584609.2012.737425

Oberfield, Z. W., and A. J. Segal. 2008. "Pluralism Examined: Party Television Expenditure Focused on the Latino Vote in Presidential Elections." In *The Mass Media and Latino Politics*, edited by F. A. Subervi-Velez, 291–308. New York: Routledge.

Oremus, W. 2016. "Who Controls Your Facebook Feed." *Slate*. Article Retrieved 02 January 2017. http://www.slate.com/articles/technology/cover_story/2016/01/how_facebook_s_news_feed_algorithm_works.html

Paivio, A. 1991. *Images in Mind: The Evolution of a Theory*. New York: Harvester Wheatsheaf.

Panagopoulos, C., and D. P. Green. 2011. "Spanish-Language Radio Advertisements and Latino Voter Turnout in the 2006 Congressional Elections: Field Experimental Evidence." *Political Research Quarterly* 64 (3):588–99. doi:10.1177/1065912910367494

Parsons, A. 2013. "Using Social Media to Reach Consumers: A Content Analysis of Official Facebook Pages." *Academy of Marketing Studies Journal* 17 (2):27–36.

Pew Research Center. 2016. "Candidates Differ in their use of Social Media to Connect with the Public." Retrieved 18 August 2016. http://www.journalism.org/2016/07/18/candidates-differ-in-their-use-of-social-media-to-connect-with-the-public/

Pew Research Center. 2017. "Social Media Fact Sheet." Retrieved 28 April 2017. http://www.pewinternet.org/fact-sheet/social-media/

Ridout, T. N. 2014. "The Market Research, Testing and Targeting behind American Political Advertising." In *Political Marketing in the United States*, edited by J. Lees-Marshment, B. Conley, and K. Cosgrove, 220–36. New York: Routledge.

Rosenberg, S., S. Kahn, and T. Tran. 1991. "Creating a Political Image: Shaping Appearance and Manipulating the Vote. *Political Behavior* 13 (4):345–67. doi:10.1007/bf00992868

Sabate, F., J. Berbegal-Mirabent, A. Cañabate, and P. R. Lebherz. 2014. "Factors Influencing Popularity of Branded Content in Facebook Fan Pages." *European Management Journal* 32 (6):1001–11. doi:10.1016/j.emj.2014.05.001

Sanson, A. 2008. "Facebook and Youth Mobilization in the 2008 Presidential Election." *Gnovis Journal* 8 (3):162–74.

Schill, D. 2012. "The Visual Image and the Political Image: A Review of Visual Communication Research in the Field of Political Communication." *Review of Communication* 12 (2):118–42. doi:10.1080/15358593.2011.653504

Schleifer, T. 2016. "Univision Anchor Ejected from Trump News Conference." *CNN*. Article Accessed 26 May 2017. http://edition.cnn.com/2015/08/25/politics/donald-trump-megyn-kelly-iowa-rally/

Shearer, E. 2016. "Candidates' Social Media Outpaces their Websites and Emails as an Online Campaign News Source." Pew Research Center. Retrieved 18 August 2016. http://www.pewresearch.org/fact-tank/2016/07/20/candidates-social-media-outpaces-their-websites-and-emails-as-an-online-campaign-news-source/

Silver, N., and A. McCann. 2014. "How to Tell Someone's Age When All You Know Is Her Name." *FiveThirtyEight*. Article Retrieved 29 April 2017. http://fivethirtyeight.com/features/how-to-tell-someones-age-when-all-you-know-is-her-name/

Skelley, G. 2015. "Democrats 2016: The Primary Map Still Favors Clinton." *Rasmussen Reports*. Article Retrieved 29 April 2017. http://www.rasmussenreports.com/public_content/political_commentary/commentary_by_geoffrey_skelley/democrats_2016_the_primary_map_still_favors_clinton

Small, T. 2012. "Are We Friends Yet? Online Relationship Marketing by Political Parties." In *Political Marketing in Canada*, edited by A. Marland, T. Giasson, and J. Lees-Marshment, 193–208. Vancouver: UBC.

Smith, R. J., P. Crutchley, H. A. Schwartz, L. Ungar, F. Shofer, K. A. Padrez, and R. M. Merchant. 2017. Variations in Facebook Posting Patterns Across Validated Patient Health Conditions: A Prospective Cohort Study. *Journal of Medical Internet Research*, 19 (1).

Spiller, L., and J. Bergner. 2014. "Database Political Marketing in Campaigning and Government." In *Political Marketing in the United States*, edited by J. Less-Marshment, B. Conley, and K. Cosgrove, 44–60. New York: Routledge.

Stenberg, G. 2006. "Conceptual and Perceptual Factors in the Picture Superiority Effect." *European Journal of Cognitive Psychology* 18 (6):813–47. doi:10.1080/09541440500412361

Subervi-Velez, F., and S. L. Connaughton. 2008. "Democratic and Republican Mass Communication Campaign Strategies: Historical Overview." In *The Mass Media and Latino Politics*, edited by F. A. Subervi-Velez, 273–90. New York: Routledge.

Towner, T. L., and D. A. Dulio. 2011. "An Experiment of Campaign Effects during the YouTube Election." *New Media & Society* 13 (4):626–44. doi:10.1177/1461444810377917

Turcotte, A., and V. Raynauld. 2014. "Boutique Populism: The Emergence of the Tea Party Movement in the Age of Digital Populism." In *Political Marketing in the United States*, edited by J. Less-Marshment, B. Conley, and K. Cosgrove, 61–84. New York: Routledge.

United States Census Bureau. 2015. "FFF: Hispanic Heritage Month 2015." Website accessed 27 April 2017. https://www.census.gov/newsroom/facts-for-features/2015/cb15-ff18.html

United States Hispanic Chamber of Commerce. 2012. "New Report Finds Spending on Spanish-language Advertising Significantly Lagging." *PR Newswire*. Article

Accessed 26 April 2017. http://www.prnewswire.com/news-releases/ new-report-finds-spending-on-spanish-language-advertising-in-2012-election-significantly-lagging-172089111.html

Vesnic-Alujevic, L., and S. Van Bauwel. 2014. "YouTube: A Political Advertising Tool? A Case Study of the Use of YouTube in the Campaign for the European Parliament Elections 2009." *Journal of Political Marketing* 13 (3):195–212. doi:10.1080/15377857.2014.929886

Williams, C. B., and G. J. Gulati. 2013. "Social Networks in Political Campaigns: Facebook and the Congressional Elections of 2006 and 2008." *New Media and Society* 15 (1):52–71. doi:10.1177/1461444812457332

Zhang, W., T. J. Johnson, T. Seltzer, and S. L. Bichard. 2010. "The Revolution will be Networked: The Influence of Social Networking Sites on Political Attitudes and Behavior." *Social Science Computer Review* 28 (1):75–92. doi:10.1177/0894439309335162

Populism and Connectivism: An Analysis of the Sanders and Trump Nomination Campaigns

MICHAEL J. JENSEN and HENRIK P. BANG

This paper is an analysis of the Trump and Sanders' campaigns for the presidential nomination of their respective parties. It studies the structure of the relationship between the campaign and its supporters through communication on each candidate's Facebook page. While both campaigns have been termed populist, we differentiate populism from connectivism and develop an account of a connective campaign as a species of connective action. Whereas populism is predicated on a singular people, connectivity involves the acceptance and recognition of difference as a resource for political activity. Whereas populism involves a hierarchical authority relationship, connectivity is based on a reciprocal authority relationship. Finally, populism articulates an anti-establishment demand while connective campaigns demand for citizens to have the capacity for consequential engagement with political life. The empirical results demonstrate that connectivism and populism are distinct in practice and that these attributes hang together as two separate concepts. Further, we find that Trump's campaign communications emphasize populist themes, for Sanders such themes are limited and in the shadow of connectivism.

Color versions of one or more of the figures in the article can be found online at www.tandfonline.com/wplm.

INTRODUCTION

Populism has been on the rise in recent years and has played a significant role in the 2016 American campaign for the Presidency. The growth of populism reflects long-term trends in the decline of party identification and the growth of apartisanship, declining trust in politicians, and political institutions (Dalton 2013; Mair 2013). Commentary by pundits (Baggini 2016; Eiermann 2016), scholars (Bonikowski and Gidron 2016; Inglehart and Norris 2016), and public intellectuals (Sandel 2016) have all populism as a force behind the campaigns of Donald Trump and Bernie Sanders. While Hilary Clinton campaigned on her experience and competence due to her time in the political establishment, her two main rivals in the general election and the Democratic primary, Trump and Sanders, respectively, campaigned against the economic and political establishment.[1]

Although populism has a long tradition in American politics going back to its founding (Cornell 2012), it is not the only American political tradition that helps explain the Trump and Sanders campaigns. Alexis de Tocqueville in his account of *Democracy in America* (2010) argued that American democracy has survived due to a tendency in American culture for citizens to address and attempt to resolve political matters on their own rather than rely on authorities. Tocqueville's observations about citizen's capacities through the practice of political association have a long history in political science going back to Aristotle who defined it as the essence of political community (Bang 2016). Similarly, Dewey's (1954) notion of the great society and Lasswell's (2009) approach to policy also emphasized an active role for citizens as the driver of democratic politics and policymaking. In an era of ubiquitous digital networks and social media, Bennett and Segerberg (2013) have termed this capacity for self-organization "connective action." While social media facilitate populist media logics with leaders able to speak directly with supporters, bypassing broadcast media outlets (Moffitt 2016; Reinemann et al. 2016), they also enable networks of citizens to organize in political associations without dependence on formal organizations and leadership (Castells 2010; Bennett and Segerberg 2013).

This paper examines the messaging of each campaign with respect to their emphasis of populist and connective themes through their Facebook communications. The findings indicate that while both campaigns exhibit attributes of populist and connective campaign styles, populism is far more prevalent in Trump's communications and connective action is more common among Sanders' posts. Furthermore, the results problematize prevailing definitions of populism which equate the concept with popular content. In contrast to the connective logic which emphasizes action by citizens on their own, populist themes, whether articulated by Trump or Sanders, are constituted around the figure of a leader who acts in their name. These findings aid in the conceptual development of both populism and connectivism as explanatory accounts of political phenomena.

POPULISM AND CONNECTIVISM IN POLITICAL CAMPAIGNS

Populism and connective action have long histories in American politics. Trump's populism finds affinities with the know-nothings of the nineteenth century and his critique of financial interests might resonate with the anti-Federalists who opposed the Constitution (Cornell 1990, 2012). While populism has always retained a notion of "the people" which legitimates the aims of a populist figure, democratic theory has historically emphasized a differentiation between populism and democracy. In the first instance, it is antipluralist as the leader is positioned as a manifestation of "the people" (Moffitt 2016, 147–48). With the projection of a cultural sameness among the people, this would quickly give rise to a political sameness which rejects independent expertise, debate, and dissention (Wolin 2006, 595). Tocqueville saw these risks as somewhat endemic to democracy though the American experience was somewhat insulated due to its widespread practice of political association where persons readily band together across social and economic differences to solve common problems. However, without this practice, Tocqueville argued, populism would give way to democratic despotism as, "the clever man who seeks to establish absolute power among a democratic nation will demand only one thing from citizens: that they do not get involved in the government and contract none of the habits that can...lead men to get involved in it" (2010, 1253). For Tocqueville, the centrality of strong leadership in political life gradually erodes the place of citizens giving rise to a form of despotism.

While alternative definitions of populism which overlap with democratic political forms have been proffered over time (Mudde and Kaltwasser 2017), it make sense to define the term such that it (a) is applied to a distinct political logic and (b) that it differentiates that logic from other political forms. In this way, we can develop a theoretical account of populism adequate for empirical investigation. In this paper, we distinguish the logic of populism from a connective logic as these are conceptually alternative responses to the decoupling between citizens and politicians.

Defining Populism

Populism is a highly contested term. In part, this may be because few populist parties, politicians, or movements claim the title themselves and the term has taken on both positive and negative valences. Populism belies a traditional left–right differentiation as politicians on both the left and the right may be described in populist terms (Moffitt 2016). Further, political actors are normally not uniformly characterized by a singular concept. Rather, they sometimes campaign or relate as populists and other times they adopt more conventional political postures. For this reason, populism is not a property of an agent but of the communications through which political interactions occur (Laclau 2005; Moffitt 2016). Those communications come to define practices and the political logics which constitute populism or other political forms. We define populism with respect to three interdependent attributes. These include the notion of a "pure" people, an antisystem component, and the critical dependence on a leader in advancing the populist project. These attributes do not stand on their own. Rather, they constitute interrelated parts of the populist logic.

As both an empirical and conceptual matters, populists often speak of "the people" which has led some political scientists to take the construction of a people as "the undisputed core of populist communication" (Reinemann et al. 2016, 14). Populism emphasizes the unity of a people at the expense of all others: foreigners, economic elites, and so forth. As Mudde and Kaltwasser (2017, 6) define it, populism is *"a thin-centered ideology that considers society to be ultimately separated into two homogeneous and antagonistic camps, 'the pure people' versus 'the corrupt elite,' and which argues politics should be an expression of the volanté générale (general will) of the people."* Whether the people are organically or rhetorically constructed, the people are taken as a politicized collective entity which makes populism incompatible with pluralism (Mouffe 2013; Reinemann et al. 2016). The collective identity is depicted as morally pure, juxtaposed against some other, be they foreigners or elites of various sorts which are said to have subverted the people over time (Espejo 2015, 62).

There is broad agreement on populism's antisystem component. The morally deserving people are juxtaposed against "the system" or indifferent and corrupt elite. For Laclau, the antisystem aspect takes the form of a demand which constitutes "the elementary form in the building up of the social link" between persons who constitute a people (2005, 35). Since populism "revolves around a central *antagonistic relationship between 'the people' and 'the elite'"* (Abts and Rummens 2007, 408), the demand is what unites the people as a homogeneous entity. The elite need not be those members of a political system occupying formal authority roles as the differentiation of the morally deserving people distinguishes them from "enemies of the people" who the elites have allowed to create a crisis situation (Moffitt 2016, 43–44). The people's enemies are in this sense an extension of the corrupt authorities, system, or establishment.

The collective's need for rescue and protection points to a third attribute often neglected in definitions of populism: the role of a strong leader who will free them and is thus able to command the obedience and allegiance of supporters (Bos, van der Brug, and de Vreese 2011). This view differs from definitions of populism which equate it with "popular sovereignty" and which draw support from a normative vision of democracy rooted in Rousseau's account of citizens engaged self-governance (Mudde and Kaltwasser 2017, 17). In practical terms, however, populism depends on the role of the leader because the generalized demand against the incumbent elites cannot be put into effect otherwise. If the sovereign people on their own could redress the matters which keep them asunder, those in positions of authority could not be regarded as indifferent and unresponsive. As populism concerns a unified people rather than recognition of the plurality, the populist leader has a role in rhetorically calling forth and constituting the people (Urbinati 2013; Espejo 2015). The leader is therefore the figure who defines the people and tasks him or herself with their redemption.

Populist leaders do not represent the interests of the people so much as they embody the people as they are seen as extraordinary with the unique capacity to fix the system themselves. Populist leaders "perform" their identities presenting themselves as emerging from outside "the system" which is held accountable for whatever ails the people. Hence, populist movements involve a special connection between leaders and the people they represent whereby the citizens' capacities to act are ceded to the authority (Madsen and Snow 1991). Moffitt (2016, 55) notes the centrality of leaders to populism: "while we can imagine populism without a party … or populism without a movement (that is, a politician who claims to speak in the name of 'the people' but without a popular base behind them), it is rather difficult to imagine contemporary populism *without any leadership at all*."

These attributes are interconnected. The leader executes the demand of the people against an indifferent or corrupt system or establishment. Movements like the 15M movement or Occupy Wall Street involved a people but were not populist in the sense that they resisted both the creation of leadership as well as the issuing of demands (Mouffe 2013, 112–14). While some scholars emphasize the "thinness" of the concept as little more than an ideational map through which political life is ordered with respect to a conflict between the people and the elite (Mudde 2004; Inglehart and Norris 2016; Mudde and Kaltwasser 2017), such a definition is of little use as that conflict may take on mutually exclusive political forms, describing equally anarchist as well as fascist movements. The fact that both may claim to embody the "will of the people" confuses the sameness of those words while applying them to distinct concepts of political relationships and forms of organization.

Defining Connectivism

By defining populism as involving all three attributes, we are better placed to distinguish it from connectivism as an alternative form of political organization operating with a distinct logic. While populism may be thought as "of" and "for" the people, connectivism is a political logic more concerned with conducting politics "by" and "with" the people. This account draws largely on Bennett and Segerberg's (2013) conceptualization of "connective action." Connective action involves the sharing of "broadly inclusive, easily personalized action frames" as a foundation for carrying out political action (Bennett and Segerberg 2013, 2). Connectivism has largely been associated with the movements which have relied on digitally mediated networks which in large measure supplant or at least supplement face-to-face and other off-line communications through which movements have been previously organized (Bennett and Segerberg 2013, 2015). Connectivity describes an organizational logic which may be attributed to not just social movements but relationships between supporters and formal organizations including political parties and campaign organizations which afford supporters spaces to engage with the campaign on their own terms (Bennett and Segerberg 2013). Though digital communication technologies have played a significant role in the development of these movements, compensating for traditional limitations of networks as an organizational form (Castells 2005), connective action is more centrally a logic of political organization and participation than a claim about the medium of communication.

Although conceptually, communication messages are distinct from the medium of communication through which they are transmitted, the adoption of new communication technologies can over time become decisively involved in the organization of social and political life in two ways. First, they may accelerate the speed at which communications can travel, thereby reducing distance as a limiting constraint (Poster 1990; Innis 2007). Second, they may alter political practices to the extent these technologies become a more significant means of communication (Norris 2001). The combination of the "technological openness" of social media platforms and the "symbolic inclusiveness" of the action frames shared enable connective action movements to scale up quickly (Bennett and Segerberg 2013, 37). Social media play two critical roles in connective action campaigns. First, connectivity facilitates the capacity for citizens to forge a division of labor regarding concrete political matters, predicated on loose political ties. Some aspects of the mobilization process are easier to carry out through social media where people are not organized in terms of thick social identities but loose connections around common concerns (Jensen and Bang 2015). Further, organization can quickly scale upward as messages diffuse across networks of digitally connected persons (Bennett and Segerberg 2013). Second, social media are interactive which provide political leaders and their supporters with symmetrical communication capacities. The communication affordances of social media therefore enable campaigns to empower campaign supporters by responding to and amplifying their supporters' voices (Jensen 2017).

Populist and connective political forms often emerge under similar conditions of a breakdown in the political relationship between authorities and citizens, a growing individuation in society, and the collapse of the cleavage system which parties used to represent (Mair 2013). For connective action movements, "these very individuation processes … lead people to seek more personalized paths to political engagement" (Bennett and Segerberg 2013, 56). However, the connective and populist logics differ in terms of their approach to the nature of the people, the issuing of demands, and their role in relationship to leaders. Connective action involves a political association between movement supporters who are engaged in a "division of labor" through which a connective movement or a connective campaign carry out their aims (Bennett and Segerberg 2013, 34), whereas populism emphasizes a collective and antipluralist identity, connectivism is open and brings together a heterogeneous assemblage of persons mobilized around open and nonexclusive personalized action frames. As these frames are personal, they do not involve a collective identification. Rather than the homogenous identity of a singular people constructed by populist movements, a connective action involves a logic of political association which identifies persons not their common origins as a people but with their participation in a common set of political structures, which also means they "share[] a common political fate" (Easton 1965, 185). Hence, while populism is organized around organic and social grounds of identity, connectivity is organized around the logic of political association.

The relationship between supporters a connective campaign is one of reciprocity whereby leaders seek to create transformative capacities for supporters to effect change rather than represent them and effect change in their name. This means while populist relationships between leaders and supporters are hierarchical, connective authority relationships are circular, with the exercise of authority depending on its acceptance by supporters. Within a connective political relationship, leaders take on the role of capacity building for their supporters who engage politics in a democratic matter manner rather than leaving the development of political strategies, messaging, tactics, and policies to the elites. We summarize these differences between connective and populist politics in Table 1.

Our aim is to demonstrate that populism and connectivism meaningfully distinguish the Trump and Sanders campaigns, and that their differing authority relationships give rise to differences in the discourses articulated by supporters of each candidate. Specifically, we expect to find differences in the distributions of communication topics across these two campaigns. Despite some similarities in policy platforms and the way they critique establishment elites representing global financial interests, Trump and Sanders represent significantly different approaches to the decoupling between citizens and political authorities. These differences are indicated by Trump and Sanders' respective campaign slogans: "make America great again" and "a future to believe in," whereas Trump's campaign sought to return America to an imagined past, Sanders' campaign was forward looking,

TABLE 1 Attributes of Connectivism and Populism

	Populism	Connectivism
Role of leaders		
Structure of authority	Hierarchical	Circular
Political connection	Representation	Reciprocity
Leadership	Leader central	Leader as capacity builder
Culture		
Consistency	Homogeneous/singular	Heterogeneous
Ties	Thick/social	Thin/political/personal
Attitude toward difference	Subversion/rejection	Acceptance and recognition
	Anger/resentment	Emotionally optimistic
Demand		
Content	Antiestablishment	Create capacities for consequential engagement in political life
Emotional valence	Anger/resentment	Disenchantment

seeing itself as a vehicle to imagine and construct a future achieved together in virtue of our differences rather than despite them.

In addition to the expectation that Trump waged a more populist campaign while Sanders' campaign had more of a connective logic, if populism and connectivism constitute distinct logics, the attributes which adumbrate each logic should appear together in practice. Hence, populist communications which emphasize the need for strong authority should also involve appeals to a collective entity and be directed against an establishment. At the same time, we should expect connective communications to simultaneously relate to supporters as participants in a political association where citizens have power to effect change embracing their differences. Finally, given that connectivism holds citizens are capable of making a difference in political life, we expect that reactions to connective campaign communications will be optimistic in tone, whereas populist campaigns should give rise to more fear as supporters are told they are threatened by the establishment and unable to save themselves.

DATA AND METHODS

Populism and connectivity are properties of communicative performances. While digital media and social media in particular are far from the only mediated spaces in which these appeals are made, they are particularly important today in the construction of populist and connective campaigns. For populist campaigns, they are a means for leaders to reach the people directly (Moffitt 2016). This direct connection serves two functions. First, it enables a leader to communicate without dependence on broadcast media which may independently filter and frame candidate messages. The Trump campaign in fact targeted mainstream media as a part of the establishment (Hensch 2016).

Second, these spaces are not subject in the same degree to the political correctness and civility which pervades other mediated spaces; hence, populist leaders may be able to forge an "authentic" identity and relationship with supporters through social media (Dryzek 2016; Moffitt 2016).

To analyze populism and connectivity in the Sanders and Trump campaigns, we focus on Facebook communications collected during the 2016 primaries. We select Facebook rather than other social media such as Twitter for two reasons. First, candidate communications and responses by supporters, opponents, and bystanders are more accessible in Facebook. Connecting candidate tweets with responses to those tweets can be complicated as locating those responses among several months of tweets can be a prohibitively large computational task for desktop computers. Second, tweets are comparably short compared to Facebook messages. Facebook permits the communication of multiple sentences or paragraphs in which ideas can be developed and related. As one of our interests is determining whether and how the attributes of populism hang together, the longer messages permitted on Facebook are preferable to tweets which are constrained to 140 characters.

The data were collected from January 26, 2016 to May 15, 2016 which covers the majority of the nominating contests from before the Iowa Caucuses through the contests in West Virginia and Nebraska (Republican Only). By this point, all of Donald Trump's competitors had left the race and Hillary Clinton achieved a near insurmountable lead in the delegate count. There were 629 and 929 Sanders and Trump posts, respectively, during this time. The number of daily posts for each of the campaigns is presented in Figure 1. This period covers the growth and peak of activity for the Trump campaign with little change in the overall activity of the Sanders campaign.

Our aim is to conceptually differentiate two approaches to political life which draw upon distinct political traditions so our data analysis identifies the extent to which each campaign exhibits attributes of these concepts as well as the extent to which these concepts hang together empirically. Posts were coded using natural language processing. Coding dictionaries for the natural language processing were created using words and phrases identified from reading through each of the posts. The coding was carried out using Python programming language script developed by the authors and made use of functions from the Natural Language Toolkit (Bird, Klein, and Loper 2009). Posts by each candidate were coded for attributes of connectivity and populism. To test the reliability of coding, 10% of the posts, 63 posts from the Sanders campaign and 93 posts from the Trump campaign, were human coded and compared against the computer results. The number of variables which the human and computer coded in agreement was summed across each of the variables and divided by the total number of posts. The results yielded a computer coding success rate of at least 80% agreement

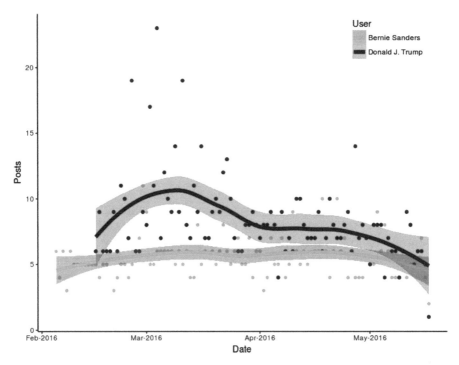

FIGURE 1 Distribution of Facebook posts in Trump and Sanders' primary campaigns.

with human coding across all variables. Such indicators included statements to the effect that the candidate cannot bring about change without the movement acting to pressure other officials which creates a condition of circularity in the authority structure between authorities and supporters. Strong authority, on the other hand, was denoted by comments emphasizing the role of the leader as an agent of change and the need for strong action in our politics. In addition, the centrality of the leader was operationalized in terms of the number of references to Sanders or Trump by name or as the pronoun "I." Finally, the constitution of the people was coded in terms of its exclusivity, denoting a singular people as opposed to some other entity such as foreigners or foreign countries as well as the need to abandon political correctness which has been criticized by Trump as placing the interests of minorities above those of an imagined dominant culture. The acceptance and recognition of difference was coded as appeals to work together across racial and ethnic lines as well as one's origins having been born in USA or immigrated from elsewhere.

Our interest is not only to demonstrate that the campaigns themselves exhibit aspects of populism and democratic connectivism but also that these approaches give rise to different responses among supporters as evidence of the consequences of differing authority structures. Therefore, we examine responses to Sanders' communication of a horizontal or circular authority structure to describe relations between citizens and elites versus Trump's emphasis on strong hierarchical authority. Comments are not necessarily written by persons who support the candidate. However, two factors tend to mitigate the risk that comments are predominantly from nonsupporters. First, we found the comments tended to be less negative than the replies on the comments, particularly on Trump's page (and we came across few negative comments or replies to comments on Sanders' page), which suggests that the Trump campaign, and perhaps Sanders' as well, tended to delete negative comments but were unable to also delete negative replies. Second, research shows that online persons are more likely to consume information which confirms their preferences (Bennett and Iyengar 2008; Garrett, Carnahan, and Lynch 2013). Even if there are some opponents of these candidates visiting and commenting on their Facebook pages, the majority will likely be supporters. To the extent we find distinct patterns in the replies on these pages, we can be more confident in this conclusion.

In addition, the comments on three exemplars of strong authority from the Trump campaign and connectivity from the Sanders campaign were collected. In all, 12,000 comments on Trump's posts and 2,186 comments on Sanders' posts were collected for analysis. The difference in the level of comments is at least in part explained by the difference in the number of fans, i.e., the number of persons who have liked each candidate's page, thereby opting in to receive their posts. At the start of the data collection on January 26, 2016, Sanders had 2,462,794 fans versus Trump's 5,442,545. Some comments could not be retrieved due to user privacy settings; however, these comments represent over 90% of all comments on these posts.

The comments were coded for emotional tone using the NRC Emotions Lexicon which has been developed for social media to identify their emotional content and valences (Mohammad, Kiritchenko, and Zhu 2013). Optimism was coded as a summation of terms by the NRC coding which denotes positive emotions: joy, anticipation, surprise, and trust. For negative emotions, we focused on "fear" in particular as the populist discourse is organized around fear of some other (Moffitt 2016). This coding was implemented using the syuzhet library in R (Jockers 2017). In addition, the comments were coded for the incidence of "democracy" to determine the relevance of this term to differing concepts of authority. These data provide evidence of the emotional valance of the response to circular and hierarchical authority patterns communicated through each campaign's Facebook posts.

RESULTS

Analyzing the Campaign Posts

In broad terms, we can identify the orientation of the Trump and Sanders campaigns by considering the frequency by which attributes of democratic connectivism and populism are found in their social media communications.

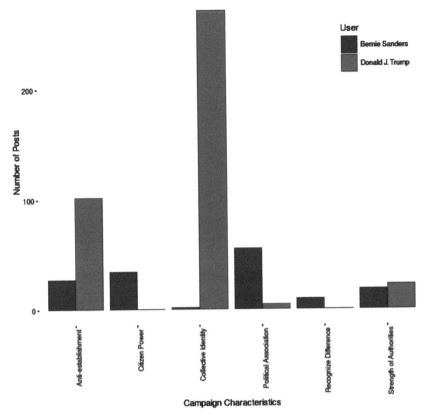

FIGURE 2 Distribution of connective and populist campaign communications.

Distribution of each of these traits in the Facebook communications of both candidates are presented in Figure 2. These data indicate the number of posts containing at least one instance of each attribute. Though both Sanders and Trump campaign on antiestablishment themes, this is far more common within Trump posts than Sanders' posts. Further, when Sanders speaks of taking on the "establishment," it is couched in terms of people taking action rather than elites.

To get a better sense of the discourse in these posts, we take some examples of posts which score high on the antiestablishment scale. Sanders posts on April 7, 2016, "We are fighting against an inherently corrupt campaign finance system that privileges the wealthy and encourages the billionaire class to pool its money to gain access to candidates. We do it differently. Watch how this corrupt system works and join our campaign if you want our way to come out on top."[2] Here, he is taking on the establishment for its loss of democratic credentials and speaks of attempting to get rid of it so that ordinary citizens may have influence in governing. Further, he contrasts his way of raising funds with what he terms the "corrupt" manner in which other candidates raise funds. Elsewhere, he boasts of receiving no support from political action committees. Similarly, Sanders challenges media and political elites stating on February 10, 2016, "The people of New Hampshire have sent a profound message to the political establishment, to the economic establishment and, by the way, to the media establishment. The people want real change."[3]

This is a contrast with Trump's antiestablishment message which approaches the establishment in terms of what he will do in office with respect to current programs or the character of other elites. He writes on February 26, 2016, "WASTE, FRAUD and ABUSE. We will cut so much of it your head will spin!"[4] Even when he speaks of a movement operating within the campaign, Trump describes himself as the locus of activity: "I have brought millions of people into the Republican Party, while the Dems are going down. Establishment [sic] wants to kill this movement! Failed candidate mitt [sic] Romney, who ran one of the worst races in presidential history, is working with the establishment to bury a big "R" win! #MakeAmericaGreatAgain #Trump2016."[5]

More broadly, there are differences in the roles ascribed to citizens by each of the campaigns. Figure 2 indicates that overall, Sanders emphasizes the power of citizens to effect change ("citizen power"). Change in Sander's view does not come from elites representing citizen interests as traditional accounts of democratic pluralism posit, but instead from the people demanding change: "It wasn't Governor Cuomo who had the idea to raise the minimum wage. It was the people telling him what to do. That's how change happens."[6] Sanders does not claim to derive power from the movement behind his campaign. Rather, he claims it is the supporters of the movement themselves who have demonstrated their capacity to dislodge the establishment: "Nine months ago, we began our campaign here in the Granite State. We had no campaign organization. We had no money. And we were taking on the most powerful political organization in the United States of America .... Tonight we served notice to the political and economic establishment of this country. This is your movement."[7]

Sanders binds his understanding of political change with the need for citizens to accept and recognize difference to work together as members of a political association in addressing common concerns. He explains, "What I believe is that this country, if we stand together and not let the Trumps of the world divide us up, can guarantee healthcare to all people as a right. Can have paid family and medical leave. Can make public colleges and universities tuition free. Can lead the world in transforming our energy system and combating climate change. Can break up the large financial institutions. Can demand that the wealthiest people in this country start paying their fair share of taxes. Millions of people must stand up, fight back and create a government that works for all of us."[8] Against Sanders' politics which places citizens at the center of political change, Trump argued in a tweet shortly before the election, "Get out and vote! I am your voice and I will fight for you."[9] The change described comes not from Trump's "movement" but from Trump himself.

These differences are also reflected in average number of references to citizens' capacity to effect change the number of references to "I" or the candidate (Trump or Sanders) himself in the text of Facebook messages. Nearly one in four (23.7%) of Trump posts reference himself either by name or by the first person subject pronoun, "I" as the subject of the sentence according to the NLTK part of speech tagger. This compares with 15.4% of the Sanders posts and t-tests show this difference between the two accounts is statistically significant ($t = -4.183$, $p = 0.000$).

Trump's figure of identity is not a diverse group of individuals working together to address common concerns. Rather, he posits an overarching American identity which he seeks to return to its latent greatness. This is suggested by the phrase "make America great again" which appeals to a cultural image of America which is claimed to have once existed. According to the Trump narrative, the threat is enabled by corrupt and indifferent elites from which the country must be rescued: "This is a movement. We are getting closer every day to taking our country back from the corrupt establishment. To do this, we all need to get out and vote. Together we will MAKE AMERICA GREAT AGAIN!"[10] Within this movement, Trump fashions himself at the center, positing an idealized American citizen juxtaposed against a multicultural and diverse America.

There is no indication of the political role associated with Trump's "movement" beyond voting for him as he is the principal agent in his account of political change: "What kind of country treats illegal immigrants better than their Veterans? I will straighten this out immediately!"[11] Throughout his Facebook posts, Trump presents an image of the pure nation, differentiated from often dangerous Muslim and "illegal" immigrants, and often imbricated with contrasting references to members of the military: "Nobody will protect our Nation like Donald J. Trump. Our military will be greatly strengthened and our borders will be strong. Illegals out,"[12] and "Incompetent Hillary, despite the horrible attack in Brussels today, wants borders to be weak and open- and let the Muslims flow in. No way,"[13] These posts create a sense that America is under siege by a foreign threat which seeks to destroy its character. Part of the problem the establishment faces, according to Trump, is their concern with "political correctness" which becomes an impediment countering the perceived threat of a multicultural America: "I would rather be CORRECT than politically correct!"[14] and "a Trump presidency won't only wipe out political correctness in America; it'll wipe it off the face of the earth."[15]

We also analyze the extent to which the theoretical attributes of populism and connectivism hang together across the campaigns. Posts are coded in terms of frequency counts across each of the six attributes with scores ranging from 0 to 8. Using a principal components analysis, we selected a two-component solution as subsequent components had eigenvalues below 1. Table 2 displays the results of a principal component analysis identifying the relationship between each of these attributes in campaign posts.

TABLE 2 Principal Component Analysis (a) Trump Campaign Communications (b) Sanders Campaign Communications

Attribute	Component 1	Component 2
(a)		
Strong authority	−0.07	0.40
Collective identity	0.13	0.54
Recognize and accept difference	0.03	−0.57
Antiestablishment	0.01	0.50
Citizen power	0.85	−0.03
Political association	0.85	0.04
(b)		
Strong authority	0.77	0.01
Collective identity	0.71	−0.05
Recognize and accept difference	−0.07	0.78
Antiestablishment	0.48	0.01
Citizen power	0.03	0.81
Political association	0.24	0.21

Two components were selected on the basis of both visual inspection of scree plots and at least one eigenvalue of variance accounted for. The Trump and Sanders models account for 42 and 45% of the cumulative variance, respectively.

In Trump's posts, collective identity, strong authority, and an antiestablishment rhetoric line up together. When Trump invokes an antiestablishment attitude, it is on behalf of the morally deserving collective and involves his strong authority to in some way counter or destroy the establishment on their behalf. These three also line up together among Sanders' posts indicating that these three elements both conceptually and in practice are interrelated attributes of populism. However, the candidates differ in terms of how they understand the role of political association. For Sanders, the transformative capacity of citizens ("citizen power") also involves that people recognize and accept difference, working together across their differences rather than allowing those differences to divide them. Separately, he talks about the "we" of the movement he is attempting to effect and its capacity to bring change. Although he addresses the movement and individual citizens separately, in both cases, he emphasizes a sense of working together as a political rather than social association. And in neither case do we find attributes of political association lining up on the same component as collective identity. These data show there is a distinct political or "connective" logic rather than collective logic operating here.

Analyzing Reactions to the Campaigns

Connective and populist communications translate into differences in the responses of the public to each of these demands. To highlight these

TABLE 3 Mean Distributions of Democracy and Collective Capacity in Candidate Comments

Attribute	Sanders mean	Trump mean	t-test
Democracy mentions	0.019	0.002	3.965 ($p = 0.000$)
Citizen power	0.046	0.022	3.250 ($p = 0.001$)

differences, we examine the divergent responses to Trump's communications insisting on the necessity of a strong authority to bring about change and to the comments on Sanders' posts which invite supporters to become involved in political life highlighting their power or transformative capacity to bring about change. This is not meant to provide a systematic accounting of all replies to Trump and Sanders' comments but is instead done for conceptual development by illustrating the differences in the operation of the populist and connective approach to political authority. For this reason, we select four posts which scored the highest for the level of connectivity and two Trump posts which score highest for their emphasis on strong authority. The reason for the difference in the number of posts selected is the large imbalance between the level of commenting on Trump and Sanders posts as Trump's page has significantly more activity. These data provide evidence of differential reactions to contrasting authority styles.

We measure reactions in three ways. First, we count the number of references to democracy as an indication of the importance of democracy in the responses to Sander's calls for a circular authority relationship and Trump's calls for strong hierarchical authority. Second, we look for evidence for each commenter's belief in their ability to bring about change. These results are presented in Table 3. The data indicate statistically significant differences along all three attributes. In each case, Sanders' communications affirming citizens' transformative capacity is met with more frequent references to democracy and expressions of their belief in their capacity to bring about change. These results suggest that the nature of the authority relation articulated in these communications does matter for the kinds of responses they receive. It may be the case that not all of these replies to candidates' posts come from supporters and it is often the case that the comments do not directly respond to the specific post. However, both of these conditions would increase the amount of noise in these findings and, given the consistency and strength of the findings, the conclusion that different campaign communications give rise to different communicative relationships with supporters is a reasonable inference.

In addition to the differing orientations to political authority between each campaign, we examine the emotional valances articulated in the comments on campaign posts. We expected that there would be a positive emotion valance associated with that aspect of connectivism associated with the collective capacity of citizens to take consequential action as these comments express a belief in the capability of oneself and others to make

TABLE 4 Emotional Valance of Authority Types

Attributes	Sanders	Trump
Citizen power * Positive emotional valance	0.119 ($p = 0.003$)	0.0252 ($p = 0.370$)
Strong authority * Fear	0.393 ($p = 0.000$)	0.140 ($p = 0.000$)

a difference and that fear of threat and loss would guide populists. As more than one word operationalizing each of these emotional dispositions may appear in any given post, we analyze the relationship of these attributes by the correlations of the appearance of these terms in posts. An additive index captures the intensity of each emotional disposition as more terms communicate a more intense emotional disposition. Given that we are looking for relationships between additive scales, a Pearson r correlation is used to determine the relationship between the items. These data are presented in Table 4. Table 4 shows that indeed discussions of citizens' power to deliver political change is correlated with positive emotions in the case of Sanders' comments but not Trump's, whereas reliance on a strong authority is correlated with the communication of fear among both candidates' supporters.

DISCUSSION

Populism represents a grave danger to democratic pluralism today while connectivism may be a path to democratic renewal. Connectivism and populism both emerge from the condition of a decoupling and alienation between citizens and the political establishment; however, they constitute different political logics and produce distinct political consequences in organizing the authority relationship between political leaders and their supporters. Populism cannot be reduced to the claim of a popular will in governing or campaigning but instead depends on hierarchical authority issuing a demand and taking action to emancipate a homogeneous and legitimized identity group from corrupt elites. Nor can populism be reduced to an antiestablishment position as antiestablishment thinking encompasses a wide range of political phenomena ranging from anarchism to fascism, and anarchy and fascism have both distinct causes and political consequences. Connectivism and populism both take aim at the establishment, but populism seeks its destruction at the hands of a populist leader, whereas connectivism focuses on reconnecting citizens, elites, and institutions, working with and against them to address common problems.

We found populist statements from both the Sanders and Trump campaigns but there were clear differences in the pervasiveness of such statements. Nonetheless, our evidence shows that populism, whether articulated by Trump or by Sanders, involves not only an antiestablishment demand but that this is attached to the notion of a singular people and the need for an authority to effect the desired change. Hence, in theory and in practice, populism is irreducible to an antiestablishment perspective. It operates with a consistent logic appearing as the dominant approach in Trump's campaign while operating in the shadow of a democratic connectivism in the Sanders' campaign.

The three attributes of populism and the contrasting attributes of connectivism empirically hang together. Trump's populist account revolves around an external threat to American identity that exists due elites who are either unable or unwilling to protect the collective from internal and external threats. Given Trump's account of the threat posed by multicultural-ism, citizens on their own are not in a position to defend a collective national identity and therefore depend on a strong leader to protect and rescue them. This links the issuance of a demand against the establishment with a necessity of protecting a collective identity and the dependence of a leader to bring about the desired change. Connectivism instead emphasizes the role of citizens acting on their own accord to bring about political change. As concrete problem-solving is the end goal, there is not the same emphasis on overthrowing the establishment that populists champion.

The differences between the Trump and Sanders campaigns are not limited to ideological, policy, and metapolitical differences in their particular approaches to politics, they also have consequences for how their supporters approach politics. Sanders' supporters communicate a greater concern for democracy, and belief in their capacity to make a difference in political life. Further, we find evidence that populist and connective politics are char-acterized by different emotional valences: Sanders' supporters tend to voice optimism when they speak of their collective capacities to make a difference in political life while instance on the need for strong authority to resolve problems tends to conjure the expression of fear among Trump supporters.

CONCLUSION

Populism and democratic connectivism create different relationships between citizens and leaders. Populism emphasizes a hierarchical structured performance and acceptance of political authority. For this reason, Tocqueville (2010) feared populism would give rise to democratic despotism as citizens receded from participation in governing. While motivated from the same starting point of political alienation between political authorities and citizens, populism appears to sustain or exacerbate that division. Without the connective aspect, there seems no way forward for populist politics to recouple citizens and political authorities.

The research presented here finds evidence that a populist packaging of a candidate as a strong leader who will fight against an establishment can be an effective message. However, connectivism may also be a viable alternative approach to campaigning. Connective messages find resonance with at least a progressive political constituency which appears activated by calls to shape political life on their own terms. This may have applications beyond electoral campaigns as the same connective logic may be harnessed with respect to specific issue campaigns and more generally the organization of the "resistance" which has emerged in the wake of the Trump presidency. These findings are limited to the extent we only capture populist and connective logics in campaign discourses and their immediate responses. The extent to which a connective political movement behind a candidate or issue can become sustained remains to be seen. Subsequent research might consider what happened to Sanders' supporters after his campaign ended and what role they may be playing now with groups such as Indivisible (The Indivisible Project 2017).

Given the long-term trends which have produced the current populist moment, demands for greater responsiveness by political authorities and governments will likely persist. It remains to be seen how long populists in government can sustain support or whether they become seen as a part of the system they once campaigned against. However, connectivism provides another alternative for politicians confronting disaffected citizens. While Sanders' campaign failed to capture the Democratic nomination, much less the White House, his campaign provided evidence of that latent culture of citizen-level political association which Tocqueville took to be distinctive of Americans.[16] Recapturing that spirit of connective political association may be a path forward, innovating democratic political life.

NOTES

1. Representative posts from Trump's Facebook page include message ID 153080620724_10156678234995725, message ID 153080620724_10156851000155725, message ID 153080620724_10156882124280725, and message ID 153080620724_10156960039970725. Representative posts from Sander's Facebook page include message ID 124955570892789_972506252804379, message ID 124955570892789_974352199286451, message ID 124955570892789_1019079561480381, and message ID 124955570892789_1047051288683208.

2. Message ID: 124955570892789_1024143807640623.

3. Message ID: 124955570892789_977935538928117.

4. Message ID: 153080620724_10156688041040725.

5. Message ID: 153080620724_10156712805285725.

6. Message ID: 124955570892789_1025058957549108.

7. Message ID: 124955570892789_977619848959686.

8. Message ID: 124955570892789_1029216750466662.

9. https://twitter.com/realdonaldtrump/status/790927104921767940.

10. Message ID: 153080620724_10156678234995725.

11. Message ID: 153080620724_10156942901590725.

12. Message ID: 153080620724_10156836399595725.

13. Message ID: 153080620724_10156813075250725.

14. Message ID: 153080620724_10156815489210725.

15. Message ID: 153080620724_10156815489210725.

16. In developing this conceptual history, we bracket the question of whether Tocqueville might actually endorse Sanders' political program. This is due to the rather complicated engagement Tocqueville has with the idea of equality of conditions which operates quite differently in the Old World and the New World as to belie casual categorizations of contemporary policies (Wolin 2002, 125, 144, 322–23, 528–29).

REFERENCES

Abts, K., and S. Rummens. 2007. "Populism Versus Democracy." *Political Studies* 55 (2):405–24. doi:10.1111/j.1467-9248.2007.00657.x

Baggini, J. 2016. "How Rising Trump and Sanders Parallel Rising Populism in Europe." *New Perspectives Quarterly* 33 (2):22–25. doi:10.1111/npqu.12031

Bang, H. P. 2016. "Interactive Governance: A Challenge to Institutionalism." In *Critical Reflections on Interactive Governance*, edited by J. Edelenbos, 66–92. Cheltenham, UK: Edward Elgar.

Bennett, W. L., and S. Iyengar. 2008. "A New Era of Minimal Effects? The Changing Foundations of Political Communication." *Journal of Communication* 58 (4):707–31. doi:10.1111/j.1460-2466.2008.00410.x

Bennett, W. L., and A. Segerberg. 2013. *The Logic of Connective Action: Digital Media and the Personalization of Contentious Politics*. New York: Cambridge University Press.

Bennett, W. L., and A. Segerberg. 2015. "Communication in Movements." In *The Oxford Handbook of Social Movements*, edited by D. della Porta and M. Diani, 367–82. New York: Oxford University Press.

Bird, S., E. Klein, and E. Loper. 2009. *Natural language processing with Python*. Sebastopol, CA: O'Reilly Media.

Bonikowski, B., and N. Gidron. 2016. "The Populist Style in American Politics: Presidential Campaign Discourse, 1952–1996." *Social Forces* 94 (4):1593–621. doi:10.1093/sf/sov120

Bos, L., W. van der Brug, and C. de Vreese. 2011. "How the Media Shape Perceptions of Right-Wing Populist Leaders." *Political Communication* 28 (2):182–206. doi:10.1080/10584609.2011.564605

Castells, M. 2010. *The Rise of the Network Society: The Information Age: Economy, Society, and Culture*. Sussex: John Wiley and Sons.

Castells, M. 2005. "The Network Society: From Knowledge to Policy." In *The Network Society: From Knowledge to Policy*, Washington, DC: Center for Transatlantic Relations, JHU_SAIS, 3–22.

Cornell, S. 1990. "Aristocracy Assailed: The Ideology of Backcountry Anti-Federalism." *The Journal of American History* 76 (4):1148–72. doi:10.2307/2936593

Cornell, S. 2012. *The Other Founders: Anti-Federalism and the Dissenting Tradition in America, 1788–1828*. Chapel Hill: University of North Carolina Press.

Dalton, R. J. 2013. *The Apartisan American: Dealignment and Changing Electoral Politics*. Washington, DC: CQ Press.

Dewey, J. 1954. *The Public and Its Problems*. New York: Swallow Press.

Dryzek, J. S. Forthcoming. The Forum, the System, and the Polity Three Varieties of Democratic Theory. *Political Theory*. doi:10.1177/0090591716659114

Easton, D. 1965. *A Systems Analysis of Political Life*. New York: John Wiley & Sons.

Eiermann, M. 2016. "How Donald Trump Fits Into the History of American Populism." *New Perspectives Quarterly* 33 (2):29–34. doi:10.1111/npqu.12033

Espejo, P. O. 2015. "Power to Whom? The People between Procedure and Populism." In *The Promise and Perils of Populism: Global Perspectives*, edited by C. de la Torre, 59–90. Lexington: University Press of Kentucky.

Garrett, R. K., D. Carnahan, and E. K. Lynch. 2013. "A Turn toward Avoidance? Selective Exposure to Online Political Information, 2004–2008." *Political Behavior* 35 (1):113–34. doi:10.1007/s11109-011-9185-6

Hensch, M. 2016. "Report: Trump meeting with media a 'f---ing firing squad.'" Text. *TheHill*. November 21. http://thehill.com/homenews/administration/307127-report-trump-media-meeting-a-f-ing-firing-squad.

Inglehart, R., and P. Norris. 2016. "Trump, Brexit, and the Rise of Populism: Economic Have-Nots and Cultural Backlash." SSRN Scholarly Paper ID 2818659, Social Science Research Network, Rochester, NY. https://papers.ssrn.com/abstract=2818659.

Innis, H. A. 2007. *Empire and Communications*. Toronto: Dundurn Press Ltd.

Jensen, M. J. 2017. "Social Media and Political Campaigning." *The International Journal of Press/Politics* 22 (1):23–42.

Jensen, M. J., and H. Bang. 2015. "Digitally Networked Movements as Problematization and Politicization." *Policy Studies* 36 (6):573–89. doi:10.1080/01442872.2015.1095879

Jockers, M. 2017. *Syuzhet: Extracts Sentiment and Sentiment-Derived Plot Arcs from Text (Version 1.0.1)*. Retrieved from https://cran.r-project.org/web/packages/syuzhet/index.html.

Laclau, E. 2005. "Populism: What's in a Name?" In *Populism and the Mirror of Democracy*, edited by F. Panizza, 32–49. New York: Verso.

Lasswell, H. D. 2009. *Power and Personality*. New Brunswick: Transaction Publishers.

Madsen, D., and P. G. Snow. 1991. *The Charismatic Bond: Political Behavior in Time of Crisis*. Cambridge: Harvard University Press.

Mair, P. 2013. *Ruling The Void: The Hollowing Of Western Democracy. London*; New York: Verso.

Moffitt, B. 2016. *The Global Rise of Populism: Performance, Political Style, and Representation*. Stanford: Stanford University Press.

Mohammad, S. M., S. Kiritchenko, and X. Zhu. 2013. "*NRC-Canada: Building the State-of-the-Art in Sentiment Analysis of Tweets.*" arXiv:1308.6242 [Cs], August. http://arxiv.org/abs/1308.6242.

Mouffe, C. 2013. *Agonistics: Thinking the World Politically*. New York: Verso Books.

Mudde, C. 2004. "The Populist Zeitgeist." *Government and Opposition* 39 (4):542–63. doi:10.1111/j.1477-7053.2004.00135.x

Mudde, C., and C. R. Kaltwasser. 2017. *Populism: A Very Short Introduction*. New York: Oxford University Press.

Norris, P. 2001. *Digital Divide: Civic Engagement, Information Poverty, and the Internet Worldwide*. New York: Cambridge University Press.

Poster, M. 1990. *The Mode of Information: Poststructuralism and Social Context*. Chicago: University Of Chicago Press.

Reinemann, C., et al. 2016. "Populist Political Communication: Towards a Model of Its Causes, Forms, and Effects." In *Populist Political Communication in Europe*, edited by T. Aalberg et al., 12–28. New York: Routledge.

Sandel, M. 2016. "Bernie Sanders and Donald Trump Look like Saviours to Voters Who Feel Left out of the American Dream | Michael J Sandel." the Guardian. http://www.theguardian.com/commentisfree/2016/feb/28/bernie-sanders-donald-trump-populist-moment-in-american-politics (July 14, 2016).

The Indivisible Project. 2017. *Indivisible Guide*. https://www.indivisibleguide.com/ (April 30, 2017).

Tocqueville, A. D. 2010. *Democracy in America: In Four Volumes. Bilingual edition*. Indianapolis: Liberty Fund Inc.

Urbinati, N. 2013. "The Populist Phenomenon." *Raisons politiques* 51:137–54.

Wolin, S. S. 2002. *Tocqueville between Two Worlds: The Making of a Political and Theoretical Life*. Princeton: Princeton University Press.

Wolin, S. S. 2006. *Politics and Vision: Continuity and Innovation in Western Political Thought*. Princeton: Princeton University Press.

Intraparty Hostility: Social Identity, Subidentity, and the Hostile Media Effect in a Contested Primary

AARON S. VEENSTRA

BENJAMIN A. LYONS

İ. ALEV DEGIM FLANNAGAN

The hostile media effect (HME) has generally been tested in terms of in-groups and out-groups, with a "neutral" story in between. This ignores the nature of many social groups as comprising subgroups, often but not always sharing feelings of connectedness and purpose. In cases when bounded subgroups are at odds with one another, HME provides little guidance. A contested partisan primary provides such a case. This study takes identity centrality, candidate favorability, and perceived social network homogeneity as measures of partisanship and involvement, hypothesizing relationships between each and perceived bias against one's candidate and party. Findings show that markers of candidate-focused social identity predict greater perceived bias against one's candidate during the 2016 primary season, while party-focused identity fails to predict perceived bias against one's party. This suggests that candidate support identity overrides plain partisanship during primaries, supporting concern that a heated primary might damage general election party unity. Subsequent

Color versions of one or more of the figures in the article can be found online at www.tandfonline.com/wplm.

postconvention findings suggest that the salience of candidate-focused identity fades, while homogeneity of one's network regarding party support helps to make perceived hostility toward one's party identity more salient. However, as campaigns become more candidate-centered, the contestation between nested candidate and party identities may grow fiercer.

Investigations of the hostile media effect (HME) stretch back decades, but as Perloff (2015) points out, these perceptual biases may play out differently in a media landscape vastly changed from the concept's origin in the mid-1980s. With this in mind, this study extends the HME literature in a few ways with special relevance to understanding the 2016 U.S. presidential campaign. Two of this campaign's hallmarks were hotly contested primaries within both parties, and the ascendancy of candidate-centered social media communities as key sources of information and opinion for the public. In this study, we examine how these developments impact voters' perceptions of media bias.

HME research has focused on identification mechanisms such as "partisanship" and "involvement." These have also sometimes been conceptualized as social identities (Reid 2012). However, they have generally been tested in terms of in-groups and out-groups, with a "neutral" story in between. This ignores the nature of many social groups as comprising subgroups, often but not always sharing feelings of connectedness and purpose. In cases when bounded subgroups are at odds with one another, HME provides little guidance. A contested partisan primary provides such a case, and particularly one defined by social media clustering among candidate-supporting subgroups. While HME suggests that Democrats and Republicans should find neutral coverage of the campaign to be biased against their parties, it is unclear how that might interact with bias perceptions by supporters of particular candidates seeking each party's nomination, especially when that candidate support is filtered through social media communities that highlight claims of "bias" against their preferred candidate. Social media thus present a challenge to literature on both HME and "relative HME" (Gunther et al. 2001), in which actual slant is seen as neutral by the favored party and especially hostile by the opposed party.

The 2016 U.S. presidential primaries specifically elevated tensions between party subgroups, as supporters of Hillary Clinton and Bernie Sanders, and "establishment" and "outsider" Republicans frequently clashed, especially in social media. Perhaps owing to the personalized marketing and virality social media affords, enhancing identification with a candidate above and beyond baseline party loyalty (Enli and Skogerbø 2013), the

2016 candidates developed fiercely loyal online followings that drew news coverage themselves (e.g., Dewey 2016; Ohlheiser 2016).

But beyond the hardcore adherents of Bernie Sanders' Dank Meme Stash or Donald Trump's Pepe the Frog army, social media may impact the way average voters perceive media bias. Nested within ideological echo chambers (Bakshy, Messing, and Adamic 2015), partisans may cluster further, creating mediated opinion climates with fairly homogeneous support for one candidate or another. Intraparty division is not unique to the primary context. For example, the Tea Party represented a broad, identity-driven challenge to Republican leadership in 2009–2010, also aided by social media. Indeed, social media introduces the ability to purposively curate one's social network, potentially based on shared political preferences and norms. Because HME is a mechanism relying on a distinct in-group affiliation, group members who identify with a subgroup should be especially likely to perceive media bias, particularly when the subidentity is salient and has the potential to positively define the broader group both in the population and within one's social network. On that measure, primaries provide an especially good setting in which to examine nested political identities.

This study takes identity centrality, candidate favorability, and perceived social network homogeneity as measures of partisanship and involvement, hypothesizing relationships between each and perceived bias against one's candidate and party. Using these measures, we specifically address these research questions: Does the candidate-centered context of the primary season lead to HME based on candidate support rather than party affiliation? Does the party-centered context of the general election make party more salient? Are these mechanisms enhanced when exposed to actually slanted news content? Using social identities as a candidate supporter and party affiliator as the mechanism of interest, our findings support a role for partisan identity based around candidate support and shed light on the potential downstream effects of candidate-centric marketing.

LITERATURE REVIEW

HME

First identified, tested, and clarified in a series of studies about perceptions of news coverage of Middle Eastern conflicts (Vallone, Ross, and Lepper 1985; Giner-Sorolla and Chaiken 1994; Perloff 2015), the HME hinges on the mechanism of high-involvement issue partisanship. In those early studies, highly involved partisans from both sides consistently rated broadcast news stories as hostile to their position. Subsequent studies expanded this model into other issues (e.g., genetically modified organisms in Gunther and Liebhart 2006) and other media (such as newspapers, in Gunther et al. 2001). In each case, partisans in particular find news stories to be biased against their position. This basic finding goes back to a 1980 U.S. presidential election survey finding that, of those who perceived press bias, 89 percent perceived it to be against their preferred candidate (Vallone et al. 1985). It has been shown to be a robust phenomenon across media and in both survey and experimental studies (Hansen and Kim 2011). Indeed, the effect is strong enough for Hansen and Kim's (2011) meta-analysis to identify it as existing among the entire population and to simply be moderated by, rather than dependent on, issue involvement. The effect also manifests on a relative basis when news stories exhibit manifest evidence of bias; that is, a story manifestly biased in favor of a group will be seen as neutral to that group but as especially hostile by an opposing group (Gunther et al. 2001; Gunther and Christen 2002).

Several mechanisms have been proposed as playing a role in the HME and of explaining different causes of the effect. An early explanation suggested that biased assimilation, over time, led partisans to bring different standards to bear when assessing news. However, it could be further argued that a different standards explanation is simply an extension of the biased assimilation process and, indeed, is affected by biased assimilation in a way that should produce selective recall of story information (Vallone et al. 1985). Subsequent findings went against the selective recall hypothesis (Giner-Sorolla and Chaiken 1994), suggesting a real-time evaluative mechanism instead. Selective categorization of story components into favorable and unfavorable groups is one such mechanism that has found consistent support (Gunther and Liebhart 2006).

Understanding the mechanics of the HME has particular importance today given the tendency of partisans to cluster in homogeneous social networks (Iyengar and Westwood 2015), which can foster selective exposure and oppositional media hostility (Arceneaux, Johnson, and Murphy 2012). Although Kim (2011) finds evidence that social network site use increases exposure to viewpoint heterogeneity, it is unclear whether this is specifically true for the highly involved partisans expected to be more vulnerable to the HME. Discussion networks can moderate the HME, strengthening it in a nurturing environment in which one's views are frequently validated (Eveland and Shah 2003). As such, the high-involvement and polarized environment of a candidate's social media setting, whether official or unofficial, is a space that may be expected to boost the HME among its participants, regardless of whether they see the media as biased in favor of a different party or a different candidate within the same party.

A reciprocal relationship between social network setting and social identity could also contribute to this phenomenon. Building on Choi, Yang, and Chang's (2009) work using social judgment theory (Sherif, Sherif, and Nebergall 1965) as a basis for the idea that perceived ego distance drives perceived attitude difference with a news source, Reid (2012) made a case for a self-categorization explanation (Turner et al. 1987). This could also be thought of as a social identity explanation. Because social identity has been demonstrated as a driver of motivated reasoning in other contexts (Hindman 2009; Veenstra, Lyons, and Fowler-Dawson 2016), the expectation that it plays a role in the HME is logical. However, conceptualizing social identity is a complicated endeavor, particularly given the potential for nested or overlapping identities.

Social Identity, Groups, and HME

It has been long understood that political partisanship and ideology can act as markers of social affiliation as much as of overarching belief systems (Conover and Feldman 1981) and that as that affiliation integrates into the self-concept as a social identity, it may affect attitude formation and maintenance (Huddy 2013). In this study, we examine three mechanisms that may account for social identity-driven HME: centrality, in-group affect, and perceived network homogeneity (Cameron 2004; Obst and White 2005). This follows work supporting a tripartite model of social identity, accounting for cognitive, affective, and social elements of its overall gestalt.

Although numerous approaches have been developed for conceptualizing social identity, most research identifies centrality to the self-concept as one of its components (Cameron 2004; Leach et al. 2008); centrality is also an important overlap between social identity and self-categorization theory. Because centrality impinges on an identity's cognitive salience, it should make people especially attuned to group-sensitive events happening both within and without and particularly to in-group threat (Sellers et al. 1998), including that potentially posed by the media.

In-group affect is also an important component of social identity, referring to the positive feelings members associate with the group. While centrality equates to the prominence of the group in one's self-concept, in-group affect translates to the value given to it—its emotional valence (Tajfel and Turner 1979; Cameron 2004). In political contexts, party favorability stands as a marker of affect. In-group affect also prompts people to seek what they perceive as social homogeneity (Simon and Pettigrew 1990), in order to better express the identity they share with that network. Being surrounded by like-minded individuals leads to greater attitude polarization (Paicheler 1979), and homogenous groups may increase motivated reasoning through increased salience of a shared identity and its accompanying normative motivation (Wojcieszak 2010). Further, attitudinally congruent networks, such as those constructed by most social media users, decrease ambivalence and boost certainty (Huckfeldt, Mendez, and Osborn 2004; Visser and Mirabile 2004). In terms of HME, this means voters in homogenous networks may be more likely to perceive bias against their preferred candidate, because even minor criticism or failure to praise would diverge sharply from the positivity they encounter in their personal echo chamber.

However, social identities are not often cleanly distinct from one another, nor strictly internally one-dimensional. Research drawing on self-categorization theory (Turner 1985) has shown that people adopt a multiplicity of identities that are activated when changing social contexts make them salient. Essentially, people construe social stimuli differently based on different self-conceptions in different situations. Because people are unlikely to "cease perceiving and using social categories" (Transue 2007: 79; also see the minimal group paradigm, e.g., Diehl 1990) and because they perceive more heterogeneity in in-groups than out-groups, subgroup identities may become salient in the absence of an out-group.

The relativity of group relations means that differing effects on cognition can come from within a single source, as the nature of a source changes in relation to others, in other words, as some in-group subsets become out-groups. In Turner and Onorato's (1999) example, "feminist" can define the complete group in relation to non-feminist out-groups or the moderate majority in relation to a more radical minority in an intra-feminist group context. This means the meaning of "feminist" changes with the restriction or expansion of the category, and different messages are accepted or rejected as congruent with "feminist" as relative prototypicality changes (32). In these shifts of group definitions, the actual underlying cognitive representation changes. Perceptions of the source (e.g., credibility and bias) can subsequently shift.

Of importance, however, just as subgroup identities are made salient in intragroup contexts, their boundaries and effects can be erased by the salience of an intergroup conflict. The presence of a competing out-group can make the overarching superordinate identity the dominant category.

The potential for perceptual shifts between an individual's subgroup and superordinate identities is unlimited. Christians, for example, might perceive themselves as denominational subgroups internally, but as one religious group in other social contexts. Citizens of European nations might identify as German or French in local continental matters but as Europeans in broader international contexts (Luedtke 2005). We extend this logic to partisan identities. In more enduring ways, partisans can identify with both subgroup party factions and a "big tent" party that subsumes them (Boucek 2009). In part, the ability of voters to identity with these kinds of subgroups (i.e., intraparty legislative factions) depends on cleavages that may be episodic or otherwise structurally absent. Moreover, they may be largely nonsalient for all but the most politically interested voters.

Conversely, presidential primaries and caucuses reliably provide temporary windows of intraparty divisions. These high-profile competitions, often between or among leaders representing opposing wings of the party, make intragroup differences more noticeable. Momentarily, co-partisans become the out-group. Likewise, neutral news stories describing the primary may appear hostile to one's favored candidate. This effect may be strengthened by a preponderance of like-minded supporters in the individual's network. However, self-categorization theory suggests that these effects would fade with the increased salience of the superordinate party identity, thanks to the intergroup conflict of the general election.

Because of this potential for a multifaceted political identity, with contours changing as events make different components more or less salient, we expect the influence of identity driving perceived media hostility to vary during the campaign season. Specifically, when candidate-focused intraparty dispute is salient during the primaries, we expect candidate-related identity to enjoy primacy and for party-related identity to be less accessible. These identities manifest in multiple ways, which we expect to be distinct but related, and that likely have reciprocal strengthening relationships in highly homogeneous social media environments. After the party conventions, when interparty disputes are dominant and only one candidate remains active in each party, we expect the reverse.

H1: During the primaries, candidate-focused measures of partisanship and involvement—(a) identity centrality, (b) relative favorability, and (c) perceived social network homogeneity—are stronger predictors of hostile media perception than party-focused measures.

H2: During the general election, party-focused measures are stronger predictors than are candidate-focused measures.

In addition, we expect that the relative HME should be observable for both story slant in favor of a party and in favor of a particular candidate.

H3: In both cases, observable slant of a news source strengthens both sets of relationships.

METHODS

Data for this study were gathered from primary voters on February 25 and August 10, 2016, using Amazon's Mechanical Turk platform. These dates correspond with the height of the primary season ($N = 327$) and the party convention aftermath ($N = 337$), points during the campaign when we would expect especially high and especially low levels of intraparty division. At both points in time, the same experimental design was used. Participants read an analysis of the primary races, which was randomly presented as an article from *U.S. News & World Report* or as a post from a fictional liberal blog. In addition, half the participants saw "most shared stories" cues that favored either Clinton or Sanders. The story was balanced in terms of its analysis of all seven candidates remaining at the time it was fielded, contrasting the two Democrats directly, and the "outsider" and "establishment" Republican groups, as well as the two parties' prospects in November (see Appendix 1 for full text). Stimulus material focused on the Democratic candidates because of the expectation that participants recruited via Mechanical Turk would skew strongly to the Democratic side (Huff and Tingley 2015), a presumption supported by their survey responses: 69.4 percent of February participants and 70.3 percent of August participants reported voting in Democratic primaries or caucuses.

Sample demographics were younger than but generally similar to those of the American Community Survey for both February (age: $M = 36.84$, $SD = 11.71$; 49.4 percent female; 81.0 percent white; education: median = associate's or bachelor's degree; income: median = $40,000– 60,000) and August (age: $M = 37.18$, $SD = 11.82$; 56.3 percent female; 73.9 percent white; education: median = associate's or bachelor's degree; income: median = $40,000–60,000). Respondents to the first study were barred from participating in the second study.

Measures

VOTE CHOICE

Respondents in each study primarily identified as Democrats (February: 58.7 percent Democrat, 22.9 percent Republican, 5.8 percent other parties; August: 54.3 percent Democrat, 22.6 percent Republican, 7.4 percent other parties). For analytical purposes, party affiliation was determined by which major party's primary respondents said they voted in or planned to vote in (February: 69.4 percent Democrat, August: 70.3 percent Democrat). It is worth noting that retrospective non-voting in August was considerably higher than prospective non-voting in February. The February study had 423 total participants, of whom 22.7 percent indicated they would not vote in the primaries; August's sample had a total of 822, of whom 59.0 percent indicated that they had not voted in the primaries.

Reflecting the liberal tendency of MTurk samples, Bernie Sanders drew the largest support from each sample, followed by Hillary Clinton (February: Sanders 52.0 percent, Clinton 17.4 percent, Trump 17.4 percent, Cruz 6.4 percent, Rubio 4.6 percent, Carson 1.5 percent, Kasich 0.6 percent; August: Sanders 46.0 percent, Clinton 24.3 percent, Trump 17.8 percent, Cruz 5.6 percent, Rubio 3.0 percent, Kasich 2.1 percent, Carson 1.2 percent).

IDENTITY CENTRALITY

Two scales were constructed for centrality of candidate and party support to respondents' identity, each comprising four items ranging from 1 (*not at all*) to 4 (*a great deal*). These asked to what extent respondents think of themselves as a supporter/member of their candidate/party, how important being a supporter/member is to them, how well the term "supporter" or appropriate partisan label describes them, and how often they use "we" instead of "they" to describe other such people. These items were averaged to create two indices in each study (February candidate: Cronbach's $\alpha = .83$, $M = 2.83$, $SD = .65$; August candidate: $\alpha = .85$; $M = 2.78$, $SD = .74$; February party: $\alpha = .87$, $M = 2.58$, $SD = .71$; August party: $\alpha = .89$, $M = 2.54$, $SD = .79$).

RELATIVE FAVORABILITY

Respondents were asked to rate each of the seven candidates and the two major parties on a favorability scale from 1 to 4. For Democratic voters, the difference between their preferred candidate's favorability and the other candidate's favorability was measured. For Republican voters, the difference between their preferred candidate's favorability and the mean of the other four was measured. For all respondents, the difference between favorability of the party in which primary they voted or planned to vote and the other party was measured (February candidate: $M = 1.40$, $SD = .92$; February party: $M = 1.56$, $SD = 1.09$; August candidate: $M = 1.21$, $SD = .92$; August party: $M = 1.41$, $SD = 1.06$).

PERCEIVED SOCIAL NETWORK HOMOGENEITY

Respondents were asked the extent to which their social networks would agree with them about each of the candidates, ranging from 1 (*strongly disagree*) to 4 (*strongly agree*). This perception-based measurement approach is standard in studies of political networks (Huckfeldt, Johnson, and Sprague 2002; Klofstad, Sokhey, and McClurg 2013) and is consistent with the theoretical underpinnings of a tripartite social identity model (Cameron 2004). The seven items were averaged to form an index of candidate assessment homogeneity (February: $\alpha = .86$, $M = 2.74$, $SD = .69$; August: $\alpha = .84$, $M = 2.74$, $SD = .66$). Another two items asked the same regarding the two major parties, which were averaged to form an index of party assessment homogeneity (February: $r = .21$, $M = 2.76$, $SD = .70$; August: $r = .33$, $M = 2.75$, $SD = .75$).

These three social identity measures—centrality, relative favorability, and perceived social network homogeneity—were all interrelated for party identity in each study (Cent-Fav: $r_{Feb} = .43$, $p < .001$, $r_{Aug} = .48$, $p < .001$; Cent-Homog: $r_{Feb} = .22$, $p < .001$, $r_{Aug} = .24$, $p < .001$; Fav-Homog: $r_{Feb} = .20$, $p < .001$, $r_{Aug} = .20$, $p < .001$), but much less so for candidate support identity (Cent-Fav: $r_{Feb} = .21$, $p < .001$, $r_{Aug} = .03$, n.s.; Cent-Homog: $r_{Feb} = .16$, $p < .001$, $r_{Aug} = .23$, $p < .001$; Fav-Homog: $r_{Feb} = .02$, n.s., $r_{Aug} = -.05$, n.s.). This aligns with the likelihood of party identity being longer-standing and more well-founded than a candidate support identity that likely does not predate the present campaign season.

PERCEIVED NEWS BIAS

For each candidate and party, respondents were asked the extent to which the story, the author, and the site were biased for or against, ranging from −5 (*strongly biased against*) to 5 (*strongly biased for*). These three items were assigned to respondents based on their preferred candidate and party and then averaged to form indices of perceived bias in favor of their preferences, with negative numbers indicating hostility (February candidate: $\alpha = .85$, $M = -.11$, $SD = 1.84$; February party: $\alpha = .82$, $M = .21$, $SD = 2.73$; August candidate: $\alpha = .87$, $M = -.19$, $SD = 2.07$; August party: $\alpha = .86$, $M = .11$, $SD = 3.25$).

RESULTS

Hypotheses were tested using a pair of analysis of covariance models in each of the two samples. These models included as factors the two experimental manipulations (source and suggested stories) and median-split groups for identity centrality, relative favorability, and perceived social network homogeneity. They also included the two-way interactions of each of those three variables with the source manipulation and demographics (age, gender coded as female, race coded as white, education, and income) as covariates. One model tested candidate-related variables' influence on candidate bias perception, while the other tested party-related variables' influence on party bias perception.

Study 1 (February)

The source manipulations had no main or interactive effects on bias evaluations, a finding that is robust across parties and candidates. However, identity centrality, $F(1, 284) = 6.92$, $p < .01$, $M_{high} = -.31$, $M_{low} = .28$, and candidate favorability relative to others, $F(1, 284) = 3.63$, $p < .1$, $M_{high} = -.23$, $M_{low} = .20$, both predicted greater perceived bias against one's candidate, while none of the involvement and partisanship measures predicted perceived bias against one's party (see Table 1).

Study 2 (August)

In the August analysis, the suggested stories manipulation was a significant predictor of perceived candidate bias, $F(2, 311) = 3.23$, $p < .05$, $M_{none} = .03$, $M_{Sanders} = -.21$, $M_{Clinton} = -.69$, $p_{none-Clinton} < .05$. However, neither the source main effect nor any interactive effects were significant. While identity centrality and perceived social network homogeneity were not significant predictors of candidate bias perception, relative candidate favorability remained significant in the second study, $F(1, 311) = 3.48$, $p < .1$, $M_{high} = -.52$, $M_{low} = -.06$.

TABLE 1 Predictors of perceived bias in February

Source	Candidate Type III sum of squares	df	Mean square	F	Sig.	Party Type III Sum of Squares	df	Mean Square	F	Sig.
Corrected model	95.19	14	6.80	2.08	**	76.12	14	5.44	.71	
Intercept	3.19	1	3.19	.98		6.13	1	6.13	.80	
Source	1.46	1	1.46	.45		1.14	1	1.14	.15	
Suggested stories	.38	2	.19	.06		7.89	2	3.94	.52	
Identity centrality	22.56	1	22.56	6.92	**	5.78	1	5.78	.76	
Relative favorability	11.83	1	11.83	3.63	†	3.50	1	3.50	.46	
Network homogeneity	7.30	1	7.30	2.24		10.72	1	10.72	1.40	
Age	13.69	1	13.69	4.20	*	15.97	1	15.97	2.09	
Race (white)	10.36	1	10.36	3.18	†	1.29	1	1.29	.17	
Gender (female)	.57	1	.57	.17		.17	1	.17	.02	
Education	10.90	1	10.90	3.34	†	2.83	1	2.83	.37	
Income	3.15	1	3.15	.96		6.76	1	6.76	.88	
Source*centrality	2.35	1	2.35	.72		13.20	1	13.20	1.73	
Source*favorability	1.90	1	1.90	.58		.93	1	.93	.12	
Source*homogeneity	.01	1	.01	.00		4.19	1	4.19	.55	
Error	926.35	284	3.26			2270.52	297	7.64		
Total	1023.89	299				2359.69	312			
Corrected total	1021.54	298				2346.63	311			

Note. $R^2 = .093$ (adjusted $R^2 = .048$).
$R^2 = .032$ (adjusted $R^2 = -.013$).
**$p < .01$. *$p < .05$. †$p < .1$.

No main or interactive effects were found in the model predicting perceived party bias. However, perceived social network homogeneity was a significant predictor, $F(1, 310) = 3.03$, $p < .1$, $M_{high} = -.25$, $M_{low} = .40$ (see Table 2).

Taken together, these results provide support for H1 but do not provide significant support for H2 and H3. Although some results suggest support for those two hypotheses, the breadth of the findings does not support them.

DISCUSSION

This study extended the HME literature by testing whether candidate-centered subgroup identities would influence perceptions of bias more strongly than traditional partisanship during a contested primary and whether this effect would dissipate during the general election. Results largely support the former, but not the latter, despite the expectation of shifting boundaries of voters' in-groups. Party organizers may be concerned that this phenomenon will damage general election unity, as is frequently expressed during heated primaries.

The pattern detected in our two studies could suggest that something about American partisanship, its intraparty subgroups, and their effects on voters will consistently differ from the mechanics predicted by social identity theory, and this will replicate in future presidential races. However, our findings are based on a single campaign season. It is worth recalling several idiosyncrasies of the parties' convention period that may have impacted the results in Study 2, as neither convention clamped down on intraparty division very well. Ted Cruz notoriously told Republicans to "vote your conscience" in his Republican National Convention speech. Bernie Sanders delegates booed every mention of Hilary Clinton. WikiLeaks published Democratic National Committee emails. It is possible that the typical reassertion of the superordinate party identity was mitigated by these unusual, divisive events. However, the fact that candidate-based identity centrality disappeared as a predictor of perceived candidate bias provides some evidence of shifting dominance in self-categorization.

Ultimately, the potential effects of specific 2016 campaign characteristics present a major limitation to our ability to generalize from these findings. They also suggest an open question for future study and potentially for retrospective analysis. The era of "candidate-centered" campaigns has mostly coincided with an era of weak party discipline (Steger 2000); however, the parties as they have existed in the last three presidential elections have been much more ideologically sorted. In this same period, several candidates (and arguably 2008 vice-presidential nominee Sarah Palin) have taken on at least temporary "rock star" status among factions of their parties, with Barack

TABLE 2 Predictors of perceived bias in August

Source	Candidate					Party				
	Type III sum of squares	df	Mean square	F	Sig.	Type III Sum of Squares	df	Mean Square	F	Sig.
Corrected model	69.18	14	4.94	1.13		148.67	14	10.62	1.03	
Intercept	1.38	1	1.38	.32		.40	1	.40	.04	
Source	2.11	1	2.11	.48		22.94	1	22.94	2.22	
Suggested stories	28.14	2	14.07	3.23	*	4.24	2	2.12	.21	
Identity centrality	.13	1	.13	.03		14.99	1	14.99	1.45	
Relative favorability	15.15	1	15.15	3.47	†	24.32	1	24.32	2.36	
Network homogeneity	.17	1	.17	.04		31.24	1	31.24	3.03	†
Age	.00	1	.00	.00		27.58	1	27.58	2.67	
Race (white)	.44	1	.44	.10		8.19	1	8.19	.79	
Gender (female)	.81	1	.81	.19		4.86	1	4.86	.47	
Education	.51	1	.51	.12		2.19	1	2.19	.21	
Income	2.36	1	2.36	.54		1.25	1	1.25	.12	
Source*centrality	7.91	1	7.91	1.82		2.61	1	2.61	.25	
Source*favorability	7.94	1	7.94	1.82		4.47	1	4.47	.43	
Source*homogeneity	2.84	1	2.84	.65		.94	1	.94	.09	
Error	1355.77	311	4.36			3198.27	310	10.32		
Total	1437.47	326				3350.19	325			
Corrected total	1424.96	325				3346.94	324			

Note. $R^2 = .049$ (adjusted $R^2 = .006$).
$R^2 = .044$ (adjusted $R^2 = .001$).
**$p < .01$. *$p < .05$. †$p < .1$.

Obama and Donald Trump both winning the presidency. This is in sharp contrast with the enthusiasm seen for past nominees and presidents but may be a sign of things to come if the trend is driven by highly engaged, party-detached, and social media–enabled networks. In that future scenario, there is little reason to assume that party factions would gel behind a nominee in a way that was more enthusiastic than perfunctory. Indeed, 2016 and future years may experience a surge in cross-partisan primary voting, in which voting supporting a candidate in the primary does not correspond to supporting that party in the general election, and the assumption of such a connection is a limitation of this study.

This study also attempted to address HME in a transformed media landscape by gauging the increasingly relevant effects of social settings on bias perceptions. While 2016 may be remembered for colorful candidate-centric online communities that first emerged during the primaries, we find that perceived social network homogeneity only influenced perceptions of bias against one's party during the general election. The presence of this effect, but none for candidate-support homogeneity during primary season, might be driven by a broader kind of network consensus and deeper or more established norms than would likely exist for candidates alone. Regardless, this finding should spark future work on the HME that further investigates the impact of individuals' social networks.

That perceived network homogeneity predicts party bias perception only in the general election context suggests that candidates' uniquely divisive in-group-conflict-inducing narratives in mass and social media helped to downplay party unity at their time of highest salience but that homogeneous networks "came home" after the conventions. Negative media coverage of subjects that are important for a subgroup strengthens the salience of the identity in the instances of moral or ideological conflict (Hartmann and Tanis 2013), in this case weakening the superordinate party identity. The fact that candidate favorability significantly predicted candidate HME in both studies suggests that it may be at the foundation of the subgroup HME, lingering as a strong influence even after one's broader network has moved to a party identity focus in the general election.

Regarding the lack of source effects, our results may provide further evidence that average online news users are more "source-blind" than we would hope (Wineburg and McGrew 2016). On the other hand, though, the significant effect of "suggested stories" in Study 2 provides some support for a line of literature that finds users' perceptions of messages communicated in mixed and social media environments are holistic impressions in which each media component (videos, tweets, comments sections, and so on) color perceptions of others on the screen (Veenstra et al. 2015; Lyons and Veenstra 2016). The implications of these mixed findings for political marketing are unclear, in part because social media settings are to a great extent out of communicators' control; however, practitioners should err on the side of caution and remain vigilant of the potential effects of the communication environments that surround strategic messages online.

More broadly, our findings on perceptions of bias driven by candidate support suggest that individual campaigns' efforts to personalize their candidate may be successful to the point that voters identify more with them than the party with whom they have likely held a longer bond. This may be seen as good short-term news in that it generates enthusiasm among party membership, but a long-run problem for parties in a plurality-driven system. 2016 was a highly unusual case in that the "outsider" candidates in the primaries included one who had refused for decades to formally join the party whose nomination he sought and another who had never previously sought or held public office and had been registered in multiple parties during his adult life. In both cases, party establishments almost uniformly backed their opponents; each candidate and his supporters pushed back against those establishments in part by decrying their treatment by the "establishment" media.

That Sanders and Trump were able to vastly outperform expectations seems to be due at least in part to their ability to win over existing social media communities (the social democratic left and the "alt right," respectively) that take media hostility as a central assumption. Indeed, early in his term, Trump's voters identify news organizations producing "false" stories as a bigger problem than Trump making false claims by a net 77 percent margin (Sargent 2017). While these voters are likely taking cues from Trump himself, many are also engaged with a social media environment in which media hostility to Trump and to themselves is unquestioned and bolstered by the "fair" sources they select instead, such as social media stalwarts Breitbart or Infowars.

This suggests a major shift in how candidates are able to cultivate bases of personal support, either within parties or without. Creating an assumption of media hostility damages the central democratic role of the press by pushing some of the most engaged parts of the public toward distortion and outright misinformation, which candidates have every incentive to support. Candidates who see their political fortunes as more dependent on a personal brand than on party success subsequently have little incentive to wholeheartedly back whoever defeated them in a primary. Voters, for their part, face many more opportunities for disaffection if they pin their hopes on the success of individual politicians, particularly when it comes to the presidency, as the vast majority of presidential candidates face the sting of defeat.

REFERENCES

Arceneaux, K., M. Johnson, and C. Murphy. 2012. "Polarized Political Communication, Oppositional Media Hostility, and Selective Exposure." *Journal of Politics* 74 (1):174–186. doi:10.1017/S002238161100123X

Bakshy, E., S. Messing, and L. A. Adamic. 2015. "Exposure to Ideologically Diverse News and Opinion on Facebook." *Science* 348 (6239):1130–1132. doi:10.1126/science.aaa1160

Boucek, F. 2009. "Rethinking Factionalism: Typologies, Intra-Party Dynamics and Three Faces of Factionalism." *Party Politics* 15 (4):455–485. doi:10.1177/1354068809334553

Cameron, J. E. 2004. "A Three-Factor Model of Social Identity." *Self and Identity* 3 (3):239–262. doi:10.1080/13576500444000047

Choi, J., M. Yang, and J. J. Chang. 2009. "Elaboration of the Hostile Media Phenomenon: The Roles of Involvement, Media Skepticism, Congruency of Perceived Media Influence, and Perceived Opinion Climate." *Communication Research* 36 (1):54–75. doi:10.1177/0093650208326462

Conover, P. J., and S. Feldman. 1981. "The Origins and Meaning of Liberal/Conservative Self-Identifications." *American Journal of Political Science* 25 (4):617–645. doi:10.2307/2110756

Dewey, C. 2016. "How Bernie Sanders Became the Lord of 'Dank Memes'." The Washington Post. Retrieved from https://www.washingtonpost.com/news/the-intersect/wp/2016/02/23/how-bernie-sanders-became-the-lord-of-dank-memes/

Diehl, M. 1990. "The Minimal Group Paradigm: Theoretical Explanations and Empirical Findings." *European Review of Social Psychology* 1 (1):263–292. doi:10.1080/14792779108401864

Enli, G. S., and E. Skogerbø. 2013. "Personalized Campaigns in Party-Centered Politics: Twitter and Facebook as Arenas for Political Communication." *Information, Communication & Society* 16 (5):757–774. doi:10.1080/1369118X.2013.782330

Eveland Jr., W. P., and D. V. Shah. 2003. "The Impact of Individual and Interpersonal Factors on Perceived News Media Bias." *Political Psychology* 24 (1):101–117. doi:10.1111/0162-895X.00318

Giner-Sorolla, R., and S. Chaiken. 1994. "The Causes of Hostile Media Judgments." *Journal of Experimental Social Psychology* 30 (2):165–180. doi:10.1006/jesp.1994.1008

Gunther, A. C., and C. T. Christen. 2002. "Projection or Persuasive Press? Contrary Effects of Personal Opinion and Perceived News Coverage on Estimates of Public Opinion." *Journal of Communication* 52 (1):177–195. doi:10.1111/j.1460-2466.2002.tb02538.x

Gunther, A. C., C. T. Christen, J. L. Liebhart, and S. C. Chia. 2001. "Congenial Public, Contrary Press, and Biased Estimates of the Climate of Opinion." *Public Opinion Quarterly* 65 (3):295–320. doi:10.1086/322846

Gunther, A. C., and J. L. Liebhart. 2006. "Broad Reach or Biased Source? Decomposing the Hostile Media Effect." *Journal of Communication* 56 (3):449–466. doi:10.1111/j.1460-2466.2006.00295.x

Hansen, G. J., and H. Kim. 2011. "Is the Media Biased Against Me? A Meta-Analysis of the Hostile Media Effect Research." *Communication Research Reports* 28 (2):169–179. doi:10.1080/08824096.2011.565280

Hartmann, T., and M. Tanis. 2013. "Examining the Hostile Media Effect as an Intergroup Phenomenon: The Role of Ingroup Identification and Status." *Journal of Communication* 63 (3):535–555. doi:10.1111/jcom.12031

Hindman, D. B. 2009. "Mass Media Flow and Differential Distribution of Politically Disputed Beliefs: The Belief Gap Hypothesis." *Journalism & Mass Communication Quarterly* 86 (4):790–808. doi:10.1177/107769900908600405

Huckfeldt, R., P. E. Johnson, and J. Sprague. 2002. "Political Environments, Political Dynamics, and the Survival of Disagreement." *Journal of Politics* 64 (1):1–21. doi:10.1111/1468-2508.00115

Huckfeldt, R., J. M. Mendez, and T. Osborn. 2004. "Disagreement, Ambivalence, and Engagement: The Political Consequences of Heterogeneous Networks." *Political Psychology* 25 (1):65–95. doi:10.1111/j.1467-9221.2004.00357.x

Huddy, L. 2013. "From Group Identity to Political Cohesion and Commitment." In *Oxford Handbook of Political Psychology*, edited by L. Huddy, D. O. Sears, and J. Levy, 737–73. New York: Oxford University Press.

Huff, C., and Tingley, D. 2015. ""Who are these People?" Evaluating the Demographic Characteristics and Political Preferences of MTurk Survey Respondents." *Research and Politics* 2 (3):205316801560464. doi:10.1177/2053168015604648

Iyengar, S., and S. J. Westwood. 2015. "Fear and Loathing Across Party Lines: New Evidence on Group Polarization." *American Journal of Political Science* 59 (3):690–707. doi:10.1111/ajps.12152

Kim, Y. 2011. "The Contribution of Social Network Sites to Exposure to Political Difference: The Relationships among SNSs, Online Political Messaging, and Exposure to Cross-Cutting Perspectives." *Computers in Human Behavior* 27 (2):971–977. doi:10.1016/j.chb.2010.12.001

Klofstad, C. A., A. E. Sokhey, and S. D. McClurg. 2013. "Disagreeing about Disagreement: How Conflict in Social Networks Affects Political Behavior." *American Journal of Political Science* 57 (1):120–134. doi:10.1111/j.1540-5907.2012.00620.x

Leach, C. W., M. van Zomeren, S. Zebel, M. L. W. Vliek, S. F. Pennekamp, B. Doosje, … R. Spears. 2008. "Group-Level Self-Definition and Self-Investment: A Hierarchical (Multicomponent) Model of In-Group Identification." *Journal of Personality and Social Psychology* 95 (1):144–165. doi:10.1037/0022-3514.95.1.144

Luedtke, A. 2005. "European Integration, Public Opinion and Immigration Policy: Testing the Impact of National Identity." *European Union Politics* 6 (1): 83–112. doi:10.1177/1465116505049609

Lyons, B. A., and A. S. Veenstra. 2016. "How (Not) to Talk on Twitter: Effects of Politicians' Tweets on Perceptions of the Twitter Environment." *Cyberpsychology, Behavior, and Social Networking* 19 (1):8–15. doi:10.1089/cyber.2015.0319

Obst, P., and K. White. 2005. "Three-Dimensional Strength of Identification Across Group Memberships: A Confirmatory Factor Analysis." *Self and Identity* 4 (1):69–80. doi:10.1080/13576500444000182

Ohlheiser, A. 2016. "'We Actually Elected a Meme as President': How 4chan Celebrated Trump's Victory." The Washington Post. Retrieved from https://www.washingtonpost.com/news/the-intersect/wp/2016/11/09/we-actually-elected-a-meme-as-president-how-4chan-celebrated-trumps-victory/

Paicheler, G. 1979. "Polarization of Attitudes in Homogeneous and Heterogeneous Groups." *European Journal of Social Psychology* 9 (1):85–96. doi:10.1002/ejsp.2420090107

Perloff, R. M. 2015. "A Three-Decade Retrospective on the Hostile Media Effect." *Mass Communication & Society* 18 (6):701–729. doi:10.1080/15205436.2015.1051234

Reid, S. A. 2012. "A self-Categorization Explanation for the Hostile Media Effect." *Journal of Communication* 62 (3):381–399. doi:10.1111/j.1460-2466.2012.01647.x

Sargent, G. 2017. "Trump's lies are working brilliantly. This new poll proves it." The Washington Post. Retrieved from https://www.washingtonpost.com/blogs/plumline/wp/2017/04/27/trumps-lies-are-working-brilliantly-this-new-poll-proves-it/

Sellers, R. M., M. A. Smith, J. N. Shelton, S. A. J. Rowley, and T. M. Chavous. 1998. "Multidimensional Model of Racial Identity: A Reconceptualization of African American Racial Identity." *Personality and Social Psychology Review* 2 (1):18–39. doi:10.1207/s15327957pspr0201_2

Sherif, C. W., M. Sherif, and R. E. Nebergall. 1965. *Attitude and Attitude Change: The Social Judgment-Involvement Approach*. Philadelphia, PA: W. B. Saunders.

Simon, B., and T. F. Pettigrew. 1990. "Social Identity and Perceived Group Homogeneity: Evidence for the Ingroup Homogeneity Effect." *European Journal of Social Psychology* 20 (4):269–286. doi:10.1002/ejsp.2420200402

Steger, W. P. 2000. "Do Primary Voters Draw from a Stacked Deck? Presidential Nominations in an Era of Candidate-Centered Campaigns." *Presidential Studies Quarterly* 30 (4):727–753. doi:10.1111/j.0360-4918.2000.00141.x

Tajfel, H., and J. C. Turner. 1979. "An Integrative Theory of Intergroup Conflict." In *The social psychology of intergroup relations*, edited by W. G. Austin & S. Worchel, 33–47. Monterey, CA: Brooks/Cole Publishing Co.

Transue, J. E. 2007. "Identity Salience, Identity Acceptance, and Racial Policy Attitudes: American National Identity as a Uniting Force." *American Journal of Political Science* 51 (1):78–91. doi:10.1111/j.1540-5907.2007.00238.x

Turner, J. C. 1985. "Social Categorization and the Self-Concept: A Social Cognitive Theory of Group Behavior." In *Advances in Group Processes: Theory and Research*, edited by E. J. Lawler (Vol. 2, 77–122). Greenwich, CT: JAI.

Turner, J. C., M. A. Hogg, P. J. Oakes, S. D. Reicher, and M. S. Wetherell. 1987. *Rediscovering the social group: A self-categorization theory*. Cambridge, MA: Basil Blackwell.

Turner, J. C., and R. S. Onorato. 1999. "Social Identity, Personality, and the Self-Concept: A Self-Categorization Perspective." In *The psychology of the social self*, edited by T. R. Tyler, R. M. Kramer, & O. P. John, 11–46. Mahwah, NJ: Lawrence Erlbaum Associates.

Vallone, R. P., L. Ross, and M. R. Lepper. 1985. "The Hostile Media Phenomenon: Biased Perception and Perceptions of Media Bias in Coverage of the Beirut Massacre." *Journal of Personality and Social Psychology* 49 (3):577–585. doi:10.1037/0022-3514.49.3.577

Veenstra, A. S., B. A. Lyons, and A. Fowler-Dawson. 2016. "Conservatism vs. Conservationism: Differential Influences of Social Identities on Beliefs About Fracking." *Environmental Communication* 10 (3):322–336. doi:10.1080/17524032.2015.1127851

Veenstra, A. S., C. S. Park, B. A. Lyons, C. S. Kang, and N. Iyer. 2015. "Intramedium Interaction and the Third-Person Effect: How Partisans Respond to YouTube Ads and Comments." *Cyberpsychology, Behavior, and Social Networking* 18 (7):406–410. doi:10.1089/cyber.2014.0588

Visser, P. S., and R. R. Mirabile. 2004. "Attitudes in the Social Context: The Impact of Social Network Composition on Individual-Level Attitude Strength." *Journal of Personality and Social Psychology* 87 (6):779–795. doi:10.1037/0022-3514.87.6.779

Wineburg, S., and McGrew, S. 2016. "Why Students Can't Google their Way to the Truth." Education Week 36, 22, 28.

Wojcieszak, M. E. 2010. "'Don't Talk to Me': Effects of Ideologically Homogeneous Online Groups and Politically Dissimilar Offline Ties on Extremism." *New Media & Society* 12 (4):637–655. doi:10.1177/1461444809342775

APPENDIX 1. STIMULUS MATERIAL

Although just a few states have voted, it is already clear that the 2016 presidential race is full of uncertainty. Few would have predicted a year ago that Bernie Sanders and Donald Trump would have won the New Hampshire primaries, let alone that these party outsiders would be in competitive positions overall. It is hard to make predictions about where the race goes from here, because there is so little precedent for the kinds of campaigns that are being run this year.

Only Sanders and Hillary Clinton remain on the Democratic side, in what some are calling a "theory of change" race. Clinton narrowly won in Iowa, while Sanders had a sizeable victory in New Hampshire; still, less than two percent of total convention delegates were awarded in those two states, so the candidates' competing visions will continue to drive the campaign. For Sanders, that's his familiar call for a "political revolution" and a focus on the financial sector. Critics, including Clinton, say that Sanders is promising more than he can deliver – that his numbers don't add up, and his big changes would never pass with a Republican Congress. Clinton's policy proposals focus on more minor changes, and she promises to build on a foundation left by Barack Obama. But according to Sanders, Clinton's preference for incremental change is indicative of her connection to a corrupt system that will never respond seriously to the public's interests.

Two-thirds of the original Republican field has left the race, but the remaining five candidates tend to be seen as representing the party establishment – Marco Rubio, John Kasich – and party outsiders – Donald Trump, Ted Cruz, Ben Carson. For the most, they have all agreed on most issues. Their debates have focused instead on who is the most consistent, furthest to the right conservative. Ordinarily, this would seem to benefit Cruz, a self-styled "insurgent" with a strong history of opposition to the Obama administration in the Senate, or even Rubio, who was elected as a Tea Party favorite in 2010.

But Cruz has put many of his fellow Republicans off since arriving in Washington, and Rubio has misstepped on the year's biggest issue: immigration. Conversely, although Trump has major question marks on his claim to be an ideological conservative, he has been the campaign's loudest and proudest immigration opponent from day one.

Because of the competitive nature of both parties' primaries, making predictions about the general election is not easy. Obama won 332 electoral votes in 2012, meaning the Democratic nominee could lose 62 votes from that total and still win the election. That would mean that if the Republican nominee picked up Florida, Ohio, and Virginia, he would still need to pick up one more state and retain all the states won by Mitt Romney. However, it has historically been difficult for one party to win three presidential elections in a row, and preliminary polls show Democratic and Republican candidates running close in head-to-head match-ups. The fact is, a case can be made against any of the seven remaining candidates winning the election in November, but ultimately one of them will, and it will cap off the most unusual presidential race in decades.

Header design of liberal blog source condition

f Most Shared Stories

🐦 Most Retweeted Stories

Bernie Sanders Meets With Residents of Flint Before Campaign

Bernie Sanders in Atlanta: "We're Going to Win Right Here"

My Slow Turn Away From Hillary Toward Bernie

The More Voters Learn About Hillary, the Less They Like Her

The More Voters Learn About Hillary, the Less They Like Her

My Slow Turn Away From Hillary Toward Bernie

Bernie Sanders Highlights "Excitement and Energy" in Campaign

12 Examples of Hillary Violating Progressives' Trust

Independents Won't Support Hillary Clinton – Here's Why

Bernie Sanders Highlights "Excitement and Energy" in Campaign

Sanders Allies Warn Voters: "Hillary Clinton Is Not Who She Says She Is"

Sanders Allies Warn Voters: "Hillary Clinton Is Not Who She Says She Is"

Suggested stories in pro-Sanders/anti-Clinton condition

Role of Social Media in the 2016 Iowa Caucuses

DANIELA V. DIMITROVA

DIANNE BYSTROM

Social media have become an indispensable tool in modern political campaigns, yet little is known about their impact, especially at the important primary and caucus stages of the US presidential elections. This study investigates the effects of visiting political party and candidate websites as well as following presidential candidates, posting political comments, and liking or sharing political content on social media on participation in the primary stage of the 2016 US election. The results of a precaucus survey in Iowa show that active use of social media tends to have positive effects, while passive social media use has a negative impact on likelihood of caucus attendance. Recommendations for campaigns include redirecting attention away from passive website viewing and developing social media content that will generate likes and shares.

The increasing popularity of social media among the American public has made it an indispensable tool in modern political campaigns. While multiple surveys have documented the widespread use of such social media tools as Twitter, Facebook, and YouTube in recent political campaigns, research investigating the actual effects of these platforms has been relatively sparse. Recently, more studies have tried to capture social media's influence on voters at critical times during political campaigns (Vitak et al. 2011; Gil de Zuniga et al. 2013; Dimitrova et al. 2014; Skoric et al. 2016), although few studies examine the role of online media during the primary stages of the campaign.

In earlier studies (Tolbert and McNeal 2003; Mossberger, Tolbert, and McNeal 2008), scholars focused on the effects of general internet use and online news media on civic engagement and political participation, particularly in general election cycles, as the more recent social media platforms either did not exist or were not widely used by political candidates. More recent studies (Kushin and Yamamoto 2010; Vitak et al. 2011; Skoric et al. 2016) have zeroed in on the effects of social media platforms on civic and political engagement, also primarily during general election campaigns. Only a few studies (Redlawsk, Tolbert, and Donovan 2010; Dimitrova and Bystrom 2013) have examined the role that the internet, online news media, and social media play during the critical—especially in the US presidential politics—primaries' and caucuses' stage.

Historically, the Iowa caucuses have been established as the first step in the presidential nomination process in USA since 1972 and, despite skepticism, have remained the nation's "trial run" for presidential contenders in both major political parties (Winebrenner and Goldford 2010). With the exception of a one-time experiment with a primary in 1916, Iowa has always held caucuses; but they fell in the middle of the primary season until 1972. That year, in response to reforms initiated by the Democratic Party following its tumultuous 1968 national nominating convention as well as a quirk in the scheduling calendar, the Iowa Democratic Party held its caucus at the beginning of the presidential nominating process. As a result, candidates actively campaigned in the state, and the media followed.

In 1976, the Iowa caucuses gained legitimacy when outsider candidate Jimmy Carter, then governor of Georgia, focused his efforts on campaigning in the state and won the Democratic Party's caucus and, eventually, the White House. Since 1972, the winner of the Democratic caucuses has gone on to gain the party's nomination in seven of nine contested races, but just Carter in 1976 and Barack Obama in 2008 won the presidency. Among Republicans since 1980, the winner of the Iowa caucuses has gained the party's nomination twice in six contested races, but the presidency just once—George W. Bush in 2000. Although the Iowa caucuses have a poor record of picking presidents, they play the important role of winnowing the field. Only once in the history of the modern Iowa caucuses has someone finished lower than third and gone on to win a party's nomination.

Recently, scholars have examined the effects of online information sources on the Iowa caucuses with mixed results. In their study of partici-pation in the 2008 Iowa caucuses, Redlawsk, Tolbert, and Donovan (2010) found that online technologies had a positive effect on Democrats. However,

Dimitrova and Bystrom (2013) found no significant social media effects for Republicans and independents participating in the 2012 Iowa caucuses.

During the 2016 presidential campaign cycle, the Iowa caucuses were once again tumultuous and nationally newsworthy, presenting an excellent opportunity to study the impact of social media on likely participants from both the Democratic and Republican parties as well as independent voters. Former US Secretary of State Hillary Clinton narrowly won the Democratic Party caucuses, winning 49.9% of the delegates (23) compared to 49.6% of delegates (21) won by US Senator Bernie Sanders of Vermont. US Senator Ted Cruz of Texas won the Republican Party caucuses with 27.6% of the vote compared to 24.3% for New York City businessman Donald Trump, and 23.1% for US Senator Marco Rubio of Florida.

The goal of this article is to see how different media channels affect political participation. Based on the results of a two-wave telephone survey of registered Iowa voters, this study examines the effects of online media use on the likelihood to participate in the 2016 Iowa caucuses; compares the effects of online media use to those of traditional media, political advertising, and interpersonal communication; and explores whether active and passive social media use have differential effects on caucus participation.

INFLUENCE OF COMMUNICATION CHANNELS ON POLITICAL ENGAGEMENT

Researchers have examined the role and influence of various channels of communication—traditional media, political advertising, interpersonal communication, the internet, and social media—on the political engagement and participation of citizens in the USA as well as other countries. Several theoretical frameworks have been used to explain the effects of communication channels on political participation, including uses and gratifications (Shah, Kwak, and Holbert 2001); the communication mediation model (Huckfeldt and Sprague 1995); the cognitive mediation model (Eveland 2001; Eveland, Shah, and Kwak 2003); the orientations–stimulus–reasoning–orientations–response model (Cho et al. 2009; Gil de Zuniga et al. 2013); the social influence model (Kim, Atkin, and Lin 2016); and media system dependency theory (DeFleur and Ball-Rokeach 1989; Tolbert and McNeal 2003).

Our study builds upon Tolbert and McNeal's (2003) adaptation of media system dependency theory for their study on the effects of internet access and online political news on the likelihood to vote in the 1996 and 2000 US presidential elections. As proposed by DeFleur and Ball-Rokeach (1989), media system dependency theory suggests that the difference between the forms of media that have a direct impact on the public and those that do not is based on needs and resources. Drawing upon the work of DeFleur and Ball-Rokeach (1989), Tolbert and McNeal (2003) hypothesized that the variety of sources available on the internet about political candidates and elections, combined with the speed and flexibility of obtaining information online, would stimulate increased participation. That is, communication channels that provide the public with the information it needs in a quicker, cheaper, and more convenient form are more likely to be adopted and change patterns of behavior.

Similarly, we are interested in learning whether or not the speed, flexibility, and convenience of obtaining information on presidential candidates and their campaigns through online media sources, including social media platforms, would stimulate the likelihood to participate in the 2016 Iowa caucuses. In addition, we are interested in learning whether the active or passive uses of social media have different effects on the likelihood to caucus.

Studies on the effects of traditional media, primarily newspapers and television, on political participation date back to the 1940s. Some studies (Entman 1989; Fallows 1996; Cappella and Jamieson 1997; McChesney 1999) have found that traditional media coverage, especially by television, decreases political engagement and participation by focusing on the "horserace" aspects of the campaign instead of the candidates' qualifications and substantive policy positions. However, other studies (Kwak 1999; Eveland and Scheufele 2000; Pinkleton and Austin 2001) have established a strong correlation between media use and political participation, including political knowledge, efficacy, and voting behavior.

In addition to the effects of traditional media coverage of political campaigns on voter engagement and participation, much research has focused on the role played by political advertising on television. Studies have found that political advertising can increase voters' knowledge of candidate issue positions (Kaid, Fernandes, and Painter 2011), even when the tone of the message is negative (Sides, Lipsitz, and Grossman 2010); their interest in the election (Atkin and Heald 1976); their engagement (Freedman, Franz, and Goldstein 2004); their political efficacy (Kaid et al. 2007); and their turnout and vote choice (Gordon and Hartmann 2012).

Interpersonal communication also plays a role in political engagement and participation, according to several studies (Huckfeldt and Sprague 1995; McLeod, Scheufele, and Moy 1999; Nisbet and Scheufele 2004; Scheufele et al. 2004, Zhang et al. 2010). Research suggests that talking about politics contributes to a number of positive outcomes, such as greater political knowledge, participation, and civic involvement; higher self-efficacy; and better social tolerance. However, the setting and nature of the political discussion may have an impact on the level of civic engagement. For example, Scheufele et al. (2004) found that discussing politics in volunteer groups was positively and directly related to political participation, while the influence of political conversations in church and work settings was indirect and mediated by exposure to different points of view.

Since the late 1990s, the growing popularity of the internet has greatly expanded citizens' access to information on political campaigns and candidates, both in terms of the amount and variety of content available. Some researchers (Shah et al. 2005; Kenski and Stroud 2006) have argued that the internet may promote political participation partly because of its flexibility, which allows citizens to access information "on demand" based on their individual interests and needs. In addition, the internet allows users to receive news in a timely manner, learn about diverse points of view, and go into greater depth about important issues (Shah et al. 2005).

A recent meta-analysis (Boulianne 2009) of studies testing the relationship between internet use and political engagement found a positive, yet small, effect. However, Boulianne noted that the relationship between internet use and political engagement increased over time in her sample of studies and was strongest when online resources were used for informational purposes. Similarly, Shah, Kwak, and Holbert (2001) found that using the internet to search for and exchange information had a universally positive impact on civic engagement, trust, and contentment across all generational groups studied.

Internet access and the use of online political news have been positively associated with political participation during recent presidential election cycles. For example, Tolbert and McNeal (2003) examined the impact of internet access and online political news on vote likelihood and found positive effects in both the 1996 and 2000 US presidential elections. Similarly, in a study of the 2004 general election, Mossberger, Tolbert, and McNeal (2008) showed that reading online news and participating in online political discussions had a positive effect on vote likelihood. Internationally, Dimitrova et al. (2014) demonstrated that social media use was a strong and positive predictor of political participation in Sweden.

More recent studies have zeroed in on the effects of social media platforms on civic engagement and political participation, primarily during the general election stage, with mixed results. For example, Vitak et al. (2011) found that political activity on Facebook (e.g., posting a politically oriented status update, becoming a "fan" of a candidate) was a significant predictor of other forms of political participation (e.g., volunteering for an organization, signing an online petition) during the 2008 presidential campaign.

A recent meta-analysis of studies investigating the effects of social media use on social capital, civic engagement, and political participation (Skoric et al. 2016) found generally positive effects, especially when these platforms are used for informational, expressive, and relational purposes. The meta-analysis defines *informational use* of social media as seeking and gathering political information through social media, which includes getting news and campaign information and following a political issue or candidate. *Expressive use* refers to using social media to express personal opinions, ideas, and thoughts, which includes writing social media comments and liking content. Finally, *relational use* involves relying on social media to maintain and strengthen relationships with others. This meta-analysis concluded that all three types of social media use were positively related to civic engagement in the majority of the studies examined.

Other researchers (Kushin and Yamamoto 2010) who have studied the effects of social media on political participation have argued that mere access to political information through the internet only marginally increases political involvement. Instead, they found that college students who took a more active role online, e.g., by frequently expressing their political opinions on social media networks, were more likely to become involved in the 2008 presidential election. Similarly, Gil de Zuniga et al. (2013) found that only expressive (or active) uses of social media content, such as writing blog posts and comments, are predictive of both online and offline political participation—including voting in the 2008 presidential election—while consumptive (or passive) uses, such as reading posts and comments, are not. In a study on the 2012 presidential election, Pennington et al. (2015) found that merely following a candidate on Facebook (a passive use of social media) did not lead to greater engagement or efficacy among young voters. However, in a study utilizing data from the Pew Research Center's Internet & American Life Project's winter 2012 tracking surveys, Kim, Atkin, and Lin (2016) found that posting about politics on social media (an active use of social media) did not lead to political involvement without accompanying offline political discussions.

As the results of these studies show, a variety of measures have been used as to what constitutes online participatory behavior. Most studies agree that simply reading content on social media is a less engaging behavior than posting comments and exchanging ideas and opinions, which are considered active, expressive, and participatory uses (Skoric et al. 2016). Liking and/or sharing social media content falls somewhere in between passive and active online participatory behavior, since it requires less effort than posting your own ideas. However, several recent studies (Gil de Zuniga et al. 2013; Park 2015) have characterized liking social media content and sharing or retweeting as expressive, participatory behaviors.

Although recent studies have produced somewhat mixed results on the effects of internet use, including social media platforms, on civic engagement in general and participation in specific election cycles, the two systematic meta-analyses noted above show mostly positive effects (Boulianne, 2009; Skoric et al. 2016). It is also clear that US citizens are increasingly turning to online resources for political information. For example, in the 2016 election cycle, social media was tied with local television as the second most helpful source of information about the presidential race in a survey conducted by the Pew Research Center (Gottfried et al. 2016). Cable television news was rated as the most helpful information source by 24% of respondents, while 14% said social media was the most helpful. News websites ranked third, with 13% of respondents rating this internet source as the most helpful.

However, when analyzing their survey results by age, the Pew Research Center found that social media was the most helpful news source on the 2016 presidential campaign for 35% of respondents age 18 to 29, with news websites second at 18%. So, 53% of the youngest survey respondents relied on social media or news websites for their election news. Comparatively, 34% of 30- to 49-year olds, 15% of 50- to 64-year olds, and just 6% of respondents 65 years of age and older relied on social media or news websites for information about the 2016 presidential campaign. The older respondents—43% of those at the age of 65 and older and 25% of those at 50 to 64—relied more heavily on cable television news for information (Gottfried et al. 2016).

Although recent surveys have found that citizens, especially younger ones, rely more on social media and news websites for information on political campaigns and elections, does the use of the internet for such information increase the likelihood that citizens will actively participate in the political process? Given the somewhat mixed results reported in previous studies, and the dearth of effects research of primary election participants, this study sets out to investigate the effects of online and social media use, both active and passive, as compared to traditional media, political advertising, and interpersonal communication on the likelihood to participate in the 2016 Iowa caucuses. Specifically, our study is designed to answer the following research questions:

RQ1: What are the effects of online media use on the likelihood to participate in the 2016 Iowa caucuses?

RQ2: How do the effects of online media use compare to the effects of traditional media, political advertising, and interpersonal communication on likelihood of caucus attendance?

RQ3: Is there a differential impact between active social media use (such as posting or liking/sharing on Facebook or Twitter) and passive social media use (such as following a politician or political party on social media) on likelihood of caucus attendance?

METHODOLOGY

Data for this study come from a two-wave telephone survey of registered Iowa voters. A sample of 12,000 individuals was selected from the state voter registration list using a stratified systematic design referencing five variables (political party, age, gender, congressional district, and previous primary election participation). The sample included 5,000 Democrats, 5,000 Republicans, and 2,000 No Party (independents). Excluding those without available telephone numbers, 10,685 registered voters were contacted by telephone, including landlines and cell phones, by a large Midwest university survey research center. Telephone interviews were completed with 1,076 registered voters between November 2 and 15, 2015. Excluding sampled voters with no reported telephone number, the survey response rate was 10.1%; the cooperation rate was 34.4% (AAPOR 2016). The second wave of the survey was in the field between January 5 and 22, 2016, with 753 completed responses, resulting in 70% of the November 2015 respondents participating in the January 2016 survey. Our analysis is based on the data from the second survey wave.

Variables

Four sets of independent variables are utilized in this study. The first set contains the demographic characteristics of the respondents, including age, gender, education, and income levels. In terms of age, the January 2016 respondents ranged between 18- and 97-year old, with a mean age of 63.10 years (s.d. = 16.02). The sample was about evenly split by gender, with 49% males and 51% females. In terms of educational levels, the respondents were slightly more educated, with 1.8% reporting less than a high school education, 21.9% high school graduates, 32.8% with some college or technical training, 22.9% with a bachelor's degree, and 20.7% with postgraduate work or degree. Total household income before taxes was about equally split across the following five categories: 14.8% reporting less than $25,000 annual income, 24.9% with income from $25,000 to $50,000, 24% from $50,000 to $75,000, 17.7% from $75,000 to $100,000, and 18.7% with more than $100,000 annual income.

Our sample composition reflects some of the key characteristics of the 2016 Iowa caucus-goers, who tend to be older, more educated, and wealthier than Iowans overall. For example, according to entrance polls conducted by Edison Research of the 2016 Iowa caucus-goers, 64% of Democrats and 73% of Republicans were at the age of 45 or older, with 28% of Democrats and 27% of Republicans age 65 or older. Comparatively, 4.1% of our sample fell under 30-years old, 17% were between 30 and 50, with the remaining 78.9% more than 50-years old. When looking at age breakdowns by party, the percentage of older adults (65 and over) in our sample is higher than in the Edison poll, although the two surveys use different methods of data collection. See Appendix 1 for additional demographic comparisons between our sample and the Edison entrance poll data.

Although Iowa's population in 2015 was 50.4% female and 40.6% male, women comprised the majority (57%) of Democratic Party caucus-goers, whereas men made up the majority (52%) of Republican Party caucus-goers (Gamio and Clement, 2016). As shown in Appendix 1, our sample and the Edison data are almost identical in terms of gender split. In terms of the educational levels of the 2016 Iowa caucus-goers, 32% of Democrats and 33% of Republicans had some college; 27% of Democrats and 33% of

Republicans held bachelor's degrees, and 23% of Democrats and 19% of Republicans had completed postgraduate work or a degree. Our sample education levels closely match the Edison data (Appendix 1). Of the Democratic Party caucus-goers, 20% reported annual incomes of $100,000 or more, 38% reported earning $50,000 to $99,999, and 41% reported annual incomes of less than $50,000 (Gamio and Clement, 2016), which resembles our sample income levels on the Democratic side (Appendix 1). Edison Research did not poll Republican Party caucus-goers about their annual household incomes.

The next set of independent variables measured the respondents' political predispositions. Three variables were included in this block: individual ideological orientation, attention to the campaign, and interpersonal discussion about politics. Ideological orientation was captured by a five-point Likert scale, ranging from very liberal to very conservative. Of the respondents who answered that question, 11.7% identified as very liberal, 20.6% as somewhat liberal, 25.8% as moderate, 23.1% as somewhat conservative, and 18.7% as very conservative. Comparatively, the ideological orientation of participants in the 2016 Democratic Party caucuses in Iowa, as reported in the Edison Research entrance polls, was 28% very liberal, 40% somewhat liberal, 28% moderate, and 4% conservative. Of Republican Party caucus-goers, 85% said they were very conservative and 15% identified as moderate or liberal (Gamio and Clement 2016).

Another question asked how closely each respondent followed the political campaign, which was gauged with a four-point Likert scale ranging from following very closely to not at all. The majority of the sample (47.3%) indicated that they paid very close attention to the campaign, followed by 41% who said they followed it closely, 10.2% who followed it a little, and 1.5% who said not at all. Finally, we wanted to capture how often respondents engaged in political discussions with family or friends, which was measured on a four-point Likert scale ranging from never to very often. More than a quarter of the sample (26.1%) responded that they never engaged in political discussions, 53.2% responded sometimes, 15% responded often, and 5.6% said very often. Overall, the sample is ideologically balanced, paid close attention to the political campaign, and regularly engaged in political talk.

The third set of independent variables included use of traditional media for political news. Respondents were asked how frequently (never, sometimes, often, or very often) they get political news from various media channels. Traditional media included newspapers; radio; television networks, such as ABC, CBS, and NBC; cable television networks, such as CNN, FOX, and MSNBC; and local television newscasts. Here, we also included late-night television comedy shows and television campaign advertising. More information about the respondents' media diet is provided in the Results section.

The last set of independent variables was designed to capture online media use with four-point Likert scales. We asked how often respondents engaged in the following online activities: visiting a website of a political party or candidate; visiting a website of traditional media organizations, such as the *New York Times* or CNN; following a politician or political party on social media, such as Facebook or Twitter; posting a political comment on Facebook, Twitter, or other social media; and liking or sharing political content on a social media network. More details on the social media use of the respondents are provided in the Results section.

Finally, a five-point Likert-type scale was used to capture voters' likelihood to attend the 2016 Iowa caucuses, which served as our dependent variable. Respondents could choose from the following options: definitely will attend, probably will attend, are unsure, probably will not attend, and definitely will not attend a local precinct caucus.

Analytical Strategy

Since the goal of this study is to examine the effects of online media use, including social media platforms, on likelihood to participate in the 2016 Iowa caucuses, the multivariate analysis below includes only those respondents who confirmed using the internet for political information. Block linear regression models are tested with four blocks of predictor variables entered sequentially based on prior caucus research (Dimitrova and Bystrom 2013). The first block includes basic demographics, the second block contains political predisposition variables, followed by traditional media in the third block, and online media in the last block. The analysis is based on weighted data from the January 2016 survey, using a poststratification method with gender and age group based on the November 2015 survey weights and a raking adjustment on the weights with congressional district, gender, and age within each party (Solon, Haider, and Wooldridge 2013).

Multicollinearity diagnostics were run in SPSS to determine if the predictor variables in the multiple regressions are related. We checked tolerance levels in all regression models and determined they were all above 0.70. Since tolerance statistics indicate the percent of variance in the predictor variable that is not accounted for by the other predictors in the model and no small values were observed in the results, it is appropriate to conclude that predictor variables are not redundant (Allison 1999).

RESULTS

Information Channels for Political News

We first looked at the use of traditional media for political news among the sample of registered Iowa voters. Combining the response categories "often" or "very often," the results show that network television networks like ABC, CBS, and NBC were used by 64% of the survey respondents. The second most frequently cited channel for political information was local television, which was used by 52% of the respondents. Cable television networks—such as CNN, FOX, and MSNBC—ranked third and were accessed often or very often by 44% of the sample. Newspapers came in fourth with 43% using this media channel, while the internet was cited as a frequent or very frequent source for political information by 35% of the sample. About 31% of Iowa voters got political news from radio, and 27% of the sample used campaign advertising often or very often. Finally, about 10% of respondents regularly used late-night television comedy shows as an information source.

After looking at the respondents' media diet, it is helpful to examine how often respondents used online information sources during the pre-caucus season. These sources include traditional media websites; websites hosted by political candidates and parties; and social media platforms, which allowed us to incorporate measures of both passive and active social media use. Excluding those who said they never used the Internet for political information, the following pattern emerges from the remaining 457 respondents.

More than half (58%) of the respondents reported visiting traditional media websites, such as the *New York Times* or CNN, at least some of the time.[1] This online activity was followed by visiting political party/politicians' websites by 45.5% of the sample (see Table 1). The next most popular online activity was liking or sharing political content within individual's social media networks, which was common for 41.9% of the sample. Following a politician or political party on social media, such as Facebook or Twitter, was reported by 38.3% of the respondents. The least common online activity was posting political comments on Facebook, Twitter, or other social media, which was done by less than one-third (29.3%) of the sample. To summarize, while social media still lags behind traditional media as a political information source, it is gaining in popularity.

Online Media Effects

The first research question focused on the effects of online media use on potential caucus-goers in Iowa. The block regression results presented in Table 2 show some interesting trends. First, the overall effect of the online media block is significant (see Table 2 Model 4). Of the five online media factors included in the final model, three are significant. Liking or sharing online content on social media is a positive predictor of likelihood of caucus attendance $(\beta = 0.29, \text{ s.d.} = 0.09, p < 0.01)$. However, visiting candidate websites $(\beta = -0.26, \text{ s.d.} = 0.07, p < 0.001)$ and following candidates on Facebook or Twitter $(\beta = -0.20, \text{ s.d.} = 0.07, p < 0.01)$ have a negative effect on caucus attendance. Visiting traditional media websites

TABLE 1 Percentage of Users Engaged in Online Activities

Online activity	Yes	No
Visit traditional media websites	58%	42%
Visit politicians/party websites	45.5%	54.5%
Like or share political content on social media	41.9%	58.1%
Follow candidates of social media	38.3%	61.7%
Post comments about politics on social media	29.3%	70.7%

$N = 457$. Descriptive statistics based on the number of respondents who report using the Internet as a source of political information.

and posting on social media were not statistically significant predictors of likelihood to caucus.

The second research question compared the relative effects of online media use to the effects of traditional media, political advertising, and interpersonal communication. As shown in Table 2 Model 4, several traditional media channels have a significant effect on caucus attendance. They include

TABLE 2 Ordinary least squares (OLS) Regressions Predicting Likelihood of Caucus Attendance

Predictor variables	Model 1	Model 2	Model 3	Model 4
Constant	2.01 (0.30)***	0.89 (0.38)*	0.50 (0.46)	1.26 (0.52)*
Age	0.006 (0.003)*	0.007 (0.003)	0.000 (0.003)	−0.003 (0.003)
Gender	0.11 (0.10)	0.13 (0.10)	0.04 (0.10)	0.13 (0.10)
Education	−0.08 (0.06)	−0.06 (0.06)	−0.04 (0.06)	−0.07 (0.06)
Income	−0.06 (0.04)	−0.06 (0.04)	−0.06 (0.04)	−0.07 (0.04)
Ideological orientation		0.06 (0.04)	0.03 (0.04)	0.02 (0.04)
Attention to campaign		0.56 (0.08)***	0.64 (0.08)***	0.55 (0.08)***
Interpersonal discussion		−0.03 (0.06)	−0.02 (0.06)	−0.003 (0.06)
Network news			0.13 (0.06)*	0.12 (0.06)*
Cable news			0.15 (0.05)**	0.14 (0.05)**
Local TV news			0.10 (0.06)	0.08 (0.06)
Late-night comedy			−0.19 (0.07)**	−0.16 (0.06)*
Newspapers			0.08 (0.05)	0.09 (0.05)
Radio			−0.12 (0.05)*	−0.10 (0.05)*
Campaign advertising			0.09 (0.06)	0.09 (0.06)
Party/candidate websites				−0.26 (0.07)***
News media websites				0.02 (0.05)
Following politicians on social media				−0.20 (0.07)**
Posting political comments on social media				−0.14 (0.09)
Liking/sharing political content on social media				0.29 (0.09)**
R^2	0.02	0.10	0.16	0.20
R^2 change		0.08***	0.06***	0.04***

Table reports results from block regression analyses using weighted data. Estimates are unstandardized regression coefficients with standard errors in parentheses.
*$p < 0.05$, **$p < 0.01$, ***$p < 0.001$.

network news ($\beta = 0.12$, s.d. $= 0.06$, $p < 0.05$) and cable television ($\beta = 0.14$, s.d. $= 0.05$, $p < 0.01$), both of which positively affect attendance, and radio ($\beta = -0.10$, s.d. $= 0.05$, $p < 0.05$) and late-night television comedy ($\beta = -0.16$, s.d. $= 0.06$, $p < 0.05$), both of which have negative effects. Newspapers, local television networks, campaign advertising, and interpersonal discussions about politics are not statistically significant. Looking at the standardized betas, the highest coefficient for all media variables is the one for liking or sharing social media content ($B = 0.20$), which is followed by cable television ($B = 0.12$). The only other variable with a higher beta coefficient in the full model is attention to the campaign ($B = 0.27$).

The last research question asked if there is a differential impact between active and passive social media use. The results here are mixed. Posting comments on social media was not significant in our analysis, whereas liking/sharing content on Facebook or Twitter was a positive predictor of caucus attendance. Conversely, passive social media use—defined here as following a politician or political party on social media—was a negative predictor. These results seem to indicate that active use of social media has a positive influence on political participation, while passive use has a negative effect, at least for the sample of Iowa internet users in our analysis.

Looking at the first regression model, we can observe that age is the only significant predictor among the demographic block of variables, and it has a positive effect on caucus attendance. In other words, older respondents were more likely to participate in the 2016 Iowa caucuses. Age remains marginally significant in the second block, but attention paid to the political campaign emerges as a strong positive predictor ($\beta = 0.56$, s.d. $= 0.08$, $p = 0.000$). Attention remains significant in the final model, indicating that those who pay more attention to the political campaign are significantly more likely to attend the caucus than those who pay less attention.

Finally, when examining the overall explanatory power of the full regression model, one can observe a modest R^2 of 0.20, which indicates that all independent variables combined explain about 20% of the variation in the outcome variable. This is a relatively small R^2 and suggests that other factors not included in this multivariate analysis may be at play. However, the F-change statistics for each of the four models are significant, which indicates that each block of variables is significant as a whole and independently adds more explanatory power. The online media block, in particular, explains an additional 4% of the variation in caucus attendance (see Table 2 Model 4).

DISCUSSION

The results of our study of the effects of online media use, including social media platforms—as compared to traditional media, political advertising, and interpersonal communication—during the 2016 Iowa caucuses both confirm and conflict with previous research findings, which have primarily focused on the general election phase of presidential campaigns.

First, our study adds some weight to the positive findings of recent examinations of the effects of social media use on participation in the 2008 and 2012 presidential elections. Similar to the studies on the use of social media during the 2008 (Gil de Zuniga et al. 2013) and 2012 (Pennington et al. 2015) presidential elections, we found that actively liking or sharing political content on Facebook or Twitter was positively related to the likelihood to participate in the 2016 Iowa caucuses, whereas passively following a candidate on social media was not. However, whereas Pennington et al. (2015) found that following a presidential candidate on Facebook had no effect on civic engagement, we found a negative effect. That is, following a politician or political party on social media was a negative predictor of the likelihood of our sample to participate in the 2016 Iowa caucuses.

To explain these results, it may be important to go back to the conceptual distinctions between different types of social media use. Research has demonstrated that expressive, or active, use of digital media—such as posting on blogs—is positively related to both online and offline political participation while consumptive, or passive, use is not (Gil de Zuniga et al. 2013). Consistent with their study, we found that passively following politicians on social media such as Facebook and Twitter has a negative effect on voter participation.

Another important conceptual differentiation offered by Skoric et al. (2016) distinguished between expressive, informational, and relational uses of social media. Their meta-analysis showed generally positive effects of these three different types of uses of social media on citizen engagement, which included social capital, civic engagement, and political participation. Our findings corroborate their analysis since liking and sharing online content, which is an example of expressive use of social media, emerged as a significant positive predictor of caucus attendance.

As for the impact of posting comments on social media on political participation, it was bit surprising not to find a significant effect in our study. While our results conflict with the findings of Kushin and Yamamoto (2010) on the 2008 presidential election, they are consistent with the findings of Kim, Atkin, and Lin (2016) on the 2012 presidential election. Whereas Kushin and Yamamoto (2010) found a positive relationship between expressions of political opinions on social media networks with political engagement in 2008, we found no such effects in 2016 as did Kim, Atkin, and Lin (2016) in 2012. That is, posting about politics on social media did not predict the likelihood to participate in the 2016 Iowa caucuses.

There are several possible reasons for this finding. First, posting is a relatively rare activity for our sample as less than 30% of the respondents engaged in this online activity, ranking it below visiting traditional media sites and candidate sites and liking, sharing, or following political candidates on social media. Second, our survey sample overrepresented older Iowans, with about 40% of the respondents being in the 65 and over age group. Although the main effect for age is insignificant in our multivariate analyses, it is possible that traditional vehicles for expressing political opinions count more heavily with older demographics. Conversely, the effects of social media channels may be more pronounced with younger generations, especially millennials who are 2.5 times more likely to be early adopters of new technologies (Fromm 2016).

It is interesting to note that liking or sharing on social media, which takes just a few seconds, was more influential for the sample as a whole in predicting participation in the 2016 Iowa caucuses than taking the time to write a comment, which was the least common online activity for our sample of registered voters. These results seem to indicate that relatively quick active participation on social media can enhance political engagement in election cycles. These types of online activities, which may blur the lines between informational and expressive uses of social media, seem to be increasingly prominent among younger adults. In the context of recent Pew Research Center studies indicating that younger voters rely on social media and news websites as the most helpful political information sources, this finding is particularly noteworthy.

Our findings that visiting political candidate or party websites or following presidential candidates on social media had a negative impact on the likelihood to caucus might be attributed to the overall negative reactions of voters during the 2016 campaign. For example, a national survey conducted June 15–26, 2016, by the Pew Research Center found that voters' overall satisfaction with their choices for president in 2016 was at its lowest point in two decades. Less than one-half of registered voters in both parties— 43% of Democrats and 40% of Republicans—said they were satisfied with their choices for president. And, 41% said it was difficult to choose between Republican Trump and Democrat Clinton because neither would make a good president—as high as at any point since 2000 (Pew Research Center, 2016b). Another report by the Pew Research Center (2016a) found that 70% of Democrats and 62% of Republicans who were actively engaged in the 2016 presidential election were afraid of the opposing party. Perhaps, registered voters in Iowa were similarly turned off by the presidential candidates and political parties and, thus, were also negatively affected by visiting their websites and following them on social media.

Interestingly, the overall negative media coverage of both Clinton and Trump as documented by Harvard University's Shorenstein Center on Media, Politics, and Public Policy in both the 2015 "invisible primary" stage (Patterson 2016a) and 2016 primary stage (Patterson 2016b) does not appear to have affected our sample of registered Iowa voters in their likelihood to caucus. In fact, consistent with the results of previous studies (Kwak 1999; Eveland and Scheufele 2000; Pinkleton and Austin 2001) on the positive effects of the use of traditional news media on political participation, we found that accessing political information from network and cable television stations was a positive predictor of likelihood to caucus. However, newspapers and local television stations had no effect. The fact that late-night television comedy shows and radio, perhaps especially partisan leaning political talk radio, had a negative effect on the likelihood to caucus may be related to the overall negativity of these communication channels during the 2016 presidential campaign.

Unlike the results of previous research, we found that television campaign advertising (Gordon and Hartmann 2012) and interpersonal communication (Huckfeldt and Sprague 1995; McLeod, Scheufele, and Moy 1999; Nisbet and Scheufele 2004; Scheufele et al. 2004, Zhang et al. 2010) had no effect on the likelihood to participate in the 2016 Iowa caucuses. These results also may be attributed to the overall negativity of the 2016 presidential campaign and, in the case of political advertising, to the relatively low use of television spots before the 2016 Iowa caucuses as compared to 2008 and 2012. According to the Wesleyan Media Project, which tracks the use of television ads in political campaigns, the 2016 presidential candidates ran about one-half the number of commercials aired in the 2012 election, which may have blunted their impact on our sample of registered Iowa voters (Wesleyan Media Project 2016).

As for the effects of interpersonal communication on participation in the 2016 Iowa caucuses, it is relevant to note the Pew Research Center survey (2016a), which found that both Republicans (50%) and Democrats (46%) were likely to say that talking about politics with people with whom they disagreed was "stressful and frustrating" as compared to "interesting and informative" during the 2016 presidential campaign cycle. Although almost 75% of our sample said they talked about politics, the majority said it was just "sometimes" with about one in five responding "often" or "very often," perhaps indicating less robust conversations.

Limitations

Our findings should be put in the context of 2016 presidential campaign, which was quite negative at all stages (Patterson 2016a, 2016b) and unexpected in terms of predicted outcomes. The characteristics of the presidential campaign and the choices presented to voters may have a bearing on this study's results. In addition, we need to acknowledge that the way social media use was captured in our survey makes it difficult to disaggregate the effects of specific social media networks. It is possible that Twitter, for instance, was used differently than Facebook, YouTube, or other social media platforms now available to voters.

Another limitation of the survey was the fact that relational uses of social media, such as initiating and maintaining relationships with others, were not included in the questionnaire. The characteristics of the Iowa respondents who participated in the survey—particularly their age, less active social media use, and close attention paid to the campaign—also may have affected the study results.

While multicollinearity diagnostics appeared at satisfactory levels, it is important to note that some of the predictor variables included in the regression models may be interrelated. Methodologically, it is also important to point out that the overall explanatory power of the multivariate models was modest (Allison 1999).

Implications and Future Research

The findings of this study have important theoretical and practical implications. From a theoretical perspective, we extend previous research on the effects of social media on political participation during caucuses and show that certain types of social media use may lead to voter mobilization, while other uses do not.

What do our findings mean for political campaigners and political communication scholars who want to stimulate political participation? First, it is not enough to have potential followers on social media. What appears to be more important is to motivate your followers to like or share your content with others, which goes beyond informational use of digital media. Second, certain types of online media uses seem to produce more alienation or subtly suppress participation. In particular, we found that visiting candidate websites negatively affected caucus attendance. While the reasons for this finding remain unknown, we can recommend to political candidates to focus on expressive use of social media and try to encourage reposting and retweeting of content from their social media platforms rather than their personal websites.

From a practical perspective, political candidates and their campaigns should perhaps focus their efforts not so much on a static online presence, but rather on producing social media content that will motivate individuals to like and share it with others. Further research into what social media users consider motivating may be needed to capture their thoughts and reasoning for sharing certain types of social media political content with others.

It is important in future research to continue to distinguish between different types of social media use and go beyond time spent and frequency of use of social media channels. A better understanding of the differences between informational, relational, and expressive use of social media is also needed. Finally, future research should test for both direct and indirect effects of social media use on political participation using statistical techniques such as structural equation modeling.

ACKNOWLEDGMENTS

The authors would like to thank Ana Ramirez, a master's student in the Greenlee School of Journalism and Communications at Iowa State University, for her help with the article.

NOTE

1. Percentages are based on combining the "sometimes," "often," and "very often" survey categories.

REFERENCES

AAPOR. 2016. *Standard Definitions: Final Dispositions of Case Codes and Outcome Rates for Surveys*. American Association for Public Opinion Research. http://www.aapor.org/AAPOR_Main/media/publications/Standard-Definitions20169theditionfinal.pdf

Allison, P. 1999. *Multiple Regression: A Primer*. Thousand Oaks, CA: Pine Forge Press.

Atkin, C., and G. Heald. 1976. "Effects of Political Advertising." *The Public Opinion Quarterly* 40 (2):216–28.

Boulianne, S. 2009. "Does Internet use Affect Engagement? A Meta-Analysis of Research." *Political Communication* 26 (2):193–11. doi:10.1080/10584600902854363

Cappella, J. N., and K. H. Jamieson. 1997. *Spiral of Cynicism: The Press and the Public Good*. New York: Oxford University Press.

Cho, J., D. V. Shah, J. M. McLeod, D. M. McLeod, R. M. Scholl, and M. R. Gotlieb. 2009. "Campaigns, Reflection, and Deliberation: Advancing an O-S-R-O-R Model of Communication Effects." *Communication Theory* 19:66–88. doi:10.1111/j.1468-2885.2008.01333.x

DeFleur, M. L., and S. Ball-Rokeach. 1989. *Theories of Mass Communication*. 5th ed. White Plains, NY: Longman.

Dimitrova, D. V., and D. Bystrom. 2013. "The Effects of Social Media on Political Participation and Candidate Image Evaluations in the 2012 Iowa Caucuses." *American Behavioral Scientist* 57 (11):1568–83. doi:10.1177/0002764213489011

Dimitrova, D. V., A. Shehata, J. Strömbäck, and L. Nord. 2014. "The Effects of Digital Media on Political Knowledge and Participation in Election Campaigns: Evidence from Panel Data." *Communication Research* 41 (1):95–118. doi:10.1177/0093650211426004

Entman, R. M. 1989. *Democracy Without Citizens*. New York: Oxford University Press.

Eveland, W. P. Jr. 2001. "The Cognitive Mediation Model of Learning from the News: Evidence from Non-Election, Off-Year Election, and Presidential Election Contexts." *Communication Research* 28:571–601. doi:10.1177/009365001028005001

Eveland, W. P. Jr., and D. A. Scheufele. 2000. "Connecting News Media Use With Gaps In Knowledge And Participation." *Political Communication* 17:215–37. doi:10.1080/105846000414250

Eveland, W. P. Jr., D. V. Shah, and N. Kwak. 2003. "Assessing Causality in the Cognitive Mediation Model: A Panel Study of Motivations, Information

Processing and Learning During Campaign 2000." *Communication Research* 30:359–86. doi:10.1177/0093650203253369

Fallows, J. 1996. *Breaking the News: How the Media Undermine American Democracy.* New York: Pantheon Books.

Freedman, P., M. Franz, and K. Goldstein. 2004. "Campaign Advertising and Democratic Citizenship." *American Journal of Political Science* 48 (4):723–41. doi:10.2307/1519930

Fromm, J. 2016. "New Study Finds Social Media Shapes Millennial Political Involvement and Engagement." *Forbes*, June 22. Accessed May 29, 2016. https://www.forbes.com/sites/jefffromm/2016/06/22/new-study-finds-social-media-shapes-millennial-political-involvement-and-engagement/#46c0710b2618

Gamio, L., and S. Clement. 2016. "Iowa Caucus Entrance Poll Results." *The Washington Post,* February 1. Accessed April 23, 2016. https://www.washingtonpost.com/graphics/politics/2016-election/primaries/iowa-entrance-poll/

Gil de Zuniga, H., I. Bachmann, S.-H. Hsu, and J. Brundidge. 2013. "Expressive Versus Consumptive Blog Use: Implications for Interpersonal Discussion and Political Participation." *International Journal of Communication* 7:1538–59.

Gordon, B. R., and W. R. Hartmann. 2012. "Advertising Effects in Presidential Elections." *Marketing Science* 32 (1):19–35.

Gottfried, J., M. Barthel, E. Shearer, and A. Mitchell. 2016. "The 2016 Presidential Campaign: A News Event That's Hard to Miss." Pew Research Center Journalism and Media, February 4. Accessed January 15, 2016. http://www.journalism.org/2016/02/04/the-2016-presidential-campaign-a-news-event-thats-hard-to-miss/

Huckfeldt, R., and J. Sprague. 1995. *Citizens, Politics, and Social Communication: Information and Influence in an Election Campaign.* New York: Cambridge University Press.

Kaid, L. L., J. Fernandes, and D. Painter. 2011. "Effects of Political Advertising in the 2008 Presidential Campaign." *American Behavioral Scientist* 55 (4):437–36. doi:10.1177/0002764211398071

Kaid, L. L., M. Postelnicu, K. Landerville, H. J. Yun, and A. G. LeGrange. 2007. "The Effects of Political Advertising on Young Voters." *American Behavioral Scientist* 50 (9):1137–51. doi:10.1177/0002764207300039

Kenski, K., and N. J. Stroud. 2006. "Connections Between Internet Use and Political Efficacy, Knowledge, and Participation." *Journal of Broadcasting & Electronic Media* 50 (2):173–92. doi:10.1207/s15506878jobem5002_1

Kim, T., D. J. Atkin, and C. A. Lin. 2016. "The Influence of Social Networking Sites on Political Behavior: Modeling Political Involvement via Online and Offline Activity." *Journal of Broadcasting & Electronic Media* 60 (1):23–39. doi:10.1080/08838151.2015.1127242

Kushin, M. J., and M. Yamamoto. 2010. "Did Social Media Really Matter? College Students' Use of Online Media and Political Decision Making in the 2008 Election." *Mass Communication and Society* 13:608–30. doi:10.1080/15205436.2010.516863

Kwak, N. 1999. "Revisiting the Knowledge Gap Hypothesis: Education, Motivation, and Media Use." *Communication Research* 26 (4):385–13. doi:10.1177/009365099026004002

McChesney, R. W. 1999. *Rich Media, Poor Democracy: Communication Politics in Dubious Times.* Urbana: University of Illinois Press.

McLeod, J. M., D. A. Scheufele, and P. Moy. 1999. "Community, Communication, Participation: The Role of Mass Media and Interpersonal Discussion in Local Political Participation." *Political Communication* 16:315–36. doi:10.1080/105846099198659

Mossberger, K., C. J. Tolbert, and R. S. McNeal. 2008. *Digital Citizenship: The Internet, Society, and Participation.* Cambridge, MA: Massachusetts Institute of Technology Press.

Nisbet, M. C., and D. A. Scheufele. 2004. "Political Talk as a Catalyst for Online Citizenship." *Journalism and Mass Communication Quarterly* 81 (4):877–96. doi:10.1177/107769900408100410

Park, C. S. 2015. "Pathways to Expressive and Collective Participation: Usage Patterns, Political Efficacy, and Political Participation in Social Networking Sites." *Journal of Broadcasting & Electronic Media* 59 (4):698–16. doi:10.1080/08838151.2015.1093480

Patterson, T. E. 2016a. "Pre-primary News Coverage of the 2016 Presidential Race: Trump's Rise, Sanders' Emergence, Clinton's Struggle." Shorenstein Center on Media, Politics and Public Policy, June 13. Accessed January 14, 2016. https://shorensteincenter.org/pre-primary-news-coverage-2016-trump-clinton-sanders/

Patterson, T. E. 2016b. "News Coverage of the 2016 Presidential Primaries: Horse Race Reporting Has Its Consequences." Shorenstein Center on Media, Politics and Public Policy, July 11. Accessed January 14, 2016. https://shorensteincenter.org/news-coverage-2016-presidential-primaries/

Pennington, N., K. L. Winfrey, B. R. Warner, and M. W. Kearney. 2015. "Liking Obama and Romney (on Facebook): An Experimental Evaluation of Political Engagement and Efficacy During the 2012 General Election." *Computers in Human Behavior* 44:279–83. doi:10.1016/j.chb.2014.11.032

Pew Research Center. 2016a. "Partisanship and Political Animosity in 2016." Accessed January 14, 2016. http://www.people-press.org/2016/06/22/partisanship-and-political-animosity-in-2016/

Pew Research Center. 2016b. "2016 Campaign: Strong Interest, Widespread Dissatisfaction." Accessed January 14, 2016. http://www.people-press.org/2016/07/07/2016-campaign-strong-interest-widespread-dissatisfaction/

Pinkleton, B. E., and E. W. Austin. 2001. "Individual Motivations, Perceived Media Importance, and Political Disaffection." *Political Communication* 18:321–34. doi:10.1080/10584600152400365

Redlawsk, D. P., C. J. Tolbert, and T. Donovan. 2010. *Why Iowa? How Caucuses and Sequential Elections Improve the Presidential Nominating Process.* Chicago: University of Chicago Press.

Scheufele, D. A., M. C. Nisbet, D. Brossard, and E. C. Nisbet. 2004. "Social Structure and Citizenship: Examining the Impacts of Social Setting, Network Heterogeneity, and Informational Variables on Political Participation." *Political Communication* 21 (3):315–38. doi:10.1080/10584600490481389

Shah, D. V., J. Cho, W. P. Eveland Jr., and N. Kwak. 2005. "Information and Expression in a Digital Age: Modeling Internet Effects on Civic Participation." *Communication Research* 32:531–65. doi:10.1177/0093650205279209

Shah, D. V., N. Kwak, and R. L. Holbert. 2001. "Connecting and Disconnecting with Civic Life: Patterns of Internet Use and the Production of Social Capital." *Political Communication* 18 (2):141–62. doi:10.1080/105846001750322952

Sides, J., K. Lipsitz, and M. Grossman. 2010. "Do Voters Perceive Negative Campaigns as Informative Campaigns?" *American Politics Research* 38 (3):502–30. doi:10.1177/1532673x09336832

Skoric, M. M., Q. Zhu, D. Goh, and N. Pang. 2016. "Social Media and Citizen Engagement: A Meta-Analytic Review." *New Media & Society* 18 (9):1817–39. doi:10.1177/1461444815616221

Solon, G., S. J. Haider, and J. Wooldridge. 2013. "What Are We Waiting for?" NBER Working Paper No. 18859, National Bureau of Economic Research, February. Accessed January 14, 2016. http://www.nber.org/papers/w18859

Tolbert, C. J., and R. S. McNeal. 2003. "Unraveling the Effects of the Internet on Political Participation." *Political Research Quarterly* 56 (2):175–85. doi:10.2307/3219896

Vitak, J., P. Zube, A. Smock, C. T. Carr, N. Ellison, and C. Lampe. 2011. "It's Complicated: Facebook Users' Political Participation in the 2008 Election." *Cyberpsychology, Behavior, and Social Networking* 14 (3):107–14. doi:10.1089/cyber.2009.0226

Wesleyan Media Project. 2016. "Presidential Ad Volume Less Than Half of 2012." Accessed January 14, 2016. http://mediaproject.wesleyan.edu/releases/oct-2016/

Winebrenner, H., and D. J. Goldford. 2010. *The Iowa Precinct Caucuses: The Making of a Media Event.* Iowa City: University of Iowa Press.

Zhang, W., T. J. Johnson, T. Seltzer, and S. L. Bichard. 2010. "The Revolution Will be Networked: The Influence of Social Networking Sites on Political Attitudes and Behavior." *Social Science Computer Review* 28:75–92. doi:10.1177/0894439309335162

APPENDIX 1 Sample Demographic Comparisons by Gender, Age, Education, and Income

	Democrats		Republicans	
Party	Our sample (%)	Edison sample (%)	Our sample (%)	Edison sample (%)
Gender				
Male	42.4	43	51.2	52
Female	57.6	57	48.8	48
Age				
Under 30	13.8	18	13.5	12
Age 30–44	14.6	19	12.1	16
Age 45–64	30.6	36	33.9	46
65 and older	41.0	28	40.5	27
Education				
High school or less	16.8	18	21.9	16
Some college	32.7	32	32.5	33
College graduate	22.4	27	32.5	33
Postgraduate study	28.0	23	13.0	19
Income				
Less than $50,000	45.4	41	28.1	N/A
$50,000–100,000	36.9	38	46.3	N/A
More than $100,000	17.7	20	25.7	N/A

Source for Edison data: Survey of Iowa voters as they entered randomly selected caucus voting places on February 1, 2016, including 1,794 Republican caucus-goers and 1,660 Democratic caucus-goers. The poll was conducted by Edison Media Research. The results have a margin of error of +/−4%. More at: https://www.washingtonpost.com/graphics/politics/2016-election/primaries/iowa-entrance-poll/.

Index